THE EQUITABLE GUIDE TO
INVESTMENT AND SAVINGS

THE EQUITABLE GUIDE TO INVESTMENT AND SAVINGS

Lorna Bourke

BLOOMSBURY

First published 1993 by Bloomsbury Publishing Limited, 2 Soho Square, London W1V 5DE

British Library Cataloguing in Publication Data
A CiP record for this book is available on request from the British Library

ISBN 0 7475 1476 3

Typeset by Hewer Text Composition Services, Edinburgh
Printed and bound by Clays Ltd, St Ives plc

CONTENTS

INTRODUCTION

The ancient Chinese curse, 'May you live in interesting times,' has a peculiarly apposite ring at the moment. Anyone trying to make financial provision for the future faces an investment landscape the like of which has not been seen since before the Second World War.

On the plus side, mortgage rates and bank base rate have not been at such low levels since the 1960s, and inflation is down to 2 per cent or thereabouts. But the other side of the coin is that unemployment, bankruptcies and public spending are all running at record levels, world trade is in the doldrums, and companies, squeezed by the longest recession since the 1930s, face a long haul back into profitability. The UK has been forced to devalue out of the European Exchange Rate Mechanism and the pound is once again floating. Though not an exact parallel with the slump of the 1930s, there are alarming similarities.

All our long-held beliefs in the value of real assets like property and equities have been turned on their heads, and investors have every reason to question whether things will ever be the same again.

What we have witnessed in the past few years has been a total upheaval in world financial markets and a fundamental sea change in the way we perceive property, equities and virtually all assets as a store of wealth. There has been a massive downward readjustment in values, and we have to face the fact that prices may not recover in real terms in the foreseeable future.

For the first time since the Second World War house prices have fallen dramatically – in some areas by as much as 40 per cent. And for the first time in nearly 50 years we have seen a five-year period (1987–92) when equities have not outperformed cash on deposit at the building society. Indeed, taking into

1

account inflation over the past five years, equities are now some 30 per cent below their 1987 value. So should we all panic?

As somebody once said to me, 'You have to be grown up about money'. Most of us have learnt that the future does not necessarily take care of itself financially, and if we want to live comfortably, have enough spare cash to enjoy life, deal with emergencies and retire in comfort, we have to make sensible provision for these eventualities.

And although the recent past has been traumatic for investors, you have to accept that all investment is risky. Even if you put your money in a building society, there is the risk that inflation will eat away at its purchasing power.

The challenge for private investors is to maximize the potential returns while minimizing the risk. And on that score the recent upheavals have not been all bad.

If it has taken five years of volatile equity markets and negative long-term returns from shares to produce the 'no risk' equity bond (which guarantees to return your cash after a given period, or a profit equivalent to the increase in one of the published stock market indices), then there has been some benefit to the consumer from what otherwise has been a disastrous recent past. At last the big financial institutions are providing what the customer wants, rather than what they can profitably sell.

We all tend to have short memories too. You may have lost some money in shares or property during the late 1980s – most of us have – but where did that money come from in the first place? Probably profits on earlier property or share deals, or inherited assets like the family home. Thirty years ago you might have expected to inherit little or nothing.

Home ownership has risen from 46.6 per cent in 1966 to 67 per cent in 1992, and an increasing number of people find themselves inheriting property which they don't need for their own use. A recent survey carried out among Nationwide Building Society members revealed that one in twelve customers (8 per cent) received an inheritance in the past five years. But what is so surprising is that the average amount was £33,857. Among the wealthier middle classes the figure could well be dramatically higher.

The value of inheritance is set to grow by 50 per cent in the next 10 years. The Henley Centre for Economic Forecasting estimates that the value of inherited wealth in the UK will rise from 12 billion to 18 billion a year in real terms between now and the end of the decade. Around 60 per cent of legacies will come in the form of cash and investments and the remainder in property.

Henley estimates that three million people will benefit from inheritance over the next 10 years, with the average amount being approximately £40,000. This sounds conservative, given the figures produced by Nationwide, but it is clear that many of us will have considerable sums to invest.

Educating children is almost always a strain on resources, and no doubt some parents will need to use any inherited money to subsidize school fees. But even in the relatively stable area of education there have been changes.

Parents with children at fee-paying schools will be resigned to the financial strain of educating children privately. But any parent who wants a child to go on to further education should now be thinking about how that will be financed.

Grants for higher education have been frozen since 1990, and in any case, only 25 per cent of students qualify for a full grant. Most parents will have to make a significant contribution to their offspring's maintenance. How will you find an estimated £3,000 a year to keep a child at university?

Those people who inherit and are lucky enough to be through the pain of paying for education, will probably use some money to pay off a mortgage or other debts (probably acquired while educating children) and to provide security in retirement.

The past few years have seen a big change here too. Investing in pensions is no longer a simple business. The advent of Personal Equity Plans (PEPs) and the earnings cap on the amount of money which can be put into a personal pension have altered our view of retirement provision.

If the Maxwell scandal has served any useful purpose, it is to make us all more aware of the huge sums of money tied up in occupational pensions – an estimated £320 billion at the time of writing – and the value of these pensions to individual employees. New legislation incorporating a compensation scheme, which will almost certainly follow the publication of the Goode Committee report, should ensure that we have no worries about whether these pensions are actually paid.

However, the spotlight thrown on occupational pensions by the Maxwell affair will inevitably make us more aware of any shortfall in retirement provision. An Additional Voluntary Contribution scheme is probably the answer but how much should you invest to top up your pension and how do you choose one?

The self-employed and those in non-pensionable employment also face a difficult choice. Do you put as much as you can afford into a personal pension, or should you diversify into PEPs?

It is arguable that the tax-free income which can be taken from a PEP is as valuable as the tax relief given on contributions to a personal pension. Both investments roll up tax-free, but the PEP is infinitely more flexible than a pension. For a single person with no dependants it is a difficult decision.

If we are inheriting more and are thus better able to provide for retirement, it follows that more of us will need to take avoiding action if we are not to pass a large proportion of our wealth to the tax man rather than our children and grand-children. Straight life cover is usually the answer, and the younger you are when you buy, the cheaper it is.

Changes here make the decision more complicated too. In the past you bought convertible term insurance or whole life insurance for a fixed sum and paid a level premium throughout the term of the policy. Today an increasing number of policies offer a range of options (you can usually increase the cover, which is useful) but the premium varies to reflect your age and the mortality risk. There are also 'hybrid' policies offering a range of savings and life-cover options. Are they good value?

Independent taxation, while almost universally welcomed – disgruntled husbands no longer have to pay tax on a wife's investment income, while women of an independent nature no longer have to reveal details of their finances to their husbands – complicates tax and estate planning. The mathematical gymnastics necessary to ensure that full advantage is taken of a non-working wife's personal tax allowance have kept many of us occupied on a long winter evening.

We all know the problem. If money in the building society is earning 7 per cent gross, how much should be transferred into a wife's account to ensure that her income does not exceed the 1993–94 personal tax allowance of £3,445? And what is the answer when rates are changing, as they inevitably do?

The difficulty most people have with investment and financial planning is one of identification; the big financial institutions think in terms of products (life assurance, pensions, PEPs, unit trusts, bonds), while most ordinary people think in terms of financial problems. We have to provide a home, pay school fees, save for a daughter's wedding, deal with divorce, invest for retirement and prevent the tax man from slicing off a large chunk of our hard-earned income and capital.

Never before in recent history has the investment scene appeared so uncertain, and rarely has planning for future financial requirements been so challenging or complex.

This book aims to deal with problems in the order they are likely to confront you – raising a mortgage, providing for dependants, putting money away for school fees, or investing for retirement – with specialist chapters on the products available, and how they can be used to solve your particular problem.

1

THE FAMILY HOME

The last few years have witnessed an upheaval in the housing market, the like of which has not been seen since the Second World War. House prices have crashed by as much as 40 per cent in London and the southeast, 30 per cent elsewhere, and all our long-held notions about the security of property as an investment and store of wealth have been undermined. The table below shows just how much home-owners have suffered.

But is it all bad? Many economists have long held that too much of the nation's wealth is locked up in domestic property and that this adjustment could have beneficial effects. If people revert to seeing their homes as somewhere pleasant to live, rather than an investment, it is probably a good thing. Cash will be released for investment or expenditure on other things, both of which will give a positive boost to the economy. And

Regional House Prices
Average and percentage change 31 March 1992–31 March 1993

	Price £	Change %
Greater London	86,575	−9.2
Southeast	74,788	−8.8
Southwest	59,750	−8.1
East Anglia	54,522	−6.6
East Midlands	50,659	−5.6
West Midlands	59,599	−6.3
Yorks/Humberside	52,065	−5.6
Northwest	55,711	−6.0
North of England	48,586	−3.6
Wales	50,664	−5.7
Scotland	56,074	0.3
Northern Ireland	38,836	−1.1

Source: Halifax Building Society

you cannot ignore the fact that while falling house prices are depressing for home-owners, they are definitely good news for young people trying to get a foot on the home-owning ladder.

Despite the crash in property values home ownership is still preferred by the majority of householders. A recent survey carried out by the Council of Mortgage Lenders revealed that the underlying demand for owner-occupation has not diminished; some 83 per cent of non-owners hoped to buy within 10 years, and 76 per cent wanted their own home within two years. Nearly seven out of ten families in the UK own their own home and the proportion is still growing.

Negative Equity

The fall in property values has produced some unique problems. An estimated 1.5 million home-buyers have mortgages which are larger than the value of their property, which has led to the unfortunate buzz phrase 'negative equity' entering our vocabulary. However, the fall in mortgage rates has meant that if you find yourself in this situation, or have a son or daughter caught in the negative equity trap, it is now possible to do something about it.

For example, in 1990 when the mortgage rate hit 15.4 per cent, the monthly interest charge on a £100,000 loan, after tax relief, worked out at £1,187. There would have been life or pension premiums on top of that. With the mortgage rate now practically halved, roughly the same monthly outlay would cover the payments on a 10-year straight repayment loan. For example, at a mortgage rate of 7.99 per cent, the monthly payments on a 10-year repayment mortgage work out at £1,209 – just £22 a month more than the loan interest was costing in 1990. In addition, those still in work have probably seen salary increases of 7 per cent or more, while inflation has fallen to under 2 per cent (as at April 1993).

An alternative method of reducing your mortgage debt is to save regularly in something like a building society high-interest account and to pay off a lump sum of the mortgage once a year. The ready availability of fixed-rate mortgages of anything from one to ten years makes it possible to lock into current low rates to ensure that the loan can be repaid or reduced within a planned timescale.

Taking Advantage of the Situation

But while buyers in trouble hit the headlines, the fact remains that, of 15.5 million home-owners, over 5.6 million have no mortgage at all, and of the 10 million owner-occupiers who are still paying for their homes, the average loan outstanding is around £32,500.

With the price of the average property standing at £65,000 or thereabouts (more in London and the southeast), most families clearly have a considerable amount of equity in their homes and are almost certainly showing a profit on the price paid.

If you are thinking of moving house, now is a good time to do it. You probably won't make as much profit on your existing property as you expected, but if you are trading up to a more expensive house, the amount you save on the new property will be greater.

Perhaps the mistake we have all made is in regarding our homes as a profit centre. We have become used to the idea that we are building a store of wealth which can be called upon to help pay for unexpected items like private medical care or longer-term expenditure on school fees. This will have to change. Ever-rising prices are a thing of the past and home-owners must face reality. House prices will probably never recover to the level hit in the boom years of 1987–88 in the foreseeable future. But there is still money to be saved if you have a mortgage, and many ways in which the equity in your property can be accessed.

The positive aspect of the late 1980s' house price explosion is that there has never been such a wide variety of mortgage offers available – and interest rates are now at their lowest level since the mid-1960s. The table below shows just how low interest rates are historically.

What is immediately apparent from the table is how relatively stable mortgage rates were during the 1960s and early 1970s. From 1963 to 1973 the mortgage rate rose from 6.0 per cent to 9.5 per cent, but there were only six changes during that 10-year period. By comparison there have been 25 changes in the past decade, and the mortgage rate has fluctuated wildly from 11.25 per cent in 1983 to 15.4 per cent in 1988 and back down to 7.99 per cent in early 1993. No wonder the experts are advising home-buyers to opt for capped or fixed-rate mortgages.

Mortgage Rate Changes, 1963–93

Date of Change	Rate (%)
February 1963	6.0
February 1965	7.125
May 1968	7.625
April 1969	8.5
November 1971	8.0
September 1972	8.5
April 1973	9.5
August 1973	10.0
September 1973	11.0
April 1976	10.5
October 1976	12.25
April 1977	11.25
June 1977	10.5
September 1977	9.5
January 1978	8.5
June 1978	9.75
November 1978	11.75
July 1979	12.5
November 1979	15.0
December 1980	14.0
March 1981	13.0
October 1981	15.0
March 1982	13.5
August 1982	12.0
November 1982	10.0
June 1983	11.25
March 1984	10.25
July 1984	12.5
November 1984	11.785
January 1985	12.75
March 1985	13.75
August 1985	12.75
March 1986	12.0
June 1986	11.0
November 1986	12.25
May 1987	11.25
January 1988	10.0
May 1988	9.5
August 1988	11.5
October 1988	12.75
January 1989	13.5
February 1990	14.5
April 1990	15.4
October 1990	14.5
February 1991	13.75
May 1991	12.45
July 1991	11.95
September 1991	11.5
January 1992	10.95
May 1992	10.65
October 1992	9.29
November 1992	8.55
February 1993	7.99

Source: The Council of Mortgage Lenders

A Home for Your Children?

Although there is no doubt that the fall in house prices has been particularly damaging for those who bought in the late 1980s, the news is not all bad. Before house prices really started to escalate, parents with children at university could often finance their offspring's further education by buying a house for their son or daughter. The student child would generate income by having fellow students share the cost.

As a parent, you could even get tax relief if you paid your parental contribution to the student's maintenance through a Deed of Covenant. This has now been abolished, but the large fall in property prices has made it possible once again to finance a child's further education by buying.

The income of most middle-class parents will probably preclude the child from getting much, if any, grant, and, in any case, this has been frozen since 1990 at a maximum of £2,845 for students in London, £2,265 elsewhere. If joint parental income totals £31,000 or more (as at 1992–93) the grant is wiped out.

The full cost of maintaining a child in higher education is probably around £4,000 a year. This would probably be sufficient to service a 90 per cent mortgage on a house in many university towns. For example, £50,000 would buy a two- or three-bedroomed terraced house in many Midlands or northern cities.

The annual cost of a £45,000 mortgage at, say, 8 per cent fixed for three years works out at £3,756 – less than the annual cost of financing your offspring's university career.

Your student child can obtain income by letting rooms to friends. (The current going rate is about £25 to £35 a week.) In addition it is now possible to receive the first £3,250 a year of income from lodgers tax-free. This should enable your offspring to take over the mortgage, on an existing property, or a new one if he or she needs to move when starting work.

While your child is still a student you will, of course, have to guarantee the mortgage, and the property should be bought in joint names so that the mortgage qualifies for mortgage interest relief.

The same situation applies if you simply want to help out a child who has insufficient earnings to purchase on his or her own. You will have to put down the deposit, guarantee the mortgage, and the property will need to be purchased in joint names to obtain tax relief.

Some lenders, notably the Woolwich, have formal schemes whereby parents can use the security in their own homes to guarantee part of a loan on their child's property, which enables younger buyers with negative equity to move home. Check whether your lender operates a similar scheme.

Changes in the Mortgage Market

The massive rise in house prices during the 1980s, followed by the sudden readjustment, has produced a number of changes in what had previously been a dull mortgage market. The high street banks are now a major force accounting for around 30 per cent of all new mortgages, and for a while centralized lenders were taking a substantial slice of lending business.

But the property collapse precipitated by the rise in mortgage rates from 9.8 per cent in 1988 to 15.4 per cent in 1990 resulted in record repossessions. In 1980 repossessions stood at 3,480, but in 1991 they had risen to 75,540 and were still high at 69,000 in 1992. The upshot has been a massive retraction in the market and a clamp-down by mortgage lenders and their mortgage indemnity guarantors who have to bear the brunt of the losses. Lenders have had their fingers burnt and are much more cautious.

From the home-buyer's point of view this means that lenders are demanding higher deposits – 100 per cent loans are a thing of the past. And the cost of mortgage indemnity premiums has risen, from a maximum of around 4.5 per cent (of the amount borrowed over 75 per cent of the purchase price) to around 7.5 per cent or more. This means that a purchaser wanting a 95 per cent loan on a £100,000 property (probably the maximum percentage available) has seen the mortgage indemnity premium rise from £900 to a hefty £1,500. Add to this stamp duty of £1,000, an arrangement fee of around £150 to £250 which most lenders demand for 'special offers' such as fixed, capped or discounted loans, plus life assurance, pensions or general insurance that is often a condition of the loan, and buying a house is now an expensive business.

First-time buyers have been particularly hard hit, with lenders being very cautious – some demanding deposits of 10 per cent and making valuations well below the asking price. This effectively prevents many first-time buyers from entering the market. If the borrower puts up a deposit of £2,500 on a £50,000 property which is subsequently valued by the building society at £45,000, the extra cash of £4,750 required to complete the purchase is usually beyond the means of most first-time buyers.

Other home-buyers may encounter difficulties too. Remortgaging a recently purchased property to obtain a better interest rate has been priced out of the market for most. The combination of falling house prices, increased indemnity premiums and early repayment penalties makes it uneconomic for a large proportion of home-buyers. For example, a buyer who originally had a 70 per cent home loan on a £100,000 property may find when remortgaging that the property's value has fallen to £80,000, resulting in a mortgage of 87 per cent. Remortgaging will involve a large indemnity guarantee premium – probably £750 – plus legal, valuation and arrangement fees, even if there are no early repayment penalties on the existing loan.

It is worth adding a warning here about mortgage indemnity guarantees. First-time buyers contemplating purchasing with a high percentage loan should be aware that if they default on the loan and the property is repossessed and sold for insufficient to cover the loan, they cannot just walk away from the debt. Although the home-buyer pays the mortgage indemnity premium, the lender claims the benefits from the insurance company, and the borrower can and will be pursued by the insurance company for any losses.

Further Advances

Gone too are the days when you could use the equity in your home to speculate in shares. During the 1980s' privatization programme, many further advances were made to home-buyers wanting to stag an issue, but not today. However, it should still be possible to release some of the equity in your property to pay personal pension premiums, as most banks and building societies are hungry for the commissions.

Further advances for home improvements are still freely available, but few lenders are willing to let you have more than 70 per cent of the property's value, taking into account any existing loan.

To Pay Off or Not to Pay Off?

High interest rates over the past three years and falling house prices coupled with uncertainty over unemployment have made home-buyers very conscious of the cost of borrowing. Increasingly, people in their forties and fifties are inheriting lump sums from parents, which gives them the option of repaying all or part of their mortgage.

Mortgage interest tax relief on the first £30,000 of your loan makes this the cheapest form of borrowing. For the basic-rate taxpayer it is, therefore, generally profitable not to pay off the last £30,000 of your home loan because the money can usually be invested at a profit on the net cost of borrowing. However, the margin is small – usually less than 1 per cent after tax – and if you prefer the peace of mind of having no borrowings at all, you should repay your loan in full. But do bear in mind the flexibility that keeping that last £30,000 in the bank gives you. In an unexpected emergency you will not have to worry about where you can lay your hands on some instant cash.

For a higher-rate taxpayer the situation is different. Higher-rate mortgage interest relief was abolished in 1991, so it is difficult for those paying tax at 40 per cent to find an investment which shows a profit over the net cost of borrowing – but not impossible. It is worth looking at Business Expansion Scheme (BES) investments which give higher-rate tax relief on up to £40,000 of investment. Something like an assured tenancy, guaranteed exit is not a high risk and can even be backed by a bank guarantee (see Chapter 6).

If you are self-employed you could put £30,000 into a personal pension (provided you have sufficient unused tax relief), rather than use it to pay off the loan. Tax relief on the premiums make this a better investment than paying off the loan in full.

Using the Family Home as Security

Generally speaking, it is a dangerous tactic to remortgage or take out a second loan on the family home in order to finance a business. Any bank manager will tell you that if the business gets into difficulties and the loan is called, you not only lose your livelihood but also your home and often your marriage too.

Having said that, if you have no other assets and are keen to set up a business, there is virtually no alternative. This kind of financing is carried out almost exclusively by the banks and they will insist on a charge on your property before they will lend. You should pay around 2.5 to 3.0 per cent over bank base rate for this type of borrowing – more if it is a second mortgage.

Using the equity in your home to finance expenditure on things like school fees is less risky because the outgoings are quantifiable and are spread over a clearly defined period. If you have no mortgage, or a small loan in proportion to the value of the property, many lenders will make an advance for this purpose. Your existing lender is probably the best place to start, as the charges associated with taking out a further advance will be less than for a complete remortgage for a larger amount with a different lender, unless of course you can obtain a significantly lower interest rate. You will pay a valuation fee of around £195 on a £150,000 house (the table below shows typical lender's charges for valuation), but if you take a further advance with your existing lender, there should be no other charges.

A new lender will need to check title to the property and there will be the usual legal fees associated with a new mortgage, plus valuation fees and possibly an arrangement fee of anything up to £250.

If you are borrowing to finance school fees, the difficulty is

Cost of Valuation

Purchase price not exceeding £	Fee £
50,000	125
100,000	165
150,000	195
200,000	225
250,000	255
300,000	285
350,000	315
400,000	345
450,000	375
500,000	405
Exceeding 500,000	by arrangement

Source: Halifax Building Society

that most lenders want you to draw down the loan in full from day one, even though the school fees fall due termly over a 5- to 13-year period. Interest charges will be high if you are forced to take the loan in full immediately. School fees specialists can usually recommend a lender prepared to allow you to draw down the cash as needed.

Home improvement loans are a standard product available from most lenders. Here, again, if you have a mortgage, approaching your existing lender will almost certainly be the cheapest route. (Note that tax relief on home improvement loans was abolished in 1988.)

Whatever the purpose of a further advance – whether to finance a business, pay school fees, undertake home improvements or other major expenditure – the maximum you can borrow is usually up to 70 per cent of the value of the property, including any existing mortgage, provided you have sufficient income to service the debt.

Your Home and Inheritance Tax (IHT)

In spite of recent falls in house prices, the family home is likely to be the most valuable asset you will have to leave to your partner, children or grandchildren.

For obvious reasons, most people leave their home to their spouse, in which case there will be no Inheritance Tax payable. All transfers between husbands and wives are free from IHT (assuming they are both domiciled in the UK), but transfers between unmarried couples living together are not.

But when your spouse dies, IHT could become payable under certain circumstances. If the property is worth less than £150,000 (as at 1993–94) and there are no other assets, there will be nothing to pay. If the property is worth more than £150,000 and there are other assets, any excess of the estate over £150,000 will be charged to Inheritance Tax at 40 per cent.

You cannot avoid IHT on the family home by giving it away to your children or grandchildren if you continue to live in it. This is called a 'gift with reservation' and does not escape Inheritance Tax. (See Chapter 7 for full details on Inheritance Tax and ways of avoiding it.)

An Income From Your Property

Many home-owners, particularly the elderly, have large sums locked up in their homes and often little income. There are a number of schemes on the market which combine a loan, secured against the property, and an annuity, which increase spendable income. The loan is repaid when the owner dies and the property is sold.

Since the 1992–93 tax year it has also been possible to earn up to £3,250 tax-free from letting rooms to lodgers (provided the house is your principal private residence). This is worth considering too if you need extra income at any stage.

Some home-buyers who have been unable to sell have bought a new property and let out their existing one. Under the new assured tenancy rules you should have no problems obtaining repossession of your property, provided the tenancy is for a minimum of six months. (You will need to consult your solicitor or the letting agent about a proper lease.) All the mortgage interest paid on the tenanted property becomes eligible for tax relief against the rental income. You must obtain permission to do this from your lender, who may charge you a higher rate of interest, and you will need to check on insurance too.

What Mortgage?

Whether you are buying for the first time, remortgaging, or moving house, there has never been such a wide variety of financing schemes on offer.

First-Time Buyers

Nobody buying for the first time need pay the quoted mortgage rate – currently 7.99 per cent. Discounts of up to 2 per cent are available from all lenders and at least 1 per cent is the norm. *Blay's Mortgage Guide* (available from Blay's Guides Ltd, Blay's House, Churchfield Road, Chalfont St Peter, Bucks SL9 9EW; tel. 0753 880482) monitors all lenders, and the terms and conditions of loans, including discounts. The guide is a good way of finding out the best deals. A copy should be available at your local public library.

Shop around among the lenders or consult a mortgage broker.

He should be prepared to act for a negotiable fee of around 1 per cent of the mortgage, or if you take out associated life or pensions policies, he should act for the commission earned on these products. The maximum percentage loan is currently 95 per cent, and with some borrowers, like the self-employed, less.

All Borrowers

The range of mortgage products now available is daunting, and it is important to understand how the different schemes work. Gone are the days when you had only a simple repayment, endowment or pension-linked loan to choose from.

In addition, the process has been complicated by the requirements of the 1986 Financial Services Act. Most of the large lenders, with the notable exception of the Bradford & Bingley Building Society, are 'tied' to an insurance company and can sell only that company's products. You are no longer offered a choice of policies.

Conditional Lending

Increased competition between the lenders has led to 'bargain offers', with discounts of up to 2 per cent for first-time buyers and larger-than-average borrowers. But nothing is for nothing. The lenders now carry out up to 80 per cent of their business on special packages offering fixed rates, discounts and other bonuses, but they all require you to take out associated life or pension policies, or buildings and contents insurance. These 'bargain' packages can turn out to be expensive, particularly if the lender is tied, as most are, to one insurance company.

The associated life or pension policies may be very poor value for money and you should take advice before signing up. The Office of Fair Trading is supposed to be monitoring 'conditional lending', and it is probably time it had a closer look. Over 50 per cent of all home loans are granted to existing home-owners, most of whom will be precluded from taking advantage of 'special offers' if life assurance is a pre-requisite of obtaining the loan. They will probably already have sufficient life cover.

Whether or not it is part of a package, all lenders will try to sell you life, pensions, or buildings and contents insurance with the loan. This may or may not be good value, but do not be persuaded to have cover you don't need. A single person with no dependants arguably needs no life cover at all. If you die the property can be sold and the mortgage repaid from the proceeds. The lender, however, prefers you to have life cover, assigned to the bank or building society, because then the lender does not have to wait for the property to be sold to get the money back. They also earn commission on the sale of the policies.

The only life policy that everybody needs is 'convertible-term' (see Chapter 4), which insures your life and your ability to get further life or savings-type policies at a later date when you may not be in good health.

Indeed, now is probably the time to take a fresh look at the old-fashioned repayment mortgage. Many home-buyers are discovering that paying off debt has an appeal in terms of peace of mind and is probably, in a low-inflation era, one of the soundest investments you can make.

Repayment Loans

The straight repayment, usually the cheapest method of paying off a mortgage, is enjoying a revival. Buyers who have seen the ghastly effects of 'negative equity' are keen to make sure that their loan is repaid. For the uninitiated, each monthly payment on a repayment mortgage consists of part repayment of capital and part interest. At the end of the agreed term the loan is repaid and you own your home outright.

Most repayment loans are sold in conjunction with a mortgage protection insurance policy, which provides a sum of money sufficient to repay the outstanding debt should the borrower die before the term of the loan has expired. It is probably better value in these circumstances to pay a little more and purchase convertible-term insurance (see Chapter 4) because of the flexibility it gives.

Endowment or Pension-Linked Loans

Some 80 per cent or more of all new home loans are now linked to a life or pensions policy. The borrower pays interest only for the term of the loan and a life or personal pension policy runs alongside, maturing at the same time as the loan. The proceeds from the life policy, or the tax-free cash lump sum which can be taken at retirement from a personal pension policy, is used to repay the loan.

There is no longer any tax relief on life policy premiums (except for those taken out before March 1984), but the proceeds are tax-free. To date, all life policies have provided sufficient cash to pay off a mortgage and there has usually been a significant cash surplus.

With falling investment returns and the pressure on life companies' bonus rates, it has never been so important to make sure you choose the right savings policy (see Chapter 6). If you are buying a house now with a 25-year endowment or pension-linked loan, you need to make doubly sure that the policy will provide sufficient cash to pay off your loan on maturity.

Mortgage Comparison*

Monthly cost of a 25-year £50,000 mortgage for a single man aged 28 next birthday, net of basic-rate tax relief. Mortgage rate 7.99%.

	Repayment £	Endowment £	Pension† £
Interest	337.99	282.98	282.98
Life/pension premium	5.06	163.00** 81.17††	113.33 gross
Total estimated residual benefits after repayment of loan	None	131,000** 39,300††	1350pm

Monthly cost of a 10-year £50,000 mortgage for a married man aged 50, net of basic-rate tax relief. Mortgage rate 7.99%.

	Repayment £	Endowment £	Pension £
Interest	554.41	282.98	282.98
Life/pension premium	16.33	460.00** 344.83††	860.00 gross
Total estimated residual benefits after repayment of loan	None	34,300** 12,400††	1480pm

* Figures from Equitable Life.
† The figure for the pension loan is a combined life and pensions premium. Residual benefits are estimated after repayment of the £50,000 loan and assume an investment return over the 10-year period of 10.5 per cent on the life policy, 13 per cent on the personal pension.
** With-profits endowment policy.
†† Low-cost endowment.

Personal pension policies attract tax relief at your highest rate paid on the premiums (see Chapter 5), and up to one quarter of the accumulated cash can be taken at retirement. This is used to repay the mortgage, and the balance provides a pension. The table above gives an example of the relative costs of the three types of mortgage.

In the late 1980s an increasing proportion of lenders were prepared to consider interest-only loans and leave it up to the borrower to decide how the loan was repaid. Others accepted unit or investment trust regular savings schemes or PEPs as the vehicle for repaying a loan. Although some lenders still accept this type of arrangement (most notably the Cheltenham & Gloucester Building Socicty), it is now more difficult to negotiate and is generally only on offer to those who need to borrow less than 70 per cent of the purchase price.

Fixed-rate Mortgages

Perhaps the biggest single innovation in the mortgage market in recent years has been the introduction of fixed-rate loans. Recent statistics show that nearly 30 per cent of mortgages taken out by previous owner-occupiers (in other words, not first-time buyers) are at fixed rates. And it makes good sense to do so.

Interest rates are at their lowest for 15 years (see table on page 10), and to lock into monthly payments at these historically low levels should save you a considerable amount of money, as well as offering peace of mind.

With a fixed-rate loan (not to be confused with the dangerous fixed-repayment mortgage), the interest charge or repayments are fixed for an agreed period, generally anything from one to ten years.

The main drawback to fixed-rate loans is that if you fix at an agreed rate, say 9 per cent for three years, and there are further cuts in home loan rates, you are out of pocket on the deal. But, of course, the reverse is also true. In today's environment, when interest rates are historically very low, the certainty of such an arrangement and its accompanying peace of mind probably outweigh the limited prospect of being seriously out of pocket.

You should also be aware of the inevitable 'early redemption' penalty – usually three to six months' interest – if you repay the loan within the fixed-rate period. Take this into account if you opt for one of the longer-term fixed-rate mortgages. However, this is not usually a problem. Most fixed-rate mortgages are transferrable and can be taken to a new property, but you will have to pay the penalty if you lock yourself into a fixed rate that subsequently looks expensive and you want to remortgage and switch to a variable rate, or a lower fixed rate.

With Britain having devalued out of the European Exchange Rate Mechanism (ERM), interest rates have probably bottomed out, so higher inflation, and sooner or later higher interest rates, are on the way – if not in 1993, then in 1994. Now is a good time to fix.

If you do decide on a fixed-rate mortgage, it is probably worthwhile consulting a reputable mortgage broker, as he monitors the entire market and will know which lender has the most attractive package. Most fixed-rate loans require you to take out associated insurances, and you will need advice on this too.

Fixed-Repayment Loans and Deferred-Interest Loans

These should not be confused with fixed-rate loans, where the interest charge is fixed for an agreed term.

With a fixed-repayment loan you can choose the level of monthly payments and these will remain fixed for an agreed period, usually three to five years. The interest charge will continue to vary, and if your agreed monthly payment is not sufficient to cover this, the unpaid interest will be rolled up and added to the outstanding debt.

For example, in 1988 you could have taken out a fixed-repayment loan when the mortgage rate stood at 9.8 per cent, only to see it shoot to 15.4 per cent within two years. Clearly, the debt will increase substantially if 5.6 per cent of the annual interest charge is not being paid.

Fixed-repayment loans have been particularly dangerous for home-buyers in recent years when interest rates have shot up and house prices have fallen. Many borrowers with fixed-repayment loans now have mortgages larger than the value of their property. This type of loan should generally be avoided.

Deferred-interest loans are a variation on the same theme. Instead of agreeing a fixed monthly repayment, you defer part of the interest charge – typically 3 per cent in the first year, 2 per cent in the second and 1 per cent in the third. The unpaid interest is rolled up and added to your debt in the third year.

There is the added drawback with both fixed-repayment and deferred-interest schemes that you are not granted Mortgage Interest Relief at Source (MIRAS). As you are not paying all the interest, you have to claim tax relief at the end of the year when the amount of interest you have actually paid is known.

Cap and Collar Loan

If you can get it, a variable-rate capped mortgage is generally the best type of loan around. It has the advantage of putting a 'cap' or maximum on the amount of interest you pay, while giving you the benefits of any interest rate cuts. If there is also a minimum interest rate written into the agreement, it is known as a 'cap and collar' loan.

For example, at the time of writing, when the variable rate mortgage is 7.99 per cent, you might be offered a cap and collar loan with a 9.5 per cent cap and a 7 per cent collar. Capped or cap-and-collar loans are mostly available only through mortgage brokers, and there is often a limited tranche of funds which gets snapped up quickly.

Currency Loans

It is possible to borrow in a foreign currency to finance house purchase, although the minimum is fairly high at £100,000. The advantage is that when interest rates in the UK are high, it is possible to borrow in other currencies more cheaply. In addition, if the pound strengthens against the currency in which you have borrowed, your outstanding debt is reduced. Of course, the reverse is also true – if the pound weakens your debt will increase.

If you can live with this extra risk without having sleepless nights, then a currency loan could be a profitable alternative. Probably the best type to go for is a managed loan where a money market professional selects the currency in which you borrow and switches your money to protect both capital and interest payments. Others offer the facility to be automatically switched back into sterling should the currency in which you have borrowed move more than a pre-agreed amount against you (usually 5 per cent). Here, again, currency loans are only available through brokers.

How Much Can I Borrow?

Back in the heady boom years of the late 1980s, loans of three and a half times gross earnings, plus your partner's earnings, were not uncommon. A couple with earnings of £50,000 and £25,000 a year respectively could probably have borrowed up to £200,000. Not any more.

Lenders have had their fingers burned with record repossessions and arrears, and they are now much more conservative. They are also well aware of the fragility of the employment market and are keen to encourage home-buyers to be cautious. The maximum loan today would probably be in the range of two and a half times the higher earner's income, plus the lower income.

Lenders are also much tougher now about seeing proof of earnings and generally disregard overtime and commission unless it is guaranteed. They also take up references, which was practically unheard of in the late 1980s.

The self-employed or small business home-buyer has a particularly tough time. Non-status loans, where you verify that the mortgage repayments are within your means, are a thing of the past. Most lenders will now insist on three years' audited accounts, unless the loan you need is a small proportion of the purchase price, say, 30 to 50 per cent.

What Will it Cost?

This is not a silly question; even relatively sophisticated borrowers can be ignorant of the monthly cost of repaying a loan. The following table shows the cost of each £1,000 borrowed at varying interest rates.

The term of the loan will also have a huge effect on monthly payments. Most tables assume that everyone is a first-time buyer wanting a 25-year loan, but over half of all mortgages granted are to previous owner-occupiers. Most lenders will expect the loan to be repaid at normal retirement age, so a borrower of 45 will probably be offered a 15- or 20-year loan at most. This is no great problem. In the days when fast-rising

Mortgage Cost Per Month for Each £1,000 Borrowed Over 10 and 25 Years

Interest rate %	With 25% tax relief		Without tax relief	
	25 yrs	10 yrs	25 yrs	10 yrs
6.0	5.62	10.54	6.52	11.33
6.25	5.74	10.64	6.68	11.46
6.5	5.86	10.72	6.84	11.60
6.75	5.95	10.82	7.00	11.73
7.0	6.07	10.93	7.16	11.87
7.25	6.19	11.03	7.32	12.01
7.5	6.31	11.11	7.48	12.15
7.75	6.40	11.22	7.65	12.28
8.0	6.52	11.33	7.81	12.42
8.25	6.65	11.43	7.98	12.56
8.5	6.74	11.52	8.15	12.71
8.75	6.87	11.62	8.32	12.85
9.0	7.00	11.73	8.49	12.99
9.25	7.12	11.84	8.66	13.13
9.5	7.25	11.92	8.83	13.28
9.75	7.35	12.03	9.01	13.42
10.00	7.45	12.15	9.19	13.57
10.25	7.61	12.23	9.36	13.71
10.5	7.71	12.34	9.54	13.86
10.75	7.84	12.45	9.72	14.01
11.0	7.98	12.56	9.90	14.16
11.25	8.11	12.68	10.08	14.30
11.5	8.22	12.76	10.26	14.45
11.75	8.35	12.88	10.45	14.60
12.0	8.49	12.99	10.63	14.75
12.25	8.63	13.08	10.81	14.90
12.5	8.77	13.19	11.00	15.06
12.75	8.87	13.31	11.19	15.21
13.0	9.01	13.42	11.37	15.36
13.25	9.15	13.54	11.56	15.52
13.5	9.26	13.63	11.75	15.67
13.75	9.40	13.74	11.94	15.83
14.0	9.54	13.86	12.13	15.98
14.25	9.68	13.95	12.32	16.14
14.5	9.83	14.07	12.51	16.29
14.75	9.94	14.18	12.70	16.45
15.0	10.08	14.30	12.90	16.61
15.25	10.23	14.42	13.09	16.77
15.5	10.34	14.51	13.28	16.93
15.75	10.48	14.63	13.48	17.09
16.0	10.63	14.75	13.67	17.25

Source: The Building Societies Association

house prices produced profits that more than compensated for the cost of borrowing, a long-term loan was a good idea.

In today's market where house prices are, at best, static, and in some areas still falling, you have to look at the total cost of borrowing. A £100,000 loan over 25 years, even at today's low rate of 7.99 per cent, costs £184,750 in interest charges alone, and you have the endowment or pension premiums on top which work out at another £40,000 or so, depending on age. By comparison, the cost of a 7.99 per cent 10-year repayment loan for the same £100,000 totals £145,116.

Of course, the monthly payments on a 10-year repayment loan at 7.99 per cent are considerably higher at £1,209.30 than on a 25-year endowment, which works out at around £615 a month in interest charges and £140 for the endowment premium – a total of £755. And this is what swings the balance for most people.

Tax and Your Home

You are entitled to 25 per cent tax relief on the interest on the first £30,000 of a loan used to finance the purchase of your principal private residence (falling to 20 per cent from 6 April 1994). There are special arrangements if you are moving house and require a bridging loan, whereby you are entitled to tax relief on both loans for up to one year, longer by concession.

If you have more than one home you can nominate which loan on which property will attract the mortgage interest relief. This also has Capital Gains Tax implications. Any profits made on the sale of your principal private residence are free from CGT (although profits on second homes are not). It is possible to switch your principal private residence to minimize CGT, but you will need to take advice from your accountant before doing so. The Inland Revenue has been known to challenge the claim to exemption if the property nominated is clearly a holiday home.

If you buy a property to let, all the interest paid will be relievable against the rental income provided the property is available for rent for at least 26 weeks of the year.

Since 1983 mortgage interest tax relief has been granted at source under MIRAS, and you make repayments to the lender net of basic-rate tax. (Higher-rate tax relief on mortgage interest was abolished in 1991.) There are a few exceptions, most notably if the loan is a deferred-interest scheme, in which case mortgage repayments will generally be paid gross and tax relief claimed at the end of the tax year.

The majority of lenders use the constant net repayment method of calculating mortgage interest relief. This means that tax relief on the interest, up to the maximum of £30,000 of loan, is evened out over the term of the mortgage and monthly repayments remain constant.

The alternative method of granting tax relief under MIRAS is 'annually reviewed' where the tax relief is higher at the beginning but declines over the term of the mortgage as the capital is gradually repaid and a lesser amount of each monthly payment represents interest.

2

MARRIAGE AND DIVORCE

Marriage, like measles, is something that happens to most people. In spite of the rising incidence of cohabitation, a high proportion of couples eventually marry – if not the partner with whom they have been living, then someone else.

Estimates from the Office of Population Censuses and Surveys reveal that 93 per cent of 50-year-old men have been married at least once, as have 95 per cent of women. And more men than women remarry. For every 1,000 men who become widowers or divorced, around half remarry, while only 20 per cent of widowed or divorced women take the plunge again. You can draw your own conclusions from these statistics.

But marriage is not what it used to be. In 1990 a total of 331,150 couples married, but there were also 153,000 divorces. Women no longer regard marriage as a safe career, and this inevitably affects their attitude towards jobs, children and money. In addition, thanks to higher standards of living and often two incomes, both partners probably expect more of marriage, so disillusionment more rapidly leads to divorce than in the days when a women were financially dependent.

Whether or not this is a good or bad thing will depend on your point of view. Anyone marrying now, however, should be aware that he or she has little better than a 50–50 chance of remaining married.

Marriage – Look Before You Leap

Once you marry you confront a different set of financial and investment problems. In recent years the trend has been for women to remain working for quite a while before having children, although many return to employment after the children are born.

Independent taxation has acknowledged the increasingly important economic and financial role women play in society. Among younger couples, few would be able to afford to buy a house unless the woman was prepared to work. At the opposite end of the age spectrum, many women end up owning everything, simply because they live longer than men. Over the coming decade an estimated £6.7 billion will be inherited in the UK, with over half of it managed by women.

But whether your financial relationship with your spouse is one of dependence or independence, you have to be prepared to sit down and discuss your finances and investments if you are to make proper provision for the future. The husband who deals totally with all the family's financial affairs and leaves his wife in the dark may still exist, but in real life few couples conform to this outdated picture. Education and efficient contraception, which have allowed women to plan careers *and* families, have played an enormous part in this social revolution.

In the legal, medical and accountancy professions 50 per cent of those qualifying are women. In fact, the number of women becoming accountants has doubled in the past decade alone, and more than 40 per cent of the total UK workforce are women. Over half the total working female population of 23 million now works either full-time or part-time.

Of the 331,150 couples who married in 1990 (the latest up-to-date figures available), 67,013 were couples where one partner had been married before, and for 55,094 couples it was a second or subsequent marriage for both partners. It is hardly surprising, therefore, that couples of all ages are tending to be more practical in their approach to money and marriage. A man marrying for the second time may well be saddled with maintenance payments to a former wife, and therefore much more dependent on his second wife's earning capacity.

A recent survey revealed that around 10 per cent of married working women earn more than their husbands, and of women executives working for major companies, four in ten earn more than their partner.

A woman remarrying, whether working or not, is probably concerned to ensure that any assets she brings to the marriage are passed on to her children, not necessarily to the new spouse and/or his children.

Prenuptial Agreements

Modern attitudes to marriage have produced new problems and new solutions. Prenuptial agreements can be entered into and do exist, but as yet none have been tested in British courts. Lawyers who specialize in matrimonial work say that the likely outcome on divorce would be that the judge would take account of any prenuptial agreement and the parties' intentions when they signed it, but not necessarily feel bound by it. The reason for this is that circumstances can change dramatically during the course of a marriage, and there is always the possibility that one partner signed under duress.

However, in France for example, prenuptial agreements are commonplace. You either marry and share everything equally, or you agree before you marry on how the assets should be split on divorce. Indeed, the French marriage of Mick Jagger to his first wife Bianca got off to a stormy start because she wanted, not surprisingly, to share the assets equally, but Mick wanted a pre-agreed settlement.

While it is not very romantic when contemplating marriage to be concerned about how assets will be divided on divorce, any sensible couple will bear this in mind. It is particularly important to do so when there are considerable assets on one or both sides, and when children are involved. A trust partner at one leading firm of chartered accountants recommends an Asset Protection Trust, which is designed to benefit certain beneficiaries and place assets beyond the reach of all other potential claimants (including creditors in the case of bankruptcy). If you are interested in setting up such a trust (on marriage or for any other purpose), you can contact the Society of Trust and Estate Practitioners, (c/o George Tasher, 42 Princes Boulevard, Bebington, Wirral L63 5LW; tel: 051–645 6801). The society can recommend a solicitor and accountant in your area who specializes in this field.

Similarly, if you decide to enter into a prenuptial agreement (or need to negotiate a divorce), the Solicitor's Family Law Association (PO Box 302, Keston, Kent BR2 6EZ; tel: 0689 850227), can recommend a specialist matrimonial lawyer who has experience of these situations.

Contrary to what solicitors will tell you, not all lawyers are conversant with the details of divorce, let alone prenuptial agreements. Just as you wouldn't go to an ear, nose and throat surgeon to have open heart surgery, don't go to a solicitor specializing in property law if you have marital problems.

You cannot insure against divorce, but sorting out your finances before you take the plunge will probably give you a better chance of making a success of the relationship than just blindly hoping for the best.

The Matrimonial or Shared Home

Some 67 per cent of all homes are purchased by couples (not necessarily married) in joint names. The vast majority of these couples will be 'joint tenants' so that on the death of one partner the house belongs outright to the surviving partner (see Chapters 1 and 7 for full details).

If there are children from a former marriage or other friends or relatives you want to benefit, you may decide to own the property as 'tenants in common', in which case your share can be willed to the beneficiaries of your choice and does not revert to your partner on death.

By making a Declaration of Trust you can decide in what proportions you will both own the house. Bear in mind, however, that this may result in the house having to be sold on your death.

Couples who cohabit should be aware that if the property is held in one partner's name only, the other partner can still acquire an interest in it – particularly if they have contributed to the mortgage payments or paid all the household bills.

If both partners to a marriage have property and children, they may decide to keep their properties in their own names and pass them on to their respective offspring – in which case they should be certain to make a will so that their assets are passed on in the way they want.

Life Assurance

It is arguable that if you are single and intend to remain single you need no life assurance. Your assets will be distributed to your next of kin or to those you have made beneficiaries of your will, so there is no need to bother.

However, in the real world most of us get married at some

stage and acquire dependants for whom we want to make provision, in which case we definitely need life assurance. At a later stage we may need life assurance to cover a potential Inheritance Tax liability.

If there is one golden rule with life assurance, it is that the sooner you take out a policy, the better – the younger you are, the cheaper it is.

Life assurance should never be confused with saving, but sadly it often is. This is because in the past there have been tax concessions for saving through the life assurance route (see Chapter 4). Life assurance should be about providing for your dependants in the event that you die or are sick and unable to work.

The best policy (and arguably the only one required) for both single people and married couples is a convertible-term contract which pays out a lump sum on your death, if that occurs within the pre-agreed term. It also gives you the valuable option to convert to a whole life contract (more expensive because it pays out an agreed sum when you die, whenever that might be), or a savings-type policy, without having to prove your good health. In other words, you are insuring your ability to obtain life assurance in the future, no questions asked, at a time when your health might have deteriorated.

With the security of increasable convertible-term insurance, you can use the conversion option to switch to other types of insurance as you need it and when you can afford it. Sadly, because it is such a bargain, some insurance companies have pulled out of this market in recent years or have moved towards contracts where the premiums and the benefits are reviewed every five years or so. Generally speaking, this is not such a good deal as a fixed-premium contract where the option to increase the benefits, and the level of any extra premium, is fixed at the outset.

The first experience most young couples have of being sold life assurance is when they raise a mortgage to buy a house. In most cases you will be offered a mortgage protection policy (if it is a straight repayment loan) which provides enough cash to pay off the mortgage if either partner dies while the loan is still outstanding. The technical term for this is a decreasing-term assurance because the sum assured diminishes as you repay the loan. Endowment or pension-linked loans have term insurance included, which performs a similar function.

However, it is worth paying a little extra for convertible-term assurance taken out separately on both lives. Joint life policies produce complications if the marriage breaks down because the policy is usually discontinued and both partners have to reinsure themselves again when they are older, and the premiums are therefore more expensive. Straight mortgage protection, although it pays off the loan, will almost certainly be inadequate to provide for your dependants.

If you buy convertible-term assurance when you are young, it is cheap. For example a 25-year increasable convertible-term policy for £250,000 for a female aged 25 next birthday costs £21.52 a month. Premiums are higher for single males, but for a married man of 25 the premium is £37.02.

Older couples marrying for the first time later in life may find cover too expensive to purchase. This may not be much of a problem if both partners work or have income, and are either beyond the age of having children, or have no desire to have a family or produce more offspring.

The golden rule is to buy convertible-term insurance – preferably with the option to increase the sum assured – as early as possible, even before you marry. If you marry or remarry later in life when you still have dependants, you may not be able to afford sufficient cover, and there is very little you can do about it at this stage.

With increasable convertible-term insurance, and permanent health insurance – a policy which pays an income if you are unable to work through an accident or illness (up to retirement age if necessary) – you probably won't need any further life assurance.

Be careful when considering 'dread disease' and, generally speaking, all 'hybrid' life policies. Dread disease is very fashionable at the moment and plays on people's fear of certain illnesses. It pays out a lump sum if you are diagnosed as suffering from one of several named illnesses (typically cancer, heart disease, kidney or liver failure and others), but the exclusions are numerous and fate will dictate that the illness which incapacitates you is not one of those for which you are covered. Permanent health insurance which pays out whatever the cause of your disablement is a much better bet.

Similarly, hybrid policies, where you pay a fixed or increasing premium and choose the level of cover required for different types of insurances (whole life, term, permanent health, savings, etc.), are generally more expensive. It is usually cheaper to buy the different types of insurance separately. For full details of all insurances see Chapter 4.

Making a Will

Marriage and divorce invalidate your will, so if you haven't made one, or have become married or divorced since you had one drawn up, you should get another one made.

People who cohabit usually have no rights to their partner's assets unless they have been specifically bequeathed in a will. Married people who die intestate should not assume that everything automatically passes to their spouse on death. The laws of intestacy can leave a surviving partner very badly provided for. For example, if there are children, he or she will receive only the first £75,000 of the estate and a life interest in half the remainder. The rest goes to the children. And, of course, there are Inheritance Tax considerations to take into account.

It is worth mentioning here that on your death a current or former spouse can contest a will from which they are excluded, particularly if they have dependent children from the marriage or are dependent themselves (see Chapter 8 for full details).

Tax

Since April 1990 married couples have been taxed independently and, like single people, both have a personal allowance which can be offset against income. Before that date a wife's income was treated as though it were her husband's income, unless she opted for separate taxation. But even if taxed separately, her investment income was always treated as though it belonged to her husband. This produced considerable bad feeling among women, who didn't necessarily want their husbands to know what income they had, while men were generally not best pleased at having to foot the tax bill for their wife's investment income.

In 1990, after several consultative documents, the rules were changed, and husband and wife are now treated totally independently as taxpayers in their own right with their own personal allowance. There is also a transferable married couple's allowance which goes to the husband first, but if his income is

Personal Allowances

	1992–93 and 1993–94
Personal allowance	£3,445
Married couple's allowance	£1,720
Single parent additional relief	£1,720
Widow's bereavement allowance	£1,720
Blind person's allowance	£1,080
Age allowance:	
single person 65–74	£4,200
75+	£4,370
Married couple 65–74	£2,465
75+	£2,505
Income limit*	£14,200

* Age allowance is reduced by one half of your income above this £14,200 limit. For example, if your taxable income is £15,200, your age allowance is cut back by £500 from £4,200 to £3,700, but not below the normal personal allowance figure of £3,445.

Income Tax Rates

1992–93		1993–94	
Rate	Band*	Rate	Band*
20%	£1–£2,000	20%	£1–£2,000
25%	£2,001–£23,700	25%	£2,001–£23,700
40%	£23,700+	40%	£23,700+

* Taxable income after deduction of all allowances.

Capital Gains Tax

1992–93 and 1993–94

The rate is linked to income tax.

Individual annual exemption*	£5,800
Trusts	£2,900
Retirement relief†	£150,000

Additional retirement relief on the next £450,000 after the age of 55

* Applies to both husband and wife.
† Applies to business assets and shares in a private family company only.

insufficient to take full advantage of this allowance, the balance can be transferred to the wife.

Separate taxation offers several opportunities for investment planning. Where a wife (or husband) has little or no earned income but the couple have investment income, the joint tax bill can be reduced by transferring assets to take advantage of the non-earning partner's tax allowance.

For example, Mr Barker has taxable income of £27,500 and pays tax at 40 per cent on £3,800 of his income. However, his wife does not work and has no income.

Some £10,500 of Mr Barker's income is derived from a portfolio of shares and building society deposits worth roughly £210,000 with an average yield of 5 per cent gross.

If he transfers £76,000 worth of assets into his wife's name she will receive £3,800 a year of income, and he will be removed from the higher-rate tax bracket altogether.

The first £3,445 of Mrs Barker's income will be offset against her personal allowance and will be tax-free, and she will pay tax at only 20 per cent on the next £355. Her total tax bill will be £71 compared with the £1,520 Mr Barker was paying in higher-rate tax on the £3,800 of investment income.

Similar savings can be made on capital gains tax by transferring assets between husband and wife – and there is no liability to CGT or Inheritance Tax on the transfer (see Chapter 7 for Inheritance Tax savings).

If one partner is self-employed or owns a business and the other has no income, tax can also be saved if the non-earning spouse is employed by the earning partner. So long as the salary remains below £54 a week or £2,808 a year (1992–93), neither tax nor National Insurance contributions need be paid. The figures for 1993–94 are £56 a week and £2,912 a year.

A higher salary will incur tax at the basic rate of 25 per cent, but it may still pay to split the earnings between the two partners rather than pay tax at 40 per cent on one larger income. The Revenue will, however, want to be satisfied that the remuneration is in line with the hours worked and type of work done.

There are a host of other ways in which tax can be avoided or saved, but this book is not intended as a comprehensive tax manual. For information on tax saving, see Further Reading on page 244.

Pensions

Marriage will affect your requirement for income in retirement and is a good time to review both pensions and long-term savings. As a single person you may have been happy to contemplate retirement in a garret, or banked on winning the pools, but it is a different kettle of fish once you have dependants.

If you are an employee in a final salary-linked scheme, marriage may not make much difference, but you would still be wise to check.

Most occupational schemes are 'defined benefit' and pay a guaranteed pension, depending on your years of service with the company and your level of pay at retirement age. Typically, you will receive one-sixtieth of final salary for every year of service, so after 40 years with the same firm, you retire on the maximum allowed by the Inland Revenue – two-thirds of final salary.

If you marry, the scheme generally automatically gives you a dependant's pension – usually half the pension you receive if you die after retirement. (The maximum allowable is two-thirds of your pension, i.e. four-ninths of your final salary.) There is no extra charge for this because the cost is shared by all the members of the scheme.

If you die before retirement there is usually a lump-sum payment to your spouse of, typically, three times your annual salary (the maximum is four times salary) and there is usually an annual pension as well. The maximum widow's or dependants' pension permitted for death in service is four-ninths of the benefits, based on your earnings at the time you die, not your salary at retirement age. This may not be very much if you are young.

Nothing is straightforward, however, and you should review the terms and conditions of your pension fund on marriage, particularly if it is not your first marriage. Check if you have signed, or need to sign, an Expression of Wishes form. Many pension funds require this in order to determine to whom benefits should be paid in the event of your death. As a single person you may have nominated your parents. Once married you would presumably wish to nominate your spouse. But if you are marrying for the second time, you may want the benefits to remain with your first partner or be split between the two spouses.

Most pension fund benefits are ultimately discretionary and the trustees may decide to split the widow's pension between a first and second wife unless instructed otherwise.

Problems can arise too in the definition of a 'dependant'. A few occupational pension schemes will not accept a husband as

a dependant where he has earnings of his own, even though his
wife may have been a high earner and made a major financial
contribution to the household.

There may be difficulties too if the dependant is not married
but a cohabitee, and some pension schemes will not accept gay
or lesbian partners as dependants. Generally speaking, the
lump-sum benefit will be paid to the person nominated, who-
ever that is. But pension funds are reluctant to pay anything
other than widows', widowers' or children's benefits when you
die.

Most pension funds will continue to pay a widow's or widower's pension until she or he dies, but a few will pay only until
remarriage. This is an important consideration if, for example,
you are a civil servant. Three-quarters of all public sector
pension schemes impose the latter restriction on remarriage.

Benefits for dependent children will generally be paid only
until the child or children reach the age of 18, unless the child
is disabled. This can clearly produce financial difficulties for
your surviving spouse if you intend your children to go on to
university or other further education. In addition, few employees work 40 years with the same firm and therefore have little
opportunity to build up the maximum two-thirds of final salary
benefit.

The answer is to check the terms and conditions of your
pension scheme with the fund manager. Ask specifically what
happens to your dependants if you die in service, after retirement, and who is classified as a dependant. Also check how
much benefit you have earned to date and take advice on how
to top up your pension through Additional Voluntary Contributions (AVCs) if it is not going to be adequate.

If you are self-employed you will also need to review your
pension arrangements on marriage. Most personal pension
policies give you the option at retirement to switch to a lower
pension in return for a dependants' pension, and you may need
to boost your pension by making extra contributions. However,
if you and your partner are earning pension benefits in your
own right, it may be beneficial for you both to continue with
this arrangement rather than the arrangement for widow's or
widower's pensions.

Similarly, it may be worthwhile giving your spouse money in
order to take full advantage of the tax relief on pension con-

tributions if he or she has earnings but cannot afford to make the contributions.

If husbands or wives have no earnings (and therefore no pension), consider employing them so that they can make their own pension contributions. For the Inland Revenue to allow this, they must be paid reasonably for what they do. This can be more advantageous in terms of both tax avoidance and better benefits than forgoing some of your pension in order to provide for a dependants' pension.

Here again, you will need to review your pensions, check whether benefits are likely to be adequate and take advice on whether increased contributions are required. Remember to take into account any life assurance benefits (which can be written into the pension policy and be eligible for tax relief on the premiums) to which your spouse and children will be entitled.

Wives should not rely entirely on their husbands for income in retirement unless they absolutely have to. Proposals in the pipeline which are likely to be introduced mean that pension benefits may well be split on divorce (see page 45 for full details).

Women, whether married or not, also have to take into account the time taken off to bring up children when they probably will not be eligible to make contributions to any pension scheme. Pensions experts calculate that if a woman takes a five-year break from employment, she will have to contribute 50 per cent more than a man to a pension scheme in order to obtain the same benefits.

These are just a few pointers to the things you should be watching out for. Full details on all aspects of pensions are given in Chapter 5.

Divorce

With nearly half of all marriages ending in divorce, this is not an eventuality you can afford to ignore. Statistics show that 50 per cent of divorced or widowed men remarry, and the majority usually find themselves paying maintenance and trying to support two households on one income. (It should be pointed out here that it has been known for wealthy or high-earning women to be ordered to pay maintenance to former husbands.)

Clearly, many men find supporting two families impossible, and the former wife frequently finds herself trying to bring up children on inadequate maintenance, supplemented by part-time earnings and/or social security payments.

Of the 1.3 million single parents in the UK caring for 2.1 million children, the vast majority are single women, divorced or widowed mothers who are largely dependent on social security payments. Fewer than 10 per cent are single fathers.

In 1991 (the last year for which figures are available) 895,000 single parents were dependent on Income Support (a non-contributory benefit roughly equivalent to unemployment benefit), and another 136,000 claimed Family Credit (a top-up state benefit for those who have income from part-time earnings, maintenance or other sources). These figures demonstrate just how few divorced women rely, even in part, on maintenance payments.

Figures from the National Council for One-Parent Families (255 Kentish Town Road, London NW5; tel. 071–267 1361) reveal that only 30 per cent of single mothers receive any maintenance payments at all; the figure is 3 per cent for single fathers. The average amount paid is £16 a week per child, or £12 a week where there are three or more children. Two in five single mothers experience non-payment of maintenance at some stage. Anyone contemplating divorce should be aware of these figures, although things should improve once the new Child Support Agency becomes fully effective.

The new tax regulations on maintenance payments have not helped. In 1988 the rules were changed, making maintenance payments tax-free in a wife's hands, but abolishing all but a miniscule amount of tax relief for the husband (see page 42 for full details).

Who Gets What on Divorce?

In recent years the courts have recognized the impossibility of one breadwinner providing for two families, and since the 1984 Matrimonial and Family Proceedings Act the emphasis has been on a 'clean break' wherever possible.

Factors the court is obliged to take into account when deciding who gets what on the break-up of a marriage include:

- The current financial situation, needs, obligations and responsibilities both now and in the future of both partners.

- The ages of the two partners.
- The length of the marriage.
- The standard of living of the family before the marriage broke up.
- Any mental or physical disability of either partner.
- Any contributions whether in cash or kind made by either partner to the welfare and support of the family.
- The value of any future benefits to which either partner will lose the right on divorce (e.g. pension, life assurance, etc.).

The court will also take into account the assets and relative earning capacity of both partners: whether either or both have worked before or during the marriage, and whether or not they could reasonably be expected to continue or return to work after the divorce.

Where an older couple divorce and the wife has never worked, her future employment prospects will probably be negligible, so will usually be ignored.

Where there are no children and the marriage has lasted for only a couple of years, the settlement may be a simple share-out of joint assets acquired since marriage, particularly if the divorcing couple are both young and have considerable earning potential.

Child bride Mandy Smith tried to sue rock guitarist Bill Wyman for £5 million on the break-up of their marriage, but settled out of court for an estimated £600,000 on the advice of lawyers.

Where the marriage has lasted longer and there are children, the usual formula is based on half the joint assets, plus one third of the joint income. This is, however, just the starting point, and the eventual settlement may be more or less.

Where the woman is the higher earner, this formula can result in the former husband being asked to pay too high a proportion of his income in maintenance, so the courts will reduce the payment accordingly.

Similarly, if the wife is the sole earner, or her income outstrips her husband's by a very large amount, she could find herself paying maintenance, particularly if, for example, the children of the marriage are teenage sons and the husband maintains custody and care of them, if he is disabled, or if there is some reason why his earnings will remain low.

If giving the wife half the joint assets means the family house has to be sold, the court may order that she and the children have the right to occupy it for a specified length of time – until the youngest child is 17, for example, or until a suitable alternative can be found. A wife should not assume that she will have an automatic right to stay in the family home.

In recent years solicitors report that the dramatic fall in property values has deterred or delayed many couples from seeking a divorce. If the family home were sold, the money might only be sufficient to repay the mortgage, leaving nothing for the separating couple to purchase new homes.

Where one partner is considerably wealthier than the other, the courts will want to see that suitable provision has been made for the children and will take into account assets held by the husband or wife before marriage. They take the view that the children could have expected a certain standard of living had the parents remained married, and if the father or mother has the wherewithal to provide this, he or she should be expected to do so after a divorce.

Where the wife is the wealthier partner, any transfer of assets may be minimal since she usually has care of the children (though care and custody can be shared), and the maintenance, if any, will reflect her financial circumstances.

In some cases, however, a wife may be ordered to make a cash settlement or pay her former husband maintenance. Where considerable sums of money are involved, or it is an international divorce, you would be well advised to consult a specialist divorce lawyer – one who is a member of the International Academy of Matrimonial Lawyers (c/o Miles Preston, Radcliffe & Co, 5 Great College Street, London SW1P 3SJ; tel.071–222 7040). Be aware, however, that since these lawyers are the best in their field, they also charge the highest fees.

Incidentally, if you are the 'other woman' or 'other man' in a divorce case, you may be asked to supply information regarding your earnings and assets by the lawyers of your partner's former spouse in support of a maintenance claim. You are perfectly entitled to refuse to do so.

Tax and Maintenance

Before March 1988 the payer of maintenance (usually the former husband) was entitled to full tax relief on payments made to a former wife and children, and the money was taxable in the wife's hands.

However, by paying money direct to the children and making use of their personal tax allowances, most ex-wives (except those with huge maintenance settlements) actually paid little or no tax on maintenance received, unless they had other income from earnings or investments.

In 1988 changes were introduced which were supposed to be an improvement. The idea was to make sure that a divorced couple were not in a better tax position than married families. In reality, most divorced couples are much worse off, and there is now no tax advantage in being divorced.

If you signed a maintenance agreement before 14 March 1988, the payer will continue to be entitled to full tax relief on the payments up to the level for which tax relief was obtained in 1988–89, and the recipient pays tax on the cash received at whatever the level was in 1988–89.

Everything changed in 1988. For all maintenance orders agreed by the courts since 14 March 1988 payments are totally tax-free in the recipient's hands, but the payer (usually the husband) is entitled to tax relief on only the first £1,720 (the difference between the married couple and single tax allowances). The net result of these changes has been that fewer couples can afford divorce and/or husbands have not been able to afford to be generous with their former wives. Many middle-class couples have found themselves trapped in marriage because divorcing is not feasible financially.

After divorce one parent may claim the Additional Personal Tax Allowance (£1,720 for 1992–93), depending on who pays the greater proportion of the cost of maintaining the children, or the allowance can be split between the two parents. If both parents maintain one or more children, both can claim the full tax allowance of £1,720.

Financial Considerations in Divorce

Legal fees can be expensive; few divorcing couples qualify for legal aid, and any lawyer will tell you it is almost certainly cheaper and better to come to an amicable agreement about money than squabble.

Legal aid is means tested and the qualifying thresholds are low. To be eligible for full legal aid you must have disposable income (i.e. take-home pay plus deductions for housing expenses and dependants) of less than £3,060 a year and capital of less than £3,000. At disposable income of £6,800 a year (or capital of £6,750) all entitlement is wiped out. If you don't want the lawyers to walk off with most of your joint assets, you would be well advised to agree.

Two into one won't go, so it is no use divorcing couples expecting to live as well after the break-up as they did when married. You will have to accept this fact when agreeing maintenance payments.

If the agreement is for a clean break and no maintenance, it is worth having maintenance of, say, £1 a year written into the agreement in case circumstances change and one partner becomes sick or redundant and is forced to be dependent on the other. The courts may dismiss a later claim for maintenance if a long period has elapsed since the divorce, but without that provision written into the agreement, it will be impossible even to make a claim.

When splitting assets, much will depend on whether there are dependent children or not. If there are no children, the general rule is that individual partners usually keep assets owned in their sole name if they were owned before the marriage. Assets acquired during the marriage and jointly owned will generally be divided; the exact proportions will depend on whether they are in joint names and the relative contributions. This does not mean just the direct financial contribution. If, say, a weekend cottage is owned in the husband's name only (perhaps a hangover from the days before he was married), but the wife has paid for improvements on the property, she would be entitled to a proportion of the home. However, if there are children, assets owned by both partners prior to the marriage and acquired during the marriage are taken into account when deciding on a settlement.

Where one partner is dependent on the other for maintenance payments, the cost of paying for suitable life assurance on the spouse's life should be taken into account. If the payer dies, the recipient will be left without support in just the same way as if he or she had remained married.

It is also worth pointing out here that on divorce all life policies taken out by the divorcing partners should be written in trust for the benefit of named beneficiaries (usually the children) so that the policies are not part of your estate and thus avoid Inheritance Tax. This will, of course, be subject to any provision for their disposal made in a court order on divorce.

On death during marriage, any assets passing to the surviving spouse are free of Inheritance Tax. This is not the case if your children are the beneficiaries, either under your will (or the laws of intestacy as appropriate).

Writing policies in trust can cause problems with lenders when buying a house after the break-up, as banks and building societies generally want any life policy used as security for a loan. A policy written in trust cannot be assigned to the lender. In any event it is sensible to have separate policies if cover is required for a mortgage and to provide for dependants.

Pensions

On divorce a wife will lose all rights to a State widow's pension; a husband loses nothing since he is entitled to nothing from the State on the death of his wife anyway. Much more important for most couples is the loss of occupational or personal pension rights on divorce as they are generally worth much more.

Pensions are a tricky area as they are currently the subject of proposals for reform. On divorce, both partners generally lose all rights to any benefits from their former spouse's pension scheme.

When older couples divorce, the accumulated pension rights can be worth considerably more than the family home and all other assets put together. This usually affects former wives more seriously than former husbands, as the husband is generally the main breadwinner.

Under the current rules a wife's or husband's entitlement to a share of a former spouse's pension is only notional – neither party knows who will die first. In reality, this is nonsense, and several older women have contested divorces on the grounds that they stand to lose all support in retirement.

If there are free assets in the form of shares or bank deposits, the courts may order the divorcing husband to make over a sum to the wife to take account of her lost pension benefits. If the wife is young, able to work and likely to remarry, her potential entitlement may be negligible and the courts will ignore this.

In most divorces there are few assets other than the family home, but the husband may be entitled to benefits under an occupational pension scheme, in which case he may be able to stipulate that his former wife remains the beneficiary, or to have his pension split between his former wife and any new spouse. However, not all pension funds are prepared, or able, to do this.

If there is no occupational pension, the only course of action is for the wife to insure her former husband's life and for the maintenance payments to take into account the cost of doing so. (After divorce the former spouse would have to show insurable interest in the other party. The maintenance payments may be used to justify this.) Neither partner should rely on the other to do this as it is all too easy when money is short to cancel the policy without telling the former spouse.

New proposals on splitting pension rights on divorce have been put forward by a number of bodies, including the National Association of Pension Funds (12–18 Grosvenor Gardens, London SW1W oDH; tel. 071–730 0585) and the Pensions Management Institute (4 Artillery Lane, London E1 7LS; tel. 071–247 1452). These proposals could soon be incorporated in new pensions legislation, currently being considered by the Goode Committee in the wake of the Maxwell débâcle.

The proposals argue that pension benefits are deferred income and that a spouse would have enjoyed a higher standard of living during the marriage if the pension contributions had not been paid. On divorce, he or she is therefore entitled to a proportion of the accumulated pension fund and the benefits which it provides in relation to the number of years the marriage has lasted.

For example, it might work like this. If a husband had paid pension contributions for five years before marriage and for 10 years during a marriage, the wife would be entitled to a half share of ten-fifteenths (two-thirds) of the pension benefits earned to the date of the divorce. The big debate is whether or not she should have a capital sum transferred to her pension scheme, representing her entitlement to benefit at the date of divorce, or whether the entitlement should be determined when the former husband retires.

Most people earn much more in their later years, so a quarter of pension fund entitlement transferred at retirement age will probably be worth much more than if it is transferred when the marriage breaks up (although it would be reinvested until pension age). However, bearing in mind the courts' preference for a clean break in divorces, it seems likely that the transfer will take place on divorce.

The advent of the Child Support Agency which came into being in April 1993 will have a profound effect on divorce settlements and how maintenance for children is calculated.

The CSA has taken over from the courts on assessing maintenance for children and some experts believe that it is only a matter of time before the CSA effectively settles most maintenance disputes on divorce, with the courts simply rubber stamping the arrangements.

The government's aim in setting up the CSA was to cut the cost of legal aid in divorce cases and to ensure that maintenance is paid by the absent parent – usually the father. The CSA has tough powers to pursue an errant parent who does not support his or her children.

The formulae are complicated but the benchmark for assessments is a minimum of £15.05 a week for every child under 11, £22.15 a week for every child aged between 11 and 15, £26.45 a week for each child aged 16 or 17 and £34.80 for an 18 year old (if he or she is still in full time education up to A level – but not higher education).

A further £9.65 is added for 'family expenses', plus an extra £4.90 a week if the parent with whom the children live does not have a new partner, plus £44 a week if at least one child is under the age of 16 – less child benefit of £10 for the first child and £8.10 a week for other children. The CSA then takes into account the income of both parents and splits the cost of maintaining the children accordingly.

The absent parent (usually the father) will be expected to pay between 15 and 30 per cent of net income towards the support of children, based on the above formula but with the following deductions – £44 a week personal allowance, plus the same deductions for children of a new or previous relationship if they live with the absent parent plus £9.65 for family expenses (if there are children), plus housing costs.

A booklet, *For Parents Who Live Apart*, is available from the Child Support Agency, PO Box 55, Brierley Hill, West Midlands, DY5, helpline tel. 0345 133133.

The description given here of what happens to your finances

on divorce is only a bare outline of the basics. Remember too that there are no absolutes, and you would be well advised to take legal advice and come to an agreement rather than go through the expense of a contested divorce.

This book cannot cover in detail all aspects of divorce and separation, and you will probably need further guidance and advice.

Cohabiting

Contrary to popular belief, there is no such thing as a 'common law' wife, and couples who live together are legally in a very different position from those who marry.

There may be a number of reasons why you decide to cohabit: the loss of pension benefits which affects many civil servants; the wish to retain independence; an unwillingness to share financial resources or to take on the formal responsibilities of a step-parent; or a simple desire by one or both partners to remain unmarried.

When cohabitees separate, neither has any legal entitlement to maintenance, but if one partner dies while still living together, the surviving partner may be able to make a successful claim on the estate.

Property owned as 'joint tenants' will revert to the surviving partner on the death of the other, but the only certain way of passing on other assets to a cohabiting partner – or making sure they do not get their hands on them – is to make a will. Relatives of the deceased partner can contest any claim made by a cohabitee for support if there is no will, and they will probably be successful. They may, in fact, still contest any claim even if there is a will. In some respects cohabiting is simpler than marriage in that the situation on break-up is clear. Those assets which are in your own name will remain your property, and agreement has to be reached only where assets are owned jointly. Maintenance for any children of the relationship will be treated in a similar way to divorcing couples.

Widows and Widowers

Divorce may be optional – death is not. Neither partner knows when the other will die, so it is best to make provision for being widowed before it happens.

Take out suitable convertible-term or whole-life cover to provide sufficient cash to enable the surviving partner to manage financially. At least three times the annual income is reckoned to be the minimum. Ensure that you know to what, if any, dependant's pension rights you may be entitled from your spouse's pension scheme, and encourage your partner to make a will if he or she has not already done so. Once your partner has died, your financial position is largely immutable and State benefits (paid only to widows) are minimal.

Married couples should ensure that they have at least one bank or building society account in joint names so that the surviving spouse has access to cash in the period immediately after bereavement but before probate has been granted (see Chapter 8).

A widow whose husband dies will be entitled to a lump-sum payment from Social Security of £1,000, provided her husband had made sufficient National Insurance contributions. If she is over the age of 45, she will also be entitled to £56.10 a week (1993–94) widow's pension. A pregnant widow or widowed mother of any age will be entitled to the same weekly allowance plus up to £10.95 a week for each child (reduced by £1.10 a week for any child for whom higher child benefit is received). Child benefit of £10.00 for the first child and £8.10 for subsequent children will also be paid.

Clearly, most widows will have some difficulty surviving on this, so making financial provision during marriage is absolutely vital for both partners. Where the wife is the higher earner, or the husband has no income at all, the situation is worse since he is entitled to no widower's pension.

In the year of bereavement and the following year a widow is entitled to a Widow's Bereavement Allowance of £1,720, which can be offset against income along with the usual personal tax allowance.

The big financial problem for widows, and some widowers, even where financial provision has been made, is avoiding the sharks who will arrive soon after the death with advice on how to 'invest' the proceeds of any life policy. You will be in no state of mind to make sensible decisions at this stage, so take the safe route of putting all the cash on deposit at a bank or building society until you are in a mood to make sensible decisions about your long-term financial security.

3

CHILDREN

Children change your life. A new addition to the family is usually an occasion for celebration, but important decisions have to be made about your offspring's future, and there are a number of reasons why you might want to invest money for them. Grandparents, godparents and other relatives often like to make a gift when a new baby arrives, and you must decide how and where to invest this money.

However, one of the major decisions regarding children and finance is likely to be whether or not to opt for education at fee-paying schools.

School Fees

Of the 7 million children currently of school age, an estimated 425,000 are educated at fee-paying schools. The average cost of prep-school fees is now £1,000 a term for day pupils, £2,000 for boarders.

Termly fees of £3,000 for boarders are the norm for secondary schools, with top schools like Eton and Cheltenham Ladies' College charging £3,600 and £3,370 respectively per term.

In recent years there has been greater pressure on places for day pupils, with fees averaging around £2,000 per term. In London, where boarding is the exception rather than the rule, day-pupil waiting lists are particularly long, even though top schools like Westminster, St Pauls, and Godolphin and Latymer charge £2,300, £2,150 and £1,610 per term respectively.

Bringing up children is an expensive business, even if you decide that they should be State-educated. If you embark upon private education, the total cost per child is currently around

£100,000 at today's prices, which does not take into account inflation over the period.

Many parents have been hit by recession, redundancy, etc., all of which could be ongoing. Many children have been with-drawn from private schools, and there has been a sharp upsurge of applications for help with fees from parents in financial difficulty. In addition, school fees have escalated well ahead of inflation, at an annual rate of roughly 10 per cent, so any parents who decide on private education should be well aware of what they are letting themselves in for. It is not cheap and fees usually come out of taxed income.

It is unwise to embark on educating your children at fee-paying schools unless you are fairly certain that you will be able to continue to do so. The trauma of removing them and sending them to State schools can be very unsettling.

The table below gives some idea of what you might expect to pay.

Your children may, of course, be very bright and obtain scholarships, which would lift some of the financial burden. Contact the school or schools of your choice for details, or an educational advice agency like the Independent Schools Advisory Service (56 Buckingham Gate, London SW1E 6AG; tel. 071–630 8793).

Some parents may get help through the Assisted Places Scheme under which the State pays a proportion of the fees for parents who cannot afford them. Generally, you have to have joint incomes of less than £20,000 a year to qualify.

The Cost of Education

Fees start at £2,000 a term and escalate by 10 per cent a year

Fees start September	Fees for 1 year £	Fees for 5 years £	Fees for 7 years £	Fees for 10 years £
1994	6,000	36,630	56,920	95,620
1995	6,600	40,290	62,620	105,190
1996	7,260	44,320	68,880	115,710
1997	7,990	48,760	75,760	127,280
1998	8,780	53,630	83,340	140,000
1999	9,660	59,000	91,680	154,000
2000	10,630	64,890	100,840	169,400
2001	11,690	71,380	110,900	186,350
2002	12,860	78,520	122,020	204,980
2003	14,150	86,370	134,220	225,480

The schools that operate the Assisted Places Scheme have their own criteria for deciding which children are eligible. Priority is sometimes given to those most greatly in need – single parents, for example, who need a boarding place for their child or children in order to be able to work. There are more than 36,000 assisted places at some 350 schools. For full details check with your local education authority.

Parents looking for guidance on the choice of school and the level of fees should get hold of a copy of *The Equitable Schools Book* by Klaus Boehm and Jenny Lees-Spalding (Bloomsbury, £14.99) a sister publication to this book.

Saving for School Fees

Given the huge cost of private education, the sooner you start saving or investing for school fees, the better – if possible, before the children are born.

You have to bear in mind, too, that your liability does not end when the child leaves school. The cost of keeping a child at university is at least £3,000 a year at today's figures, even if your offspring qualifies for the maximum grant of £2,845 a year, (see page 64 for full details).

There is nothing magical about school fees plans – they are simply saving schemes to provide for a specific event. But whereas you can, perhaps, take risks with some of your investments, the need to provide up to £10,000 a year per child for something as important as school fees is not something with which you want to take chances.

Like any form of saving, the longer the money is invested, the better will be the ultimate return. You should understand too that no school fees investment plan can guarantee to pay the fees when the time comes. The plan will pay a sum of money, part of which may be guaranteed. This may, or may not, be sufficient to cover the cost of the fees.

Tax on School Fees

There is generally no tax relief on paying school fees. However, if the payment of school fees was part of a maintenance settlement on divorce and the agreement was dated before 14 March 1988, tax relief is granted to the payer on the maintenance agreement up to the level in force at that date. Agreements after that date are eligible for tax relief only up to a maximum of £1,720 – the difference between the married couple's allowance and the single person's tax allowance.

How to Invest?

Your first decision will be whether to invest any money, either a lump sum or regular savings, in the child's name or your own name.

Every child is entitled to a personal tax allowance (£3,445 for 1993–94), and the amount available to pay the school fees could be considerably more if the assets are held in the name of a child (who will probably be a non-taxpayer or basic-rate taxpayer only) rather than a wealthy grandparent or other relative who might be paying tax at 40 per cent.

If the money invested has come from a parent, the income generated will be treated as though it is the parent's income once it exceeds £100 a year. The decision on how to invest will therefore depend largely on who provides the money for the school fees scheme.

Lump Sum or Regular Saving?

You may be intending to provide school fees from a lump-sum investment, regular savings, out of income on a pay-as-you go basis, or on borrowings. (The last option should be used only as a last resort.) Most parents use a mixture of methods – saving out of income, using gifts from grandparents and other relatives to make lump-sum additions and, if necessary, topping up the school fees when they become payable out of income. Only the wealthiest can invest a lump sum at birth and fund the entire cost from investments.

If your adviser recommends insurance-based products, lump-sum one-off payments usually have lower charges than a regular premium plan, and are more flexible since there is no long-term commitment. However, some people need the discipline of regular savings, which also offers the advantages of 'pound cost averaging' when you are buying unit-linked products or making direct investments in equities through PEPs, unit trusts or investment trusts (see Chapter 6).

How Do the Different Schemes Work?

Most people take professional advice when planning for school fees. You may have an adviser – your bank manager, independent financial adviser or life assurance consultant – but there are brokers who specialize in school fees schemes. The Independent Schools Advisory Service (56 Buckingham Gate, London SW1E 6AG; 071–630 8793) will send you a list of them on request. You would be well advised to get several quotes from different sources before finally deciding.

The investments or type of scheme you choose will depend on the proportion of school fees the investments have to provide, the length of time the money can remain invested before school fees have to be paid, and the degree of risk with which you are comfortable. It's no use having a high-risk plan which may show a fantastic return, if it keeps you awake at night worrying.

Do not allow yourself to be mesmerized by salesmen's jargon. Investing for school fees is like any other form of investment – there is more than one option open to you.

Educational Trust

This is probably one of the best methods of providing for school fees if you have a lump sum to invest. It offers a high degree of security in the form of guarantees, and still shows an attractive return if there are only a few years before you need to pay school fees. A number of insurance companies and some schools run educational trusts which have the advantage of enjoying charitable status.

You can invest a lump sum in a trust to provide a pre-agreed, guaranteed level of fees for any number of terms, depending on how long you envisage your children being at fee-paying schools or in further education. For example, a lump-sum investment made in 1992 of just under £21,000 could provide school fees of £2,000 a term for five years starting in 1997. The amounts available from such plans are guaranteed but, of course, would not necessarily be sufficient to pay the fees by the time you get to 1997. It is also possible to buy with-profits and unit-linked plans which do not provide such guarantees, but do give the opportunity for growth.

On average, school fees have increased by around 10 per cent a year, and if you want to fund for such an increase, the cost

Lump-Sum Investment to Fund School Fees of £30,000

(£2,000 a term for 5 years)

Fees starting August	Total fees £	Your investment £	Net	Return 25%	40%
1995	30,000	24,470	3	7.3	10.7
1997	30,000	21,779	3.6	7.0	9.7
1999	30,000	19,383	4.1	6.8	9.0

Lump-Sum Investment to Fund School Fees of £36,630

(£2,000 a term + 10% inflation per year for 5 years)

Fees starting August	Total fees £	Your investment £	Net	Return 25%	40%
1995	48,755	39,227	3.2	7.5	11.0
1997	58,994	42,245	3.8	7.2	9.8
1999	71,382	45,493	4.2	6.2	9.1

Source: Equitable Life

escalates alarmingly. You may be better off funding for a basic amount and paying any inflationary increases out of income.

To provide school fees for five years, starting at £2,000 a term in 1995 and escalating by 10 per cent a year, you will need to invest a lump sum of £30,000. The table above shows the capital sum required to provide school fees at various dates in the future.

The figures are only an illustration. Your lump-sum investment is used to buy a deferred annuity (a guaranteed income) which pays the termly fees over the pre-agreed period. The return on a deferred annuity is influenced by the level of interest rates at the time of purchase. The best time to invest in one of these schemes is when interest rates are high, but, generally speaking, you don't have much choice.

Once a child starts at the school of your choice, cheques from the insurance company arrive just before the beginning of each term, made payable to the school, and the money must be used for the child's education. In some cases the cheque is paid direct to the school.

The advantage of the insurance company-based schemes is that you need not choose which school your children attend until just before they are due to start.

If you opt for a savings scheme run by the school of your choice, the guaranteed benefits may or may not be higher. Most schools are reasonably flexible about transferring fees to another school if, for example, your child does not meet the academic requirements for entrance.

With both types of educational trust you can usually transfer any benefits to another child (if the first child, for example, obtains a scholarship). If all your children turn out to be very bright and win scholarships, or for some other reason you decide not to send a child to a fee-paying school, the benefits can be deferred and used to provide financial support in higher education, but the money must be used at some stage for educational purposes and usually has to be paid to the educational establishment.

If a child should die before starting school, the money can be returned to you, usually with a guarantee of it being not less than your original investment or whatever the surrender value is at the time.

The table below gives an example of the type of surrender value you might receive, but this is not guaranteed.

There are some important Inheritance Tax and Capital Gains Tax implications of these educational trust schemes. For example, surrendering a scheme can result in a liability to CGT. If you choose to be a 'parent trustee', then generally there will be no liability to IHT. The position may well be different for non-parents. You should take advice on the implications before investing.

The reason these educational trust schemes are able to offer such attractive returns is because they are charities and do not pay tax. If this tax-free status is removed at some stage in the future, the returns may fall.

Surrender Value of a £10,000 Investment in an Educational Trust

End of Year	Estimated surrender value (£)
1	10,465
2	11,524
3	12,685
4	13,958
5	15,494

Source: School Fees Insurance Agency

There are other versions of charitable trust schemes where the lump sum is not used to buy an annuity but is invested in a spread of shares, gilts and other investments. The returns from these schemes are not guaranteed, and may be better or worse than the guaranteed version. However, they usually offer a better return than a lump-sum investment in an insurance company investment bond because the charitable status of the trust allows the dividends and capital gains from the underlying investments to roll up tax free. Much will depend on the investment expertise of the managers of such a charitable fund.

Composition Schemes

Many schools operate these schemes, which are, in effect, a means of getting a discount on the fees by paying in advance. For example, if you were to pay five years' fees up front at the time the child starts at the school, you might get a 15 per cent discount. If you were able to make the same capital commitment four years before the child starts, the discount might be as high as 50 per cent. Contact the bursar at the school of your choice for details. Check whether the scheme is transferrable to another child or a different school.

Ten Years or More to Invest

You may not want to invest in a guaranteed educational trust scheme, or you may need to top up the guaranteed benefits provided by such a scheme with a lump sum or regular savings out of income. Provided you have at least 10 years to the commencement of school fees, the whole spectrum of investments is open to you and what you choose will depend on the degree of risk with which you are comfortable.

Long-term, equity-based investments have produced a much higher return than straight building society deposits. The tables below show the relative returns.

The figures illustrate the benefits of investing in unit trusts, investment trusts and shares through PEPs, where both the income from dividends and any capital growth is totally tax-free.

If you can live with the risk of a straight equity investment like this, without having sleepless nights every time the value of your investment temporarily falls, then this should be your first choice – provided you have at least 10 years until school fees need to be provided.

The beauty of straightforward equity investment through a PEP is that charges are low and you have no long-term commitment, so if your circumstances change, you can opt not to send your child to a fee-paying school. There are no penalties and you can simply cash in your investment or use it for other purposes.

PEPs are very flexible; you can add lump sums when you are able (up to the current annual maximum of £6,000 per person each year for a general PEP, and £3,000 per person for a single company PEP) and you can discontinue regular savings without penalty (see Chapter 6 for full details).

Current Value of £6,000 Invested Annually Over Various Periods to 1.1.93

Commencing Years Ago	Building Society high interest account £	UK Invested equity unit trust £	UK Invested equity unit trust (PEP)* £
5	37,254	36,152	37,963
10	91,469	125,135	138,724
15	174,104	342,059	411,684

Net income is reinvested in the building society and UK equity unit trust, gross income where the unit trust is held through a PEP.
* PEPS were not available 10 years ago, but for the purposes of accurate comparison, the performance figures assume they were.

Current Value of £50 Invested Monthly Over Various Periods to 1.1.93

Commencing Years Ago	Building Society high interest account £	UK Invested equity unit trust £	UK Invested equity unit trust (PEP)* £
5	3,603	3,380	3,555
10	8,842	11,093	12,249
15	16,793	31,401	37,599

Net income is reinvested in the building society and UK equity unit trust, gross income where the unit trust is held through a PEP.
* PEPS were not available years ago but for the purposes of accurate comparison, the performance figures assume they were.

Source: Save & Prosper

Charges are relatively low, though you must check this as there are wide differentials. Equitable Life and many other unit trust managers make no charge at all for a 'wrap around' PEP when you purchase unit trusts from them. Others levy a flat annual fee which can work out much cheaper than the alternative annual charge of a percentage of the fund, particularly if your investments perform well.

PEPs also give you great freedom in your choice of investments, and you can buy and sell within the PEP without losing the tax benefits. You may, of course, decide you want a professional to make the choice for you, in which case you should take advice.

Independent investment advisers Chase de Vere produce an excellent publication *PEP Guide*, which is an annual review of the terms and conditions of all the PEP schemes on offer. It is obtainable, price £8.95, from Chase de Vere (63 Lincoln's Inn Fields, London WC2A 3JX; tel: 071-404 5766.)

If both you and your spouse have used up your PEP allowance for the current year (unlikely for those saving out of income, as it is a total of £18,000 at the moment), you can put additional funds into straight unit or investment trust regular savings schemes. There is nothing complicated about them, though you will probably need advice on which ones to choose. (For a full description of unit trusts and investment trusts see Chapter 6.)

The Association of Unit Trusts and Investment Funds (65 Kingsway, London WC2B 6TD; tel. 071-831 0898) and the Association of Investment Trust Companies (Park House, 16 Finsbury Circus, London EC2M 7JJ; tel. 071-588 5347) can recommend independent financial advisers who specialize in this field.

With-Profit Endowments

A with-profit endowment policy offers the security that annual bonuses, once added to the policy, cannot be removed. The value of your investment cannot go down.

Many school fees plans consist of a series of 10-year with-profits endowments maturing in successive years. For example, if you are saving for school fees which start in 2003, you would take out five policies maturing between 2003 and 2008. Your monthly premiums would remain constant for the first 10 years and decline from 2003 onwards as the policies matured and the fees were paid.

The difficulty with this arrangement is that you may be able to afford total premiums for the five policies of, say, only £250 a month at the moment, which may not be sufficient to provide the estimated school fees.

The alternative, to take out 10-year policies in successive years means that your contributions will increase substantially. For example, you may start off in 1993 paying £60 a month for a policy which will pay the fees during 2003. But in 1994 you will have to take out another policy for £60 a month to cover the fees for 2004, and so on. By the year 2002 your monthly out-goings will be £540 a month, declining thereafter as the policies mature and the fees are paid.

In either case you will probably need to top up the benefits out of income when the policies mature in order to fund the fees in full.

Under 10 Years to Invest

DEFERRED ANNUITIES, like with-profits endowments, can be pur-chased serially to provide fees at a guaranteed level. Generally speaking, there is no advantage in doing this yourself rather than through an educational trust, as the trust has the tax advantage of being a charity and can therefore offer a higher return.

Minimum investment in most educational trusts is £2,500 so you could save out of income in, say, a building society account, and once a year make a lump-sum contribution to the trust.

GILTS AND OTHER FIXED-INTEREST INVESTMENTS are suitable invest-ments if there are fewer than 10 years until the payment of school fees commences and a high degree of certainty is necessary.

If you and your spouse are both taxpayers and do not have a TESSA (Tax Exempt Special Savings Scheme), you should both take one out, regardless of whether it is used for school fees, as the interest on these schemes is tax-free. You can invest up to £9,000 each over five years (see Chapter 6 for full details). However, this does not apply if either of you does not pay tax, as non-taxpayers can get a similar gross return without the restrictions of a TESSA.

In the past it has also been possible to use low-coupon gilts maturing in successive years to provide a guaranteed return which forms the basis for a school fees plan. They can usually be bought at a discount to their redemption price, with a built-in capital gain which can be taken tax-free. However, there are very few low-coupon gilts currently in issue and most gilts are trading at a premium to their redemption value.

The government's requirement to fund its huge borrowing requirement over the next couple of years will probably produce new opportunities to invest again, but, at the moment, gilts are not really a suitable investment.

You can construct a similar scheme with deep-discount bonds and zero-coupon investment trust shares. You will need to take advice on these investments from a stockbroker. The Association of Private Client Investment Managers and Stockbrokers (20 Dysart Street, London EC2A 2BX; tel. 071-410 6868) can recommend one of its members.

When interest rates are high, money can be saved in bank or building society high-interest accounts, or you can purchase guaranteed growth bonds which offer a fixed, guaranteed return over one to five years. For example, a £10,000 investment in a guaranteed growth bond at 10 per cent will show a guaranteed return of £16,105 after five years. Of course, this sort of return is possible only when interest rates are high, but when they are, it is probably not worth taking a chance on the more risky equity-based investments.

For basic-rate taxpayers, and particularly those paying at 40 per cent, National Savings Certificates offer a tax-free guaranteed return over a five-year period. These too can form part of a school fees plan, as can National Savings Capital Bonds which offer a fixed return.

Last-Minute Planning

Inevitably, some parents will have little or no time to plan for school fees. You may have intended to send your son to the local comprehensive, but in the event he turns out to be a brilliant musician and clearly needs to go to a school offering specialist tuition in this field. You may have a handicapped child and there are no places available to cope with the disability in local State schools.

If you have a house with little or no mortgage, some banks

and building societies may be prepared to lend for school fees against the security of the property. However, with the current uncertainty in the housing market over property values they are not so keen to do this as they were in the 1980s, but at a push you can usually raise some cash this way. The drawback is that few have tailored their lending to the payment of school fees, and most want you to draw down the total loan at the beginning, while you need to pay the school fees in relatively small amounts. This is an expensive way to go about things as you are borrowing more than you need.

You will probably have to negotiate an overdraft-type facility or loan account with your bank manager so that you pay interest on the money only as you actually need it, not on the whole facility. A gold card overdraft facility is probably the simplest way of arranging this, in which case you need to have an income of at least £25,000 a year.

Some of the banks still offer gold card overdrafts of £10,000 (more by negotiation) at 2.5 per cent over bank base rate, but in recent years the interest has crept up, and although it is cheaper than a standard overdraft, it is rarely the bargain it used to be. Check with the lender what the interest charge will be.

Borrowing should usually be regarded as a stop-gap or top-up facility rather than the main means of paying school fees. With the total cost at a minimum of £50,000 for five years at a fee-paying school, your gold card facility, or even the equity in your home, is not going to go very far.

Insurance

With large sums of money involved in school fees provision you will need insurance. First, you must protect your ability to pay if fees are coming out of income, or regular savings are being built up to provide fees at a future date. Most school fees schemes include death and disability cover, with unemployment and redundancy cover as an optional extra.

In addition, you will need insurance in case the child dies and your money is tied up in an educational trust, and to reimburse you for fees paid if the child is off sick. Your adviser should be able to arrange this.

Conclusion

Whatever method you choose, you will undoubtedly benefit from taking advice from a specialist. He will consider the following things:

- Are you investing a lump sum or saving from income?
- How many years until fees commence?
- Would an educational trust with its guarantees suit you best?
- If school fees are at least 10 years away, do you want a with-profits endowment-based scheme or can you live with the higher risk and potentially higher returns of a PEP unit or investment trust regular savings scheme?
- If you have fewer than 10 years to go, what are the options?
- What are the tax implications of your school fees plan?
- How flexible is your preferred scheme and can you change your mind?

Higher Education

The cost of educating a child does not necessarily end at the age of 18. Research carried out by Norwich Union reveals that it costs an estimated £10,000 to fund three years in further education.

As a parent, it is no use burying your head in the sand and imagining that State grants will take care of the cost. A recent survey revealed that 84 per cent of parents had no idea how much it costs to maintain a child at university.

The student grant system has changed dramatically in the past three years. Only 27 per cent of students receive the full grant, which has in any case been frozen since 1990 at £2,845 a year for students living away from home and studying in London, £2,265 elsewhere, and £1,795 for students living with parents.

Student grants are means tested on joint parental income and start to be reduced at joint income of £13,630 a year. At just over £34,000 a year any entitlement to grant is entirely wiped out, unless you have more than one child at university at the same time.

Of the vast majority of parents who are supposed to make a contribution, or pay in full the cost of maintaining their student

Students Grants and Loans, 1993–94

Students living away from home:	Grants	Loans full year	final year*
In London	£2,845	£940	£685
Elsewhere	£2,265	£800	£585
Living at home	£1,795	£640	£470

* The amount is less in the final year, as students are expected to get a job on graduation.

Source: Department of Education

offspring, 30 per cent pay nothing at all, 10 per cent pay less than they should and 50 per cent have made no provision for making the payments anyway. As a result, most students depend on cheap student loans from the government scheme, bank over-drafts, credit cards and borrowing from family and friends. The average student leaves university with debts of around £1,100 and borrowings of £3,000 are not uncommon.

The first thing any parent should do is get hold of the publication *Student Grants and Loans* available free from your local education authority or the Department of Education Publication Centre (PO Box 2193, London E15 2EU; tel. 081-533 2000). This will enable you to work out any grant to which your student offspring may be entitled. It also sets out details of the government loan scheme. Maximum loans for the current academic year (September 1993–May 1994) are £940 for those studying in London, £800 for those studying elsewhere and £640 for students living at home.

Repayment of the loan plus interest is deferred until the student finishes at university. Interest is inflation-linked and added to the original loan each year.

If you will be expected to contribute towards your offspring's maintenance at university, then, as with school fees, the sooner you start to make financial provision for this eventuality the better. Turning a blind eye to your responsibilities is likely to leave your child in severe financial difficulties; getting a vacation job is now a rarity and you cannot rely on this as a let-out.

How Much Will It Cost?

Fees for halls of residence, which typically provide room, heating, electricity, etc. with breakfast and evening meal, vary from around £75 a week in London to £55–£65 elsewhere (£50 and £35 respectively if meals are not taken).

Renting a room after the first year works out at around £35 a week in the provinces, £50 or more in London, and your student son or daughter will have to pay for gas, electricity, telephone and food on top of this.

All students will need extra for travel, books, clothes and other living expenses. Some courses such as medicine require considerable expenditure on equipment. The real cost of maintenance is probably a minimum of £3,000 for a 30-week year.

Making Provision

All the methods of saving mentioned in the school fees section apply equally to any scheme designed to pay for further education. (Educational trusts were not designed for further education, though you can use the proceeds for this if necessary.)

Alternatively, you might like to consider the possibility of paying your parental contribution by way of guaranteeing a mortgage on a property for your student offspring. This has the advantage of providing them with one foot on the home-owning ladder while costing you no more in contributions.

Much will depend on the mortgage rate at the time and the price of suitable properties in the area where your child is studying. You will have to check it out, but it is possible to buy a two- or three-bedroomed terraced house in many towns for £50,000 or less. The repayments on a £45,000 mortgage probably won't work out any more expensive than the amount you would have to contribute towards your student son or daughter's maintenance (assuming he or she is ineligible for a grant). If the house is owned in joint names, the repayments are eligible for mortgage interest relief. You will have to guarantee the mortgage repayments.

Your student offspring can rent a couple of rooms to colleagues to provide income, which should be tax-free because it can be offset against the mortgage interest charges. In addition, as from 1992–93, the first £3,250 of income from lodgers living in your principal private residence is tax-free.) You will have to investigate for yourself to see if the figures stack up.

Investing for Children

Whether or not your children go on to further education, most parents find themselves with the problem of investing money on their behalf, even if it is relatively small amounts of birthday and Christmas money.

At the other end of the spectrum wealthy grandparents may want to pass on quite large sums to grandchildren to avoid Inheritance Tax, or you may have money you want to give to your children or put in trust.

Tax and Your Children

All children, no matter what age, are entitled to the personal tax allowance (£3,445 for 1993-94). They are also entitled to the usual Capital Gains Tax exemption (£5,800 for 1993-94). Any income above the personal allowances will be taxed in the usual way, except if a parent is the source of the income.

Any income from investments given to a child by a parent is taxed as though it were still the parent's income, once it exceeds £100 a year. However, if the income is allowed to roll up (as in an offshore roll-up fund) and is not distributed until the child is 18, it can then be treated as the child's income in the normal way.

If the source of the money is a parent, you should look at investments generating capital growth rather than income, such as growth unit and investment trusts, the capital shares of split-capital investment trusts, deep-discount bonds and the like (see Chapter 6 for full details). Children's investment needs are probably little different from those of older investors, and in many respects they are ideal investors – able to take a long-term view.

Their investments may need to generate income – to pay for school fees or further education. On the other hand, you may be looking to build up a nest egg for when the child is 18 or 21 to give them a start in life.

Where you invest will depend on the degree of risk you are

prepared to accept (although over a 10-year period you can afford to ride out the ups and downs of equity-based investments) and whether income or capital growth is required.

Most children are non-taxpayers, so if you go for bank, building society or National Savings investments, choose something that pays interest gross. Tax-free investments like National Savings Certificates and TESSAs are of no benefit unless your child happens to pay tax.

Large Sums – Trusts

If you, a grandparent or other relative want to pass on substantial sums of money you may want to do so under a trust. This can be a simple 'bare trust' with you as the trustee. This is the most common method by which shares, unit trusts or investment trusts are held for a child under the age of 18.

If relatively large sums are involved, you or the grandparents may want to set up a more formal 'Accumulation and Maintenance Trust', and there are Inheritance Tax advantages in doing so. Provided the donor survives for seven years after setting up the trust, the gift is exempt from Inheritance Tax. (This applies to all gifts, whether given in trust or directly.) Bear in mind that there is a potential liability to CGT on transferring assets into the trust.

Most private client stockbrokers have departments which will carry out simple trust work. Contact the Association of Private Client Investment Managers and Stockbrokers (see Useful Addresses) for a copy of their directory of member firms.

Your accountant or solicitor should also be able to set up such a trust for you. Generally speaking, the costs of running a trust dictate that it is not worth doing so for sums of less than £25,000.

Trusts do not, generally, save income tax, except inasmuch as the donor may have paid tax on the income generated by the investments at 40 per cent, and the recipient may be a non-taxpayer or basic-rate payer only.

The Society of Trust and Estate Planners (see Useful Addresses) are specialist lawyers and accountants with wide experience of trust law. If large sums of money are involved, you would be well advised to consult a member.

Life Assurance

You can use a life assurance policy as a way of investing for a child 'in trust' so that they cannot touch the money until a pre-agreed date. You can take out a life assurance policy in either your name or your spouse's name written 'in trust' with the child as the named beneficiary. This is a convenient and useful means of saving, which avoids the expense of setting up a formal trust, and you can use both with-profit endowment and unit-linked-type policies, as well as guaranteed growth bonds.

If the premiums are paid by you, they can be free from Inheritance Tax if they come under one of the exemptions (see Chapter 7). If the policy is handed over to the child after the age of 18, the parent should have no tax liability.

Bear in mind that the charges will be higher than holding securities like shares, unit trusts and investment trusts directly as a 'bare trustee' for the child's benefit.

Special Investments

Most banks and building societies have special accounts aimed at children. Generally, the child will be able to open the account at any age, but will not be able to sign for withdrawals until he or she is at least seven years old.

Letting the child manage small amounts of money is good practice for later life. Don't lock up all the money so the child cannot get at it. Most children enjoy going into the local building society to pay in or withdraw cash.

National Savings offers a Children's Bonus Bond designed to be used as a vehicle for gifts to children. They can be purchased for any child under the age of 16, and will continue to grow in value until the child is 21. All returns are totally tax-free. The maximum holding is £1,000 per child, and the bonds can be bought in units of £25, either by the child or the donor.

The rate of interest varies, but is guaranteed for five years at a time. National Savings tries to keep the rate competitive with other investments paying interest gross.

In order to get the advertised return the bonds have to be held for five years, after which a bonus is added. The child cannot encash the bond and receive the proceeds until he or she is 16, although the parents can encash the bond on the child's behalf at any time.

Investments for Children

Type	Age child can invest in own name	Minimum investment £	Comments
Gilts on Nat. Savings Stock Register	A	None	Fees - £1 under £250, plus 50p for every extra £125
Nat. Savings Certificates	A	£25	Not suitable for non-taxpayers
Nat. Saving Yearly Plan	A	£20 per month	Not suitable for non-taxpayers
Nat. Savings Ordinary Acct.	A	£5	Low return
Nat. Savings Investment Account	A	£5	Pays interest gross; 1 month's notice
Nat. Savings Income Bonds	A	£2,000	Pays interest gross/variable
Nat. Savings Capital Bonds	A	£100	Pays interest gross/fixed
Nat. Savings Children's Bonus Bonds	A	£25	Max. investment £1,000; return fixed 5 years
Premium bonds	A	£10*	Prizes; no return
Bank savings and deposits	A	£1	Often poor return
Building Soc. savings and deposits	B	Varies	
Gilts bought through stockbroker	18 (a)	None	£1,000 realistic minimum†
Shares	18 (a)	None	£1,000 realistic minimum
Unit and Investment Trusts	18 (a)	Varies	Often £500 minimum
Savings-type Life Assurance	Varies	Varies	Often £1,000 lump sum or £20 a month
Guaranteed Income and Growth Bonds	18 (a)	Varies	Often £1,000 minimum

A – from birth, but normally no withdrawals until age 7.
B – varies according to type of account.
(a) – can be held by parents as trustee for the child under this age.
* – £100 for children over 16.
† – stockbrokers' minimum commission usually £20 at least.

Other National Savings investments, such as Income Bonds which pay income gross (although it is taxable), may be attractive as an investment for your child, but you will have to compare rates with what the banks and building societies have to offer on their gross accounts. Capital bonds which pay a fixed, guaranteed return, might be more suitable than National Savings income bonds which offer a variable rate.

If you want to make a comparison, *Blay's Guide*, a monthly

publication, monitors all bank and building society investment accounts, and a copy should be available in your public library. It will show which is the best buy for your child.

4

LIFE ASSURANCE

Life assurance is all too often muddled up in people's minds with saving. The two things should be entirely separate. Life assurance is all about protection and providing for dependants in the event of disaster. This is absolutely fundamental to your security and peace of mind, and should be the basis of all financial planning. Do not even consider savings and investment until you have taken out adequate life assurance protection. In the event of a disaster, your life assurance policy pays out a sum of money to provide for your dependants, and buying this protection should be your top priority.

Life assurance has become inextricably mixed up with savings because of tax relief. Prior to 14 March 1984 premiums paid on a life assurance policy qualified for tax relief. This had been the situation for a very long time, and over the years the life assurance companies moved away from straight protection and introduced a savings element into life policies – the conventional with-profits endowment. They sold this very successfully, not least of all because of the tax relief, but also because this business was more profitable than straight protection.

Before 1968 you could even get tax relief on one-off lump-sum payments into a life policy – and many people rushed to invest.

From 14 March 1984 tax relief was abolished on all new life policies effected after this date (although generally relief continued to be available on existing policies). Arguably, this was not a good move as families badly need protection and tax relief on life assurance premiums was an incentive to take out cover. Perhaps the government should have removed tax relief on savings-type policies, but retained it for straight cover.

You may choose to save with an insurance company, but that

71

is not what life assurance is about. Life assurance is a means of providing financially for your dependants in the event of your death or disablement. You pay a monthly or annual premium (occasionally a one-off single premium) and when you die the insurance policy pays the guaranteed lump sum to a person named by you as the beneficiary, or to your estate. If it is a term policy and you don't die during the term, you get nothing back.

Arguably, if you have no dependants, you do not need life assurance. But most of us eventually get married and have children, and even among those who don't, we may well acquire responsibilities – a live-in partner, elderly parent, or disabled relative, for example.

Like everything else to do with providing for yourself and your dependants, the sooner you buy life assurance, the cheaper it is. Do not wait until you have acquired a family to purchase protection.

If there is one life assurance policy that everyone needs, it is convertible-term assurance. This pays a lump sum if you die during the life of the policy, but gives you the option to convert to, say, a whole-life or savings-type policy at a later date, without providing evidence of good health. This is enormously valuable. You are effectively insuring your ability to obtain life cover at a later date when you may not be in good health. It is also cheap, particularly if you buy when young, and in an ideal world every parent would give his or her offspring the first year's premium on a convertible-term policy for their 21st birthday. You couldn't have a better present.

Who Can Buy Life Assurance?

You can insure your own life, or you can buy a policy to insure someone else's life (your husband or wife, for instance). But you must have an 'insurable interest', which basically means you must suffer some financial loss or incur extra costs if the person dies.

Most life assurance is taken out by policy-holders on their own life or on the life of a spouse. But there are other situations where you might want to insure someone's life. For example, you might want to insure the life of a former spouse if you receive maintenance payments which would cease on his or her death; you might decide to take out 'key man' insurance on a key employee's life if his death would damage the business; or you might want to insure a godparent who is paying your child's school fees out of income. The godparent might want to take out life assurance to cover this risk.

Imagine your aged uncle has given you £100,000 because he has no other relatives and he wants to reduce his estate for Inheritance Tax purposes. It would make sense to insure his life for the amount of any potential Inheritance Tax liability should he die within seven years of making the gift. This type of policy is known as 'life of another'. A liability would only arise if he had made other life-time transfers during the seven years. Otherwise the transfer would be wholly within the 'zero-rate band' and so no liability would arise.

Many parents are surprised to discover that you generally cannot insure a child's life. Although a child's death would cause untold unhappiness, you generally suffer no financial loss, so you do not have an insurable interest. You might, however, be able to insure a child's life if, for example, its survival into adulthood was a condition of an inheritance from which you would benefit.

How Much Life Assurance Do You Need?

Experts argue about this, but as a general rule of thumb you should insure your life for three or four times your gross salary – more if you have a large mortgage, a huge commitment to school fees, or large borrowings to fund a family business which would eat up any cash from the insurance policy.

When working out how much life cover to buy you should take into account the following:

- The size of your mortgage.
- Any other borrowings.
- Any commitment to school fees which are being paid out of income.
- Maintenance to a former spouse and/or children.
- Any commitment to support another person (an elderly relative, for example.

On the other side of the equation you should also take into account:

- Any life cover provided by an employer – but bear in mind that this might cease on leaving the job and won't necessarily be provided by a new employer. To replace this cover yourself, late in life, could be expensive or impossible if you are by then in poor health.

The average company scheme provides life cover of three to four times gross earnings, with no requirement to produce evidence of good health. If in doubt, treat the company life assurance as a bonus and buy your own life cover on top.

- Your income now from both earnings and investments.
- Any investments you have which could be used to support your dependants.
- Any life cover which may be built into a package. For example, most with-profit endowment mortgages include mortgage protection which will provide a lump sum to pay off the mortgage should you die before the end of the term.

The amount of cover you buy will depend on individual circumstances and how much you can afford, as well as the amount of income needed by any dependants (spouse, partner, children, elderly relatives or others).

Women who do not earn, and their husbands, frequently forget the contribution they make to the household and the cost of buying the services of child-minder, cook, cleaner and housekeeper if the woman were to die. This should be taken into account and the wife's life insured – at the very least while the children are young – for a sum sufficient to hire replacement domestic help.

A single person with no dependants may feel that life cover is a waste of money. But most of us do get married and have children, and the earlier you buy life cover the cheaper. Better to over-insure when you are young than to discover at a later date that you cannot afford proper cover. The older you are, the more expensive life assurance becomes and, of course, as time goes on you may not be in the best of health. For example, 15-year convertible-term cover of £100,000 costs around £300 a year at age 29, but by the time you reach 54 the annual premium for a new policy could be around £1,500.

One life assurance company has suggested that a sum of 10 times your gross income would not be excessive if you are buying at an early age when cover is cheap. For example, your earnings might be £30,000 at age 29. If you insure for the minimum recommended, three times your gross earnings, your dependants will receive £90,000 on your death. If this money is invested at a net return of, say, 5 per cent (about what you might get from a building society today), this would produce income of only £4,500. Your dependants are not going to have much to live on.

Many life assurance contracts give you the option to increase the cover at various intervals to take account of inflation; the premium will, of course, increase too.

Single People

As a young single person, the only life assurance you need is a 25- or 30-year convertible-term policy. This provides a lump sum should you die during the term of the policy, and gives you the option of switching to, say, a whole-life or savings-type policy at a later date, without having to give evidence of good health. You are, in effect, insuring your ability to obtain life assurance at a later date. The cheapest version pays a fixed amount should you die during the term of the policy, and you pay a fixed premium.

Many policies have the option to increase the sum insured during the life of the policy. Naturally, if you exercise this option, you will pay a higher premium. Others have built-in increases in both benefits and premiums to take care of inflation, or at a pre-agreed rate.

In recent years many life companies have introduced policies which have a five-year review of premiums and benefits. The drawback with this type of policy is that you have no idea what the premium will be five or 10 years down the line. The policy with set increases in premiums and cover, or level term, gives you a known outlay.

Aids has made many of the life companies wary of insuring young single men, and most will ask you to fill in a 'lifestyle' questionnaire when you apply for life cover. Some life companies have pulled out of this market altogether and will not insure single males. Single men now generally pay a premium some 30 to 50 per cent in excess of the rate charged to single women.

If you are in a job where your employer does not pay your salary if you are off sick (or pays for only a short time), or you are self-employed, you should also consider Permanent Health Insurance. This pays a monthly income if you are unable to work through accident, disability or sickness. If you are permanently disabled, it will pay an income for the rest of your life (see page 89 for full details).

Young Married Couples

On marriage, and certainly as soon as children are born, you should review your life assurance. The main breadwinner, usually the husband, should have sufficient Life and Permanent Health Insurance cover to replace the income he is producing. A working wife should be insured in the same way.

Where the wife is a non-earner and is at home looking after children, you need to insure her life for sufficient to hire a nanny or housekeeper, should she die. A few companies will also insure her against sickness or disability, though the limits are quite low – around £10,000 a year.

Where the wife works outside the home, both partners should consider permanent health insurance if you could not survive on only one income.

You will probably be sold mortgage protection insurance as part of a package when you buy the family home. This is either term assurance or decreasing-term assurance (depending on whether you have an interest-only endowment or pension-linked loan, or a repayment mortgage). This will provide a sum sufficient to pay off the mortgage if you die before the mortgage is repaid. If the mortgage is based on both your earnings, you may be encouraged to take out a joint-life, first-death policy which will pay off the mortgage if either of you dies.

Generally speaking, it is better to take out two separate life policies, one on each partner, for the amount of the mortgage (if you don't have other life cover). With one in three marriages ending in divorce, any joint-life policy will have to be unwound if the marriage breaks up. At this point you will both have to buy separate life cover at an older age, when it will be more expensive.

Single Parents, Widows and Widowers

On divorce, or the death of a partner or spouse, you should review all your life assurance. A divorced woman needs to insure her former husband's life if he is paying maintenance, or vice versa if the wife is paying maintenance.

It is best if any divorce settlement includes a sum for the life assurance premiums and the wife maintains the policy. If the premiums are paid by the husband, he can discontinue the policy without the wife's knowledge.

Divorced or widowed mothers and fathers also need to ensure that they have sufficient life cover (term or convertible-term) on their own life. This should be sufficient to provide for the children during the years when they are still dependent – broadly, until the youngest child is aged 21.

Many wives are not insured. If, on divorce, you return to work and become the main breadwinner, you will need cover. You will also need to change existing life policies to ensure that they are written in trust for the benefit of your children, as your spouse will no longer inherit. Written in trust, the proceeds are outside your estate and free from Inheritance Tax. Any new policies taken out to top up cover should also be written in trust.

Middle-aged Couples

The middle years could be the right time to convert some or all of your convertible-term insurance to whole-life. This will pay out a lump sum to your dependants, whenever you die, at whatever age.

Even if your savings, investments and pensions would leave your spouse well provided for, you might want some whole-life insurance to cover any potential Inheritance Tax liability. If you delay making the switch until you are in your sixties (and possibly thinking of passing on assets to children and grand-children), the premiums for whole-life cover will be much higher.

For example, at age 44, you could convert £25,000 of cover to whole-life at a premium of around £400 to £450 a year. By the time you are 64, the same cover will cost approximately £1,300 a year.

The middle years are also the time when you will be reviewing your pension. If you are investing in personal pensions, you can buy life assurance cover through the pension policy and obtain tax relief at your highest rate paid on the premiums. There is a limit on the amount of life cover which can be bought through a pension policy. The maximum premium is 5 per cent of your eligible earnings up to the earnings ceiling (£75,000 for 1992–93 and 1993–94).

Older Married Couples

This is the time when you should be looking at any Inheritance Tax liability. You might want to take out a joint whole-of-life last-survivor policy on your own and your spouse's life. This will pay a sum of money, sufficient to pay any IHT liability, on the death of the second partner. It pays out on the second death because there is no IHT payable on transfers between husband and wife. The IHT liability will occur when the second partner dies. This assumes wills have been made leaving everything to the other partner.

For many couples their main asset is the family house. Philippa and Simon Fawcett are a typical example. They are 55 and 60 respectively, they have a house which is today worth £275,000 and other savings and investments of £40,000. They want to pass on the family house, tax-free, to their only daughter. If they were both to die tomorrow in a car accident, there would be an IHT liability of 40 per cent on the excess of their estate over £150,000 (1992–93). This works out at £66,000 (40 per cent of £165,000), which is more than the £40,000 cash in their estate, so their daughter would be forced to sell the family house to pay the tax bill.

The Fawcetts therefore decide to insure their lives on a joint-life, last-survivor basis for £50,000. This would mean that even if the house increases in value, there would be sufficient cash in the estate to pay the IHT bill and leave the house unencumbered. (The IHT threshold would, one hopes, rise too.) An alternative would be a with-profits, whole-of-life policy for £50,000. Hopefully the growth in death benefits would match any increase in the IHT bill.

The premium for £50,000 of cover is around £1,000 a year, payable to the date of the second death. The policy is written in trust, with the daughter as the named beneficiary, so the proceeds are outside their estate.

Retirement

This is the time when your personal pensions and self-employed retirement annuities reach maturity and you can take the accumulated fund and use it to buy an annuity or income for life. It is very important at this point to shop around because annuity rates can differ widely between insurance companies. Annuity rates are a function of your age (and the age of your partner if it is a joint-life annuity), your life expectancy, and interest rates at the time when the annuity is purchased. If possible, defer retirement when interest rates are low and wait until they have risen (see Chapter 5 on pensions). Once you have bought your annuity, you are generally stuck with the income at that level for the rest of your life, although there are now a range of annuities, such as with-profit, unit-linked, RPI linked, or conventional escalating, which provide either definitely or hopefully increasing income, although the starting annuity will generally be lower.

Buying Life Assurance

There are huge differences in the premiums charged for life assurance, so it pays to shop around or take advice. The difference in premiums between the best and the worst policies for exactly the same cover can be as much as 50 per cent or more.

Sadly, some life assurance salesmen push the savings-type contracts – with-profit endowments or unit-linked policies – because they earn higher commission on these sales. This could be dangerous. The life assurance cover contained in these packages is usually minimal so you must make sure that you get the cover that suits your particular circumstances.

The golden rule is make sure you have enough protection-type policies before you even consider endowments and savings. If in doubt, over-insure when you are young and protection is cheap, or have at least one policy where the sum insured is either index-linked, or the policy gives you the option to increase the amount of cover.

Hybrid policies which offer you the chance to buy protection, permanent health and savings all in one package may be more expensive than buying the different elements separately. Such policies are usually described as 'lifeplan' or 'lifetime' policies and may not provide good value for money.

It follows that it will pay to understand the different types of policy on offer, what they are used for and what they should cost.

Term Assurance and Convertible-Term Assurance

These policies are very similar. Both are straight protection policies which provide a lump sum, payable to named beneficiaries, or to your estate, should you die before the term of the policy expires. They are used to provide cash for your dependants should you die during the time when they are not able to look after themselves. The term of the policy may be anything from five to 25 years or longer, although you can buy very short-term cover, one year at a time, if you have a specific risk to cover.

As a single person or young parent in your mid-twenties, you would typically take out increasable convertible-term insurance for 25 years to cover the period when you are likely to have young dependent children. If you already have a family, aim to provide cover until the youngest child is 21.

The difference between term cover and convertible-term insurance is that you can, as the name implies, convert the convertible-term policy into another type of insurance. You might, for example, want to switch part of the cover to whole-life protection. This pays a lump sum to your spouse, dependants, or other named beneficiary whenever you die. Convertible-term insurance gives you the option to make the switch, without being obliged to give evidence of good health.

Unless the policy also includes options to increase the cover, you will only be able to convert it to whole-life cover for up to the original sum insured. However, this should not be a problem since whole-life cover is much more expensive than convertible-term (because the insurance company will inevitably have to pay out on your death, whereas with convertible-term there is only a possibility it will have to pay up if you die before the policy expires).

It is almost always worth paying the slightly higher premiums for convertible-term as opposed to term assurance because it gives you the added protection that if you contract an illness at a later date, you can still buy cover at standard rates without paying any extra premium. In a worst possible situation where you develop, say, cancer in your middle years, just when your family commitments are highest, without convertible-term it will be impossible to obtain life assurance at any price. Remember, convertible-term assurance insures your ability to obtain life assurance at some time in the future, whatever your state of health at the time.

Although inflation today at just over 1 per cent is not the problem it was in the 1970s and 1980s, there is no knowing what will happen in the future, particularly if you are buying long-term protection. It is therefore worth paying extra for increasable convertible-term. This usually gives you the following options:

- To index-link the premiums and benefits to the rate of inflation.
- To increase the premiums and benefits at a pre-agreed rate (say, 5 per cent a year).
- To increase the premiums and benefits at five-yearly intervals by a pre-agreed proportion of the original sum assured (a more common option).

A good policy will allow you to exercise your options to increase the benefits throughout the term of the policy.

If you want to fix the premiums from the outset but also take care of inflation, you could over-insure when you are very young and the premiums are cheap.

With convertible-term cover, price is not the only consideration. The option to switch into whole-life or a savings-type policy is worthless if the company's whole-life premiums are double the going rate, or the savings policies have poor invest-ment track records.

Best Rates for Convertible Term Assurance

Non-Smoker – £50,000. Annual Premiums – Male

Age next birthday	Term		
	5 yrs £	10 yrs £	20 yrs £
30	79.43	90.95	99.69
45	176.36	233.00	329.00
55	380.50	537.00	869.00

Source: Money Management

There is no point paying for the conversion option if the company does not have any policies into which you want to switch. In this context, the cheapest convertible-term policy might not always be the best.

If price is your main consideration, go for straight term assurance without the conversion option – the cheapest policy will be the best.

But even this is not the whole story. Different companies have varying views on what lives they are prepared to insure and the risk you present. Some will insure you almost without question up to a certain limit, say, £50,000. Others may quote a cheaper rate, but will be very selective about the risks they are prepared to take on. For example, they may insist on a full medical, or load the premiums for anyone doing anything other than a white-collar office job. Some companies will not offer cover to single males because of the Aids risk.

All companies take differing views of health risks, so if, for example, you have a heart complaint, it will pay to shop around as there are wide variations in cost. The above table shows the best rates currently available in 1993.

Uses for Term and Convertible-Term

Convertible-term is generally used for straight protection to provide for your dependants should you die when they are unable to take care of themselves.

Term assurance is used in exactly the same way, but it has other applications. You might, for example, need to provide cover on your own or someone else's life for seven years after you have given away or received assets in order to provide cash for any potential Inheritance Tax liability (see Chapter 7).

For example, you might at age 60 put £200,000 in trust for your grandson. The potential Inheritance Tax liability if you die within seven years of making the gift is between £80,000 and £16,000, depending on when you die. This assumes you have already fully utilised the zero-rate band by previously making transfers in excess of £150,000. Term assurance could be purchased to cover your life for the seven years when your estate has a potential IHT liability.

Family Income Benefit

This is a variation on straight term cover but is rarely bought or sold today. On death the policy pays your dependants monthly income, rather than a lump sum, until the end of the term of the policy. This type of policy should be written in trust.

Whole-Life

A whole-life policy has no specific term, but guarantees to pay a pre-agreed lump sum on your death, whenever that might be. If you already have term or convertible-term cover, you will only need whole-life if your partner, spouse or other dependants could not live comfortably on their own income, plus whatever other assets you will leave, after you die.

You might, for example, have a disabled child needing expensive residential care for the rest of its life, long after you have died. Whole-life cover would ensure that there would be a lump sum, payable on your death, which could be invested to produce an income to cover the cost of full-time care.

Most couples buy term or convertible-term protection to cover the risk when they are young. By the time you reach retirement, you have probably been able to make provision for your partner through savings and pensions policies, and provided these are adequate, whole-life cover will probably not be needed. Children, unless for unusual reasons they are likely to remain dependent, can usually take care of themselves by the time you are in your sixties.

Whole-life cover is more expensive than convertible-term

because the policy is guaranteed to pay out at some stage – you will inevitably die.

Whole-life cover is also used to provide for an unavoidable Inheritance Tax liability. Transfers between spouses are free from IHT, but if, for example, you want to pass the family home on to your children or grandchildren free from IHT, you may have to buy whole-life insurance to cover the liability.

Whole-life – How Much Does it Cost?

Non Profit – Non-smoker – Male

Age next birthday	Sum Assured		
	£50,000	£100,000	£150,000
	£	£	£
30	336.40	672.80	1,009.20
40	551.00	1,070.88	1,606.22
50	943.00	1,829.42	2,744.13
60	1,664.60	3,234.95	4,852.43

Source: Equitable Life

You cannot avoid Inheritance Tax by giving away the family home and continuing to live in it. This is called a 'gift with reservation', and the transfer does not avoid IHT. This problem
can be solved if you buy a whole-life (or joint-life, last-survivor policy if you are a married couple) to provide a cash sum sufficient to pay the IHT liability when you die, or in the case of a married couple, on the second death. Of course, this may not matter if the house was to be sold anyway and the proceeds split between several children or grandchildren.

Joint-Life Policies

As the name implies, two lives (usually, but not always, a married couple) are covered by joint-life policies. These come in two varieties and have two very different uses.

Joint-life, First-death

Joint-life, first-death policies provide a lump sum payable on the death of the first partner. They are most commonly used as mortgage protection policies, providing a lump sum to pay off the loan on the death of the first partner. They may be level-term if the mortgage is an interest-only endowment loan, or decreasing-term if it is a repayment mortgage.

Since most couples need two incomes to be able to buy their home, it makes sense to insure both lives. Although women usually earn less than men, their earnings make an important contribution to the family budget, so it is worth covering this risk.

However, there is a drawback to joint-life, first-death policies. One in three marriages end in divorce, and in this situation you may not want your former spouse or partner to benefit from the proceeds of the mortgage protection policy. If you have to discontinue the joint-life policy and take out separate insurance at that point, it will cost more.

It might be better to insure both lives separately for whatever proportion of the mortgage each partner is paying for. For example, John and Marianne Leighton are 30 and 25 respectively and buying their first home on a 25-year £100,000 repayment mortgage. John earns £24,000 a year and Marianne £16,000.

If they take out a joint-life last-survivor policy for the whole £100,000, the cost is £218.14 a year. But if they decide to take

Joint-life, First-death – Level-term 25 years (interest-only loan)*

Sum insured		£50,000		£100,000		£150,000	
Ages next birthday		Annual premium	Monthly premium	Annual premium	Monthly premium	Annual premium	Monthly premium
Husband	Wife	£	£	£	£	£	£
25	20	137.00	11.67	271.00	22.83	405.00	34.00
30	25	159.00	13.50	315.00	26.50	471.00	39.50
35	30	217.00	18.33	431.00	36.17	645.00	54.00
40	35	333.00	28.00	663.00	55.50	993.00	83.00
45	40	537.00	45.00	1071.00	89.50	1605.00	134.00
50	45	867.00	72.50	1731.00	144.50	2595.00	216.50
55	50	1395.00	116.50	2787.00	232.50	4179.00	348.50
60	55	2163.00	180.50	4323.00	360.50	6483.00	540.50
65	60	3239.00	270.17	6475.00	539.83	9711.00	809.50

* These figures are calculated with an interest rate of 7.99%.

Source: Equitable Life

Joint-life, First-death – Decreasing-term 25 years (repayment loan)*

Sum insured		£50,000		£100,000		£150,000	
Ages next birthday		Annual premium	Monthly premium	Annual premium	Monthly premium	Annual premium	Monthly premium
Husband	Wife	£	£	£	£	£	£
25	20	95.44	8.20	187.87	15.91	280.31	23.61
30	25	110.57	9.46	218.14	18.43	325.72	27.39
35	30	148.41	12.62	293.82	24.74	439.24	36.85
40	35	227.88	19.24	452.75	37.98	677.63	56.72
45	40	371.67	31.22	740.34	61.94	1109.00	92.67
50	45	608.17	50.93	1213.34	101.36	1818.50	151.79
55	50	984.68	82.31	1966.35	164.11	2948.03	245.92
60	55	1552.28	129.61	3101.55	258.71	4650.83	387.82
65	60			Special Rates			

* These figures are calculated with an interest rate of 7.99%.

Source: Equitable Life

out two separate mortgage protection policies for £100,000, the cost will be £93.54 for Marianne and £127.60 for John.

Joint-life, Second-death

Joint-life, second-death policies pay out on the death of the second partner, and are used almost exclusively by married

Joint-life, Last-survivor*

Sum insured		£50,000	£75,000	£100,000
Ages next birthday		Annual premium	Annual premium	Annual premium
Husband	Wife	£	£	£
25	20	44.00	64.50	85.00
30	25	45.00	66.00	87.00
35	30	47.50	69.75	92.00
40	35	56.50	83.25	110.00
45	40	81.00	120.00	159.00
50	45	141.50	210.75	280.00
55	50	277.00	414.00	551.00
60	55	537.00	804.00	1071.00
65	60	967.50	1449.75	1932.00

* These figures are calculated with an interest rate of 7.99%.

Source: Equitable Life

couples in Inheritance Tax planning where the liability to IHT does not arise until the second partner dies. You should insure for sufficient to cover any potential Inheritance Tax liability (see Chapter 7).

The younger you are when you buy joint-life cover, the cheaper it is, but the greater the likelihood of divorce. Once divorced, you will no longer want, or be able, to transfer the property to your spouse free of Inheritance Tax, so you will need single-life cover.

Mortgage Protection

Mortgage protection is just another name for term assurance. It pays out sufficient to repay your home loan should you die before the end of the term of the loan when the mortgage becomes repayable.

With interest-only endowment or pension-linked loans, level-term insurance is usually built into the package, and your endowment premiums will include a sum to cover the mortgage protection risk. With pension-linked home loans you will be entitled to tax relief on the pension premium.

If you have a repayment mortgage, you will be offered decreasing-term mortgage protection, where the sum insured decreases over the term of the loan to take account of the fact that you are repaying the capital.

For a single person with no dependants, mortgage protection is not necessary, although do bear in mind that it will be more expensive to buy if you marry and decide you need cover at a later date. Some lenders, however, make it a condition of the loan that you take out mortgage protection cover, in which case you will have no option.

If you have no life assurance, it would, however, be better to purchase convertible-term cover when buying a house (for all the reasons mentioned before) rather than take the mortgage protection which doesn't have the conversion option.

Mortgage protection should be cheaper than convertible-term, but this is not always the case because of the huge differences in the premium rates charged by varying life companies.

Annual Premiums for Mortgage Protection Cover – Decreasing-Term 25 years*

Age	20		25		30		35		40		45	
	M	F	M	F	M	F	M	F	M	F	M	F
Sum insured	£	£	£	£	£	£	£	£	£	£	£	£
£15,000	16.58	16.58	17.15	16.58	21.69	17.72	31.91	23.39	50.07	34.94	81.86	55.18
£20,000	21.11	21.11	21.87	21.11	27.92	22.62	41.54	30.19	65.76	45.33	108.14	72.57
£25,000	25.64	25.64	26.58	25.64	34.15	27.53	51.18	36.99	81.45	55.91	134.43	99.96
£30,000	30.16	30.16	31.30	30.16	40.38	32.43	60.81	43.79	97.14	66.49	160.71	107.36
£40,000	39.22	39.22	40.73	39.22	52.84	42.24	80.08	57.38	128.52	87.65	213.28	142.14
£50,000	48.27	48.27	50.16	48.27	65.30	52.06	99.36	70.98	159.90	108.82	265.85	176.93
£60,000	57.33	57.33	59.60	57.33	77.76	61.87	118.63	84.57	191.28	129.98	318.42	211.71
£70,000	66.38	66.38	69.03	66.38	90.22	71.68	137.90	98.17	222.66	151.14	370.99	246.50
£80,000	75.44	75.44	78.46	75.44	108.68	81.49	157.17	111.76	254.04	172.31	423.56	281.28
£90,000	84.49	84.49	87.90	84.49	115.14	91.30	176.44	125.36	285.42	193.47	476.13	316.07
£100,000	93.54	93.54	97.33	93.54	127.60	101.11	195.71	138.95	316.80	214.63	528.70	350.86

Annual Premiums for Mortgage Protection Cover – Level-Term 25 years*

Age	20		25		30		35		40		45	
Sex	M	F	M	F	M	F	M	F	M	F	M	F
Sum insured	£	£	£	£	£	£	£	£	£	£	£	£
£15,000	22.20	22.20	24.00	22.20	30.60	24.60	45.60	33.00	72.00	49.80	116.40	79.80
£20,000	28.60	28.60	31.00	28.60	36.80	31.80	59.80	43.00	95.00	65.40	154.20	105.40
£25,000	35.00	35.00	38.00	35.00	49.00	39.00	74.00	53.00	118.00	81.00	192.00	131.00
£30,000	41.40	41.40	45.00	41.40	58.20	46.20	88.20	63.00	141.00	96.60	229.80	156.60
£40,000	54.20	54.20	59.00	54.20	76.60	60.60	116.60	83.00	187.00	127.80	305.80	207.80
£50,000	67.00	67.00	73.00	67.00	95.00	75.00	145.00	105.00	233.00	159.00	381.00	259.60
£60,000	79.80	79.80	87.00	79.80	110.40	89.40	173.40	123.00	279.00	190.20	456.60	310.20
£70,000	92.60	92.60	98.00	92.60	128.80	103.80	201.80	143.00	325.00	221.40	532.20	361.40
£80,000	105.40	105.40	115.00	105.40	150.20	118.20	230.20	163.00	371.00	252.60	607.80	412.60
£90,000	118.20	118.20	129.00	118.20	168.60	132.60	258.60	183.00	417.00	283.80	680.40	460.80
£100,000	131.00	131.00	143.00	131.00	187.00	147.00	287.00	203.00	463.00	315.00	759.00	515.00

* These figures are calculated with an interest rate of 7.99%.

Source: Equitable Life

Hybrid Policies

Hybrid policies are a combination of straight life cover (term or convertible-term or whole-life) and a savings plan. Check whether you can buy the individual elements of the policy more cheaply if you purchase them separately.

These policies are marketed under fancy names like 'Plan for Life', 'Lifetime' or 'Passport for Life', and work like this. You pay a monthly premium. The policy gives you the option of deciding how much life cover you need, and the balance is put into the savings part of the contract. However, the insurer reserves the right to increase the premiums on the straight life cover at various stages throughout the contract, dipping into the savings part to pay for the higher premiums. You therefore cannot be certain what it is actually costing you or how much money you are saving.

Permanent Health Insurance (PHI)

After straight life cover, permanent health insurance is probably the most important protection, and a must if you can afford it – particularly for the self-employed. This type of policy pays out an income, if necessary until retirement age, if you are unable to work through sickness, accident, or disablement.

In recent years life companies have sold 'dread disease' policies, which pay out a lump sum on diagnosis of several life-threatening illnesses – certain cancers, heart, liver or kidney failure, and the like.

PHI is much more comprehensive and may be a better buy than dread disease. The illness that strikes you down and makes it impossible for you to work is not necessarily going to be one of those listed in the 'dread disease' policy.

Most people are well aware of the consequences of premature death and insure against this happening. But few realize that you are far more likely to have an accident or serious illness and be unable to work or get about than you are to die before the age of 65. Permanent health insurance provides cover for just such an eventuality. It pays a monthly income, usually up to age 60 or 65, if you have an accident or serious illness and are unable to work.

Both the employed and the self-employed can buy this cover – indeed, it is vital for the self-employed, as a sole trader, for example, may have no income at all from the first day of being unable to work. Employees, on the other hand, generally find that their employer will continue to pay them for anything up to six months of sick leave. Note, however, that PHI premiums for the self-employed are higher than for employees.

Women also pay roughly 50 per cent more than men for PHI

cover because the actuarial tables used by the life companies concerning the incidence of sickness among women are years out of date. As the number of working women buying the cover increases, the life companies are building up a broader statistical base on which they can review the incidence of claims. The situation should improve, but at the moment, women are still penalized.

Permanent health insurance varies widely in the terms and conditions of the policies available. For example, there is often a long list of exclusions, including pregnancy-related illnesses, pre-existing conditions, Aids and many others. There may be different benefits if you become long-term disabled, depending on whether you are unable to work, or unable to 'follow your usual occupation'. Some policies take into account any earnings you may have and deduct them from the benefits. Others don't pay out at all if you are able to do work of any kind. Choosing a policy is difficult, and it will definitely pay to take advice.

Underwriting on these policies can be very tough, so the insurance companies which offer this cover can be very choosy about whom they accept. This is because it is a lifetime policy – once you have taken it out, it cannot be cancelled by the company (although you can discontinue the premiums). No matter how many claims you make, even if you are unable to work for the rest of your life, the company has to pay until the benefit period expires, unless the policy has a specific limit on claims. As a result, you will generally be expected to have a medical before you are accepted by the life company, and if you have had any serious illness, you may have the premiums heavily loaded to reflect the risk. There is frequently an exclusion for pre-existing conditions. In a worst possible case you may not be able to obtain cover at all.

PHI is one area of life assurance where there is considerable scope for dispute and litigation. With straight life cover you are either dead or you are not. With PHI you might be permanently disabled, but you could be malingering. It was to cope with this problem that insurers introduced 'dread disease' or 'critical illness' cover. With this type of policy the life company's liability is limited to a one-off lump-sum payment on diagnosis of certain specific fatal conditions which are easily identifiable.

Dread disease or critical illness insurance is directed at people's fears of contracting cancer or having a heart attack, while keeping premiums at a level that makes the cover easier to sell. It is better than nothing, and is generally cheaper than full PHI cover, but it is not really very satisfactory. If you are unable to work for the rest of your life, the sickness which disabled you is immaterial. Full PHI cover is far superior if you can afford it.

Self-employed People and Non-earners

The self-employed pay more for PHI cover because the insurance companies take the view that these people may find too many incentives to remain ill. This may be justifiable. Who is going to hurry back to work if business is bad? Premiums will be loaded, depending on the job you do, and the maximum cover obtainable may be relatively low. Some companies do not offer PHI for the self-employed at all.

Cover for non-working men or women who are carers or looking after young children is available, but is more difficult to obtain. Very few companies offer it, and there is usually a fairly low maximum benefit of around £10,000 a year. This is because the insurers take a similarly sceptical view of non-working women as they do of the self-employed.

Deferral Period

With all PHI policies there is a deferral period – usually a minimum of one month – before benefits are paid. If you are able or prepared to accept a longer deferral period, the cost can be cut dramatically. Say, for example, your employer will pay your salary for up to six months of illness, you could manage with a six-month deferral period, and the premiums will be lower.

However, some self-employed people, such as sole traders, have a problem in that their earnings stop almost as soon as they are sick. One month might be the maximum deferral period. In this case you can cut the cost by insuring for a smaller proportion of your income. You might decide, for example, to insure for just enough to cover the mortgage and household bills.

How Much Can You Insure For?

Maximum cover is usually between two-thirds and three-quarters of your earnings at the time you become disabled or seriously ill. This point is important as it can lead to misunderstandings when there is a claim.

For example, you might insure for PHI benefit of £30,000 a year when you are earning £40,000, i.e. three-quarters of your earnings. However, at the time of the claim, business may be bad and your earnings are only £30,000. Your maximum claim will therefore be £22,500, three-quarters of the lower figure.

This limit is imposed because the intention is that you should not be better off financially while sick than when you are working. You cannot insure for 100 per cent of your earnings because the insurer wants to provide you with an incentive to get well and return to work.

This limit also takes into account that the benefits from a PHI policy are not taxable until they have been paid for a full fiscal year. For example, if you are permanently disabled, say, on 10 April 1995, the PHI benefits will not be taxable until 6 April 1997 – almost two years later.

The limit will also make allowances for the fact that if you are an employee, you might be entitled to statutory sick pay.

Declaring Your Income

There are several definitions of earnings or income. Some policies, for example, do not take into account bonuses, even though they may be regular, predictable and not entirely dependent on your efforts. Other companies use gross earnings as the basis for calculating maximum benefit, while others use after-tax pay. There is generally an absolute maximum amount of income you can insure – commonly around £50,000 a year – but a few companies have no limit.

How Much PHI Cover Do You Need?

When deciding on the level of cover, you should take into account any State benefits to which you are entitled. Employees will generally be eligible for Statutory Sick Pay paid by their employers for up to 28 weeks. If you are not eligible for this, you will receive Sickness Benefit, also for 28 weeks. After this period, if you are still unable to work, you will receive Invalidity Benefit. The self-employed will probably be entitled to Family Income Support.

State Sickness and Disability Payments	
Weekly Benefit	1993–94 £
Sickness Benefit	
Under pensionable age	42.70
Adult dependant	26.40
Over pensionable age	53.80
Adult dependant	32.30
Child dependant	10.95
Invalidity Pension	56.10
Adult dependant	33.70
Child dependant	10.95
Invalidity Allowance	
Higher rate	11.95
Middle rate	7.50
Lower rate	3.75
Statutory Sick Pay	
Higher rate	52.50
Lower rate	46.95
Severe Disablement Allowance Age-related	
Higher rate	11.95
Middle rate	7.50
Lower rate	3.75
Adult dependant	20.15
Child dependant	10.95

Occupation and Effect on PHI Premium

Premiums for PHI vary widely – not just between companies offering similar cover, but according to your occupation. Factory workers, for example, are much more likely to suffer an injury at work, so premiums are loaded to reflect this fact. White-collar workers, who are supposed to lead a less adventurous existence, are considered a better risk, so cover is cheaper.

Making a Claim

You cannot claim until the deferral period has expired; this may

Annual Premium for PHI Cover

Benefit, £100 a week payable to age 60 – Class 1 occupation

Age next birthday	Deferral period							
	4 weeks		13 weeks		26 weeks		52 weeks	
	M	F	M	F	M	F	M	F
	£		£		£		£	
25	150	208	114	114	114	114	114	114
30	117	249	114	131	114	114	114	114
35	209	296	115	156	114	114	114	114
40	250	358	141	195	114	125	114	114
45	306	442	175	245	116	157	114	140
50	365	530	213	302	141	194	121	165
55	341	495	191	290	138	190	121	165

NB All figures rounded to the nearest pound. Benefits illustrated based on a salary of £10,817 p.a. Cover will continue until 60th birthday.

Source: Norwich Union

be anything from one month to six months or more, depending on the terms of the policy.

Make sure you understand the conditions for claiming. These will inevitably include a doctor's certificate, but you might be required to have signed on for State sickness benefit.

When you first fall ill, there is generally no problem over the initial claim. If you have a serious car accident and you are lying in a hospital bed with broken limbs and are unable to speak, no insurance company is going to dispute your claim.

Disputes often arise when you start to get better, as the insurance company is always tempted to believe that you are dilly dallying – and no doubt some claimants do. There can be problems on claims if you are suffering from some less easily definable condition like back pain, where it can be difficult to measure your real incapacity objectively.

On making a claim, the definition of 'disability' and the level of benefits paid will vary from company to company. If you are permanently unable to follow your normal occupation, you will receive benefit, but it may not be the full amount for which you have insured. If you never fully recover but may still be able to do work of some kind, many life offices take this into account and reduce benefits pro-rata.

Some companies pay benefit even if you do get another job – albeit not your previous job and at a lower salary. More often benefit is reduced to take account of the fact that you may be able to get a suitable job which is not so well paid.

Other companies reduce your benefit by the amount of actual income you are earning once you return to work. This in itself can provide a disincentive to get better. Some companies may review each case individually and throughout the period of claim. Most will ask for medical reports if the disability looks like being permanent and having a serious effect on your earning capacity and ability to work. The majority of companies offer a waiver of premiums while you are claiming benefit.

As the evidence shows, PHI can be a minefield, so it is very important to take advice before signing up. Terms and conditions vary widely and it will pay to consult a specialist broker who knows your particular circumstances and what is available in the market.

Medical Fees Insurance

Medical fees insurance is not strictly life insurance, although it is often sold along with PHI cover. It provides a sum of money to pay for medical fees if you are treated privately outside the National Health Service.

About 80 per cent of all medical fees insurance is provided as a perk by employers through group schemes, and through affinity groups like the AA. The employer may pay all or part of the premiums. If you join through an affinity group, you will be entitled to large discounts.

In recent years premiums have rocketed to reflect the rising incidence of claims, and it is doubtful whether this cover is worth purchasing if you have to pay for it yourself.

If you are seriously ill there is no doubt that you are generally better off being admitted to an NHS hospital. Few private hospitals have accident or casualty units, and there are rarely any doctors on duty. In an emergency, you will probably be treated more quickly through the NHS.

If your illness and the treatment required is minor – varicose veins, for example – the cost of paying for the treatment outright is probably considerably less than the premiums for medical fees insurance.

The best-value policies are those, pioneered by Private Patients' Plans (PPP), which pay fees for private medical treatment, but only if the waiting time for treatment under the NHS is more than six weeks. These policies are relatively cheap and good value for money, offering the best of both worlds.

Of course, if your employer offers free medical fees insurance or discounted premiums, it is worth taking it up. Otherwise it is expensive and of dubious value.

Accident and Disability Insurance

Accident and disability insurance pays a lump sum if you are injured in an accident or permanently disabled. It pays no benefit if you are unable to work through illness.

Pure accident insurance would pay nothing if, for example, you suffered a stroke and were bedridden for the rest of your life. Accident and disability insurance may pay in these circumstances, but the definition of 'permanently disabled' can be very specific.

Accident and disability insurance is an annual contract, meaning that it has to be renewed every year. It is of limited benefit as you generally have to lose an eye, a limb or be permanently disabled by an accident (sometimes disabling illness) before any benefits are paid. It is not worth bothering with if you have permanent health insurance. You will also find that the premiums are loaded if you play sports, particularly potentially dangerous activities like skiing or bicycle racing.

Life Assurance – Medical Limits

Provided you are in good health, you should have no difficulty obtaining life assurance cover at standard rates. The one exception to this is single males where, even if you are in excellent health, you are considered an Aids risk and your premiums may be loaded. Most insurance companies now ask all applicants to fill in a 'lifestyle' questionnaire to determine whether or not you are an Aids risk. Clearly, if you are a practising homosexual or a drug user you will find it very difficult, if not impossible to obtain cover.

If you come into this category contact the Aids charity, the Terrence Higgins Trust (52 Gray's Inn Road, London WC1X 8LT; tel:071-831 0330). The trust has considerable experience of dealing with this problem and has specialist brokers who may be able to help.

All applicants for life cover will have to fill in a health questionnaire and you may be asked to undergo a medical if the sum insured is very high, or the life company wants further clarification of your health record. The questionnaire will also ask you for details of any serious illnesses.

Many insurers will provide cover of around £50,000 for anyone who claims to be in good health without a medical, although almost all now ask you to fill in a lifestyle form to establish whether there is a potential Aids risk. The precise 'non-medical-limit' varies enormously from company to company from nothing up to £250,000 or more. Above this limit, or if your health track record is not good, the company will want you to have a medical.

Medical underwriting practices vary greatly between different companies. Some are much tougher than others and their medical officers may take differing views of the same risk. Some companies, for example, won't even quote for a woman who has tested positive for cervical cancer, even though it has been treated 100 per cent successfully. Others are prepared to quote with a decreasing premium loading for every year the follow-up tests remain negative. The attitude towards various risks will depend very much on the company's own underwriting experience.

Always declare any serious illnesses on the application form. If you don't, the life company may refuse to pay the benefits to your dependants on the grounds of non-disclosure.

If you think you may be a poor risk, you would be well advised to consult an insurance broker, who will know which life companies are prepared to give a quote for someone with your particular health problem. The British Insurance and Investment Brokers Association (14 Bevis Marks, London EC3A 7LH; tel: 071-623 9043) can recommend members in your area.

Many companies offer discounts for non-smokers, but these are not necessarily the cheapest rates. The best premium from a life company that does not offer non-smoker discounts may still be cheaper than the rate quoted by another company offering discounts.

Tax on Life Premiums

Tax relief on life assurance premiums was abolished in March 1984. Policies taken out before 14 March 1984 are still eligible for tax relief on premiums and are generally worth maintaining for this reason. Do not cash them in unless you have to.

Life premiums paid under a personal pension policy also qualify for tax relief at your highest rate paid (see Chapter 5).

Tax on Benefits

The benefits paid out under most straight life assurance contracts including term, convertible-term, whole-life and endowments, are generally free of income tax and Capital Gains Tax and are known as 'qualifying' life policies.

However, you can be liable to higher-rate tax or a reduction in age allowance and consequent increased tax liability in certain circumstances on qualifying policies if you cash them in within 10 years and they have run for less than three-quarters of their term. The most common example of this is if you cash in a unit-linked Maximum Investment Plan in the first seven and a half years of its existence and it has shown substantial capital gains (see Chapter 6).

Those who are single, divorced or widowed, including single parents, should make sure that life policies are written in trust to avoid the proceeds being included in your estate and subject to Inheritance Tax. This will also apply in certain circumstances if the proceeds are intended for someone other than your spouse. For example, you may have a seven-year term policy on your own life to pay a potential Inheritance Tax liability on money given to your grandchildren. If you die within seven years, the grandchildren will be liable for any IHT charge, but if you insure your life for the potential liability, the policy can be written in trust for the benefit of the grandchildren and the proceeds will be outside your estate.

Bear in mind that, although the proceeds of a life policy are usually tax-free, the investment income generated when the money is invested is taxable in the usual way.

Savings-Type Life Policies

These should not really be regarded as life assurance, since the amount of cover is minimal and they are actually long-term savings plans. The most common are with-profit endowments and unit-linked life policies. All savings-type policies are dealt with in Chapter 6, which covers savings and investments.

5

PENSIONS AND PLANNING FOR RETIREMENT

Saving for retirement has never been more important. With both main political parties now currently reviewing the State Social Security Benefits – and in particular State pensions – we are clearly into an era of providing for ourselves. The reality of the situation is that with an increasingly ageing population the State cannot afford to provide for everyone without huge increases in taxation or National Insurance contributions. In future, State pensions may be reduced, particularly for middle-income families and above.

But even if under any new regime you still manage to qualify for a State retirement pension, it is unlikely that you will be able to do anything much more than survive on it. The vast majority of middle-income families will have to make their own provision for pensions if they are not to suffer a severe drop in living standards.

State Pensions

The basic State retirement pension currently stands at £56.10 a week for a single person, £89.80 for a married couple (1993–94) and you are entitled to the maximum only if you have made the requisite National Insurance contributions. This means that you must have paid contributions for roughly 90 per cent of your adult life.

The State retirement pension is made up of three elements:

- The basic pension based on your National Insurance contributions.
- An earnings-related supplement (SERPS) based on contributions made since April 1978.

- A third element (for older employees) based on 'graduated contributions', which were deducted from earnings between 1961 and 1975.

If you have paid contributions to SERPS (State Earnings-Related Pension Scheme), or if, between 1961 and April 1975, you paid Graduated Contributions, you will get more than the basic State pension, but it is not a lot.

The calculation of your precise entitlement is complicated but the original aim of SERPS, introduced in 1978, was to provide the average employee on average earnings who had worked and made contributions to SERPS for at least 20 years, with a pension at retirement of at least half pay. This would be made up of the basic State pension and the SERPS supplement.

Average earnings of full-time employees are only £340 a week for men, £241 for women, so even if you qualify for the maximum SERPS addition, retirement today on nothing but the State pension would be tough financially.

To make matters more difficult, not everyone is eligible for the maximum benefits. To qualify for the full basic State pension you must have made National Insurance contributions, or been credited with them, for 39 years out of the 44 between the ages of 16 and 60 if you are a woman, or 44 years out of the 49 between the ages of 16 and 65 if you are a man. This may well be altered soon, as the government is considering equalizing the pension age at 65.

Anyone who has periods of working abroad, goes to university or embarks upon a higher education course will have difficulty qualifying for the full pension. Women who have career breaks while they bring up children, or those who do not work after they are married, will find it still harder to earn maximum benefits. However, many will be entitled to a State retirement pension based on their husband's earnings. Working wives can qualify in their own right.

Since 1978, anyone who stays at home to look after children or other dependants can earn home responsibilities credits, which means you need fewer contributions in order to qualify for the State pension.

You can find out how much you might receive in State pension by filling in form BR19 (available from your local DSS office) and sending it to the Department of Social Security

Retirement Forecast and Advice Service, RPFA Unit, Room 37D, Newcastle upon Tyne NE98 1YX. The service will give you a report on the amount of pension earned to date, including SERPS and graduated contributions, and a forecast of your entitlement by retirement age.

Graduated Contributions

If you were employed between 1961 and 1975, you will be entitled to a small extra pension based on your earnings during these years. Contributions were based on earnings in excess of £9 a week.

Most people can effectively ignore any return from these contributions because it is small. For 1992-93 the *maximum* supplement to the basic retirement pension anyone could have earned from Graduated Contributions is £5.11 a week for a woman, £6.10 a week for a man. This figure is index-linked in line with inflation.

If you were in a 'contracted out' company pension scheme, you might have earned extra pension from your occupational scheme. Check with your former employer and the DSS.

State Earnings-Related Pension Scheme (SERPS)

This is an earnings-related supplement paid in addition to the basic State pension. Contributions are deducted from your pay at source, and anyone earning between the National Insurance 'lower earnings limit' and the 'upper earnings limit' (£2,912 and £21,840 for 1993-94) will be eligible for SERPs, unless any of the following circumstances apply to you:

- You belong to an occupational pension scheme which is 'contracted out' of SERPS.
- You have 'contracted out' yourself by buying a personal pension.
- You are self-employed, in which case you are not eligible to join SERPS.

While you are unemployed, you will not be given any credits for SERPS, and neither will those with home responsibilities.

It is virtually impossible for you to work out what your

entitlement to SERPS will be as the rules are unbelievably complicated, although you can use the DSS forecasting service, mentioned earlier, to do it for you. Those retiring after 1999 will not get as much as they were originally promised, as the government has cut back on SERPS benefits because of the rapidly spiralling cost.

Remember, however, that the intention of the legislation was to provide the average person on average earnings with a basic pension and SERPs supplement which would total £170 a week for a man retiring today, or £120 for a woman. Whatever the actual figure is by the time you retire, in spending power it will be roughly the same. Bear this in mind when making your own provision for retirement.

Women and National Insurance Contributions

Working women who pay the full rate National Insurance (NI) contributions qualify for State benefits and retirement pension in exactly the same way as men. However, most have career breaks to bring up children, and since 1978 it has been possible to qualify for home responsibility credits for NI contributions. Until 1977 it was possible for married women to pay reduced NI contributions, and many still do. But it has not been possible to do so since that date if you have returned to work since 1977. You will be paying the full stamp.

Reduced-rate contributions allowed married women to qualify for a State pension on their husband's record (as non-working women still do). If you come into this category, you will have to wait until your husband retires to qualify for a pension. You will not be eligible for any SERPS benefits.

Widows

Widows can qualify for a number of State benefits on their husband's contribution record. Leaflet NP45 from your local DSS office will explain your entitlement. All widow's benefits, except State retirement pension, stop on remarriage or if you live with a man as a married couple. If you do not marry but subsequently move out and live alone, you should become entitled to benefits once again. Widows benefits are index-linked, like the basic State retirement pension.

Those widowed after the age of 60 will be entitled to the basic retirement pension; those under 60 will be entitled to a widow's pension plus a widow's payment of £1,000 if the husband had not retired. They will also be entitled to a SERPS supplement, based on the husband's SERPS contributions.

In or Out of SERPS?

In 1988 the government introduced incentives in the form of National Insurance rebates and bonuses to those employees who decided to opt out of SERPS. Looking forward, the government could see that the cost of providing earnings-related pensions would eventually cripple the country; the State pension scheme is a pay-as-you-go scheme and National Insurance contributions paid by employees today are used to pay the pensions of those already in retirement. There is no element of investment.

To encourage people to opt out of SERPS and make their own pension provision the government introduced a rebate of that part of National Insurance contributions which relate to SERPS, plus a 2 per cent bonus on earnings between the lower and upper limits for National Insurance contributions, payable until April 1993. This bonus has now been reduced to 1 per cent from April 1993, and is only paid to people aged 30 and over who contract out, using a personal pension scheme. It is now usually referred to as an 'additional age-related rebate' rather than a bonus or incentive.

For most employees in final salary schemes the decision is simple, as most of these schemes are already contracted out of SERPS, so you have no choice. For the remainder – those in contracted-in pension schemes and employees in non-pensionable employment – it may pay to opt out of SERPS if you are under 45 (for men) or 40 (for women), but, as a general rule, remain in SERPS if you are over that age.

Some five million employees have already opted to contract out of SERPS, but it is not at all clear whether they have done the right thing. High charges in the early years on contracted-out personal pensions, and penalties if you discontinue them (you could change jobs to a company which has a contracted-out scheme), often eat up all the advantages of the rebate and bonus. This does not apply to contracts with Equitable Life. The best advice is, if in doubt, stay in SERPS.

The self-employed do not have to worry since they are not eligible to join SERPS in the first place, so they cannot contract out.

At the moment (Summer 1993) you have the option to go back into SERPS. If you have already opted out, say, at the age of 27 three years ago, it will be to your advantage to opt back in at the age of 45 or thereabouts (for men), or 40 (for women). Ask your pension adviser or the company that sold you the pension policy if you are in any doubt. They are obliged to give you 'suitable' advice.

Employees who are members of a contracted-in occupational pension scheme can take out a personal pension known as a MAPP (minimum appropriate personal pension) for the sole purpose of contracting out of SERPS, yet remain within the occupational pension scheme. This is often known as a 'rebate only' personal pension because the contributions consist entirely of the National Insurance rebate plus the 2 per cent incentive – (1 per cent from April 1993). If you did not opt out of SERPS in 1988 when the incentive was 2 per cent, there does not seem much point in doing so now the 'bribe' has been cut to 1 per cent.

Planning for Retirement

Clearly, with the State pension worth so little, everyone should consider making extra provision for retirement – either through an occupational pension scheme, additional voluntary contributions (AVCs), a personal pension, or other forms of long-term saving, such as Personal Equity Plans (PEPs).

The golden rule with all investment – and planning for retirement is no different – the sooner you start, the better. The longer the money is invested, the greater the return. The difficulty is that when you are bringing up a family you may have little or no spare cash to lock up long-term.

Women's pension needs may be different from men's. Women have a longer life expectation, retire earlier (although we will probably see the State retirement age equalized at 65 in the next few years), and frequently have fewer years when they are earning and can build up pension rights or save for retirement.

The effect of career breaks on pensions is dramatic, whether you are a man and the reason is unemployment or a return to academic studies, or a woman and you take time off to have children or care for an elderly relative.

The cost of providing a pension for a woman who works all her adult life, will generally be around 10 per cent more than for a man because she retires five years before her male counterpart.

If, as is common, a woman takes just five years off to have children, she will have to contribute 50 per cent more to a pension scheme than a man in order to retire on the same pension.

Occupational or Personal Pension Plan?

About half the working population, some 11 million employees, are members of an occupational pension scheme run by their employers. Since April 1988 membership of occupational schemes has been voluntary, but, generally speaking, if you have not already joined, it will pay you to become a member rather than try to provide for yourself through personal pensions. The reason is simple.

With almost all occupational schemes two contributions are made: one from the employee and another from the employer. Commonly, these are around 5 per cent of gross salary for an employee, with the employer contributing probably 8 or 9 per cent, in some cases much more.

No personal pension can begin to compensate on performance because there is usually only one contribution to a personal pension – your own – while the occupational scheme enjoys two contributions, one from you and one from your employer.

In some cases the employer may be the only contributor. If the employer makes all the contributions, it will clearly be to your advantage to join since it is costing you nothing (unless you have accepted a reduced salary to take account of the pension contributions).

The life assurance industry, which produces personal pensions, has acknowledged the fact that employees are generally better off belonging to a company scheme, and has put out tough guidelines for intermediaries who advise employees on pensions. It is almost always to your advantage to join a company pension scheme or stay with it if you are already in.

Occupational Pensions

There are two main types of occupational pension scheme – final salary and money purchase. You will have no option but to join whatever scheme your company runs, but it is worth understanding the differences because they are vitally important to how well you will live in retirement and the way in which you make extra provision.

Final Salary Schemes

The vast majority of employees in occupational pension schemes are in final salary schemes and will, typically, enjoy a pension of 1/6oth of their salary at the date of retirement for every year of employment. For the person who works for 40 years with the same firm, this works out at 40/6oths or two-thirds of his final salary at retirement age – the maximum permitted by the Inland Revenue. In less good schemes the fraction is 1/80th of final salary for each year you are employed, or even 1/120th.

For example, if Mr Simpson reaches retirement age with Scruttons Graphics Ltd on a salary of £37,000 a year and the company has a 60ths scheme, the maximum pension he can receive is £24,420 a year – two-thirds of final salary. In reality he is likely to receive considerably less than this for two reasons:

- Many final salary company schemes are 'integrated' with the State pension, and a deduction from maximum benefits to take account of State pension will often be made.
- Virtually no employees work all their life with one company, and those who leave a pension scheme before retirement age will receive reduced benefits (see Job Changers, page 111).

If your company pension scheme was set up before 14 March 1989, and you joined it before June of that year, there is no limit on the amount of your pay that can be taken into account. In other words, if you were earning £200,000 a year at retirement, you could retire on a maximum pension of £133,332 a year. Otherwise, the maximum pay which can be taken into account is £75,000 (1993–94), indexed in line with inflation most years, although it was not raised in 1993. The effect of this change in 1989 has been to make high earners and top executives less willing to change jobs.

More than nine out of 10 company pension schemes are final salary schemes, and over 82 per cent of them offer one-sixtieth of final salary, or better, for every year of service.

The big advantage of a final salary occupational pension scheme is that the employer guarantees the benefits. If you reach retirement age and the pension fund does not have sufficient money to pay your pension as promised, the employer has to pay up. Only in extreme circumstances, where paying up would bankrupt the company, are pension benefits reduced, but they cannot be cut for benefits earned to date. In practice, this does not happen often because pension schemes are reviewed regularly by the fund's actuaries to ensure that there are sufficient assets to meet the fund's liabilities.

If the assets are insufficient, the employer makes an extra contribution to cover the shortfall. Your employer has to pick up the bill and effectively 'guarantees' the pension. Very occasionally, when a company has been in difficulties, pension benefits have been reduced, but this is unusual.

The Maxwell case, where fraud is involved, is unusual. As a result of this highly publicized case, the Goode Committee is currently looking at ways of ensuring that members of occupational pension schemes are protected from fraud. A compensation scheme will almost certainly be set up.

As long as both you and the employer contribute to your pension fund, the decision about whether to join or not is quite clear-cut – join. Two contributions are always better than one. Your employer should provide you with an annual statement of your pension benefits earned to date. If he does not, or you cannot understand what the statement is telling you, contact your pension fund manager.

Money Purchase Schemes

A minority of employees work for companies that have money purchase schemes. Money purchase, as the name indicates, means that your pension benefits are related to the amount of money paid in contributions (by you and your employer) and how well these contributions are invested. The pension paid at retirement will not necessarily bear any relationship at all to the salary you are earning at retirement.

Smaller firms tend to run money purchase schemes because

the employer's liability is limited entirely to the contributions he decides to make. He may decide, for example, to put 5 per cent of the payroll into the pensions pot. However, if the pension at retirement is a quarter or less of the salary you are earning and is insufficient to live on, the employer has no obligation to do anything about it.

None the less, provided your employer is making worthwhile contributions to the scheme, it will still pay you to join, on the basis that two contributions are better than one. In addition, there will probably be valuable death-in-service benefits (typically three times your annual salary) and dependants benefits, which would cost considerable sums for you to provide yourself. Only if your employer's contribution is negligible should you consider going it alone with a personal pension. This decision is important because, once you join the company pension scheme, you will not be eligible to make contributions to a personal pension plan.

Money purchase, as the name implies, means that what you pay for is what you get. The pension it finally provides on retirement may bear no relationship to the salary you were earning: it could be more or less. There are few guarantees, and your employer's liability is limited to the contributions he has contracted to make. If this means that you end up with an inadequate pension, he has no responsibility to do anything about it.

Money purchase schemes are usually run by an insurance company (although they can be run by the employer) and operate like with-profit endowment life policies, or unit-linked life policies. With the former there are some guarantees; with the latter the value of your pension fund depends entirely on the value of the underlying investments.

The advantage of this type of pension scheme is that you derive full benefit from the contributions; you do not lose out if you change jobs. In addition, they are often easier to understand than final salary schemes, and allow you greater control and flexibility.

The disadvantage is the obvious one that the pension may not bear any relation to the sort of income you had before retirement. However, this usually becomes apparent well before retirement date (you can ask for a valuation, say, seven to 10 years in advance) and you can make extra provision through Additional Voluntary Contributions (AVCs).

The important point to bear in mind is that the pension may be more or less than you need to live comfortably in retirement – usually less. However, if you become a member of any occupational scheme, you will be able to top up your pension (whether final salary-linked or money purchase) with an AVC or Free-Standing Additional Voluntary Contributions (FSAVC) (see page 116).

Unitized With Profits

In recent years insurance companies have introduced unitized-with-profits contracts on both life and pensions policies. They provide a halfway house between the traditional with-profits and unit-linked policies, with some of the features of both types of contract.

The policy is unitized and, unlike a straight unit-linked contract, the units are guaranteed to grow at a certain minimum rate (although this is not very high – usually 3 to 4 per cent). The guarantee, however, operates only on maturity or death. If you surrender the policy early the unit price can be reduced.

The performance of the underlying investments is smoothed, and like the conventional with-profits policy, bonuses are added which cannot be taken away. This is shown as an increase in the unit price, or number of units allocated to your policy. Critics would say that this is the worst of all possible worlds.

Group Personal Pension Schemes

The aim of the original personal pensions legislation was to give employees greater control over their pensions. It was envisaged that they would opt out of occupational schemes (which did not always provide sufficient pension, particularly for early leavers, and could be very restricting in terms of job mobility) and take out personal pensions, which are portable and can be taken from job to job.

It was also envisaged that, where this happened, the contributions the employer had been making to the company scheme would be transferred to the employees' personal pensions. The government, however, did not place a statutory requirement on employers to do so. As a result, virtually no employer has volunteered to make contributions to employees' personal pensions – not least because of the administrative nightmare of making thousands of one-off payments to hundreds of different schemes.

However, some companies have set up group personal pensions whereby you can have a personal pension to which the employer makes a contribution, but the policies are all with one insurance company for ease of administration. Whether it is a good idea to join such a scheme will depend on the level of your employer's contributions and the company with which the personal pension is arranged. If the employer is making a worthwhile contribution – say, 5 per cent of your gross salary or more – it will probably pay you to join, even if the insurance company has a poor track record. You can always move the accumulated fund to another company when you change jobs, although there will almost certainly be penalties for doing so.

Hybrid Schemes and Others

Increasing numbers of employers are reluctant to commit themselves to a full final salary scheme because of the unknown cost. Many are introducing hybrid schemes, which have an element of final salary linking and an element of money purchase, the exact proportions dependent on the employer's expected ability to fund an unknown commitment to final salary benefits. The money purchase element may contain some guarantees, as in a with-profits endowment, but this is likely to be low.

A very few employers operate a 'flat-rate' scheme where benefits are guaranteed, but bear no relationship to your final salary. These are usually based on deferred annuities.

Job Changers – Early Leavers from a Final Salary-linked Pension Scheme

Few employees retire on the maximum pension of two-thirds final salary because job-changing is common and, until relatively recently, had a detrimental effect on pension benefits.

Changing jobs before 1978 generally meant that your pension benefits would be frozen within the scheme. You might, for example, have been with your employer for seven years, in which case you would have earned a pension of 7/60ths, but based on your salary at the date of leaving rather than on retirement. There was, and still is, no legal requirement to uprate this to take account of inflation.

For those who have left a company since 1 January 1991, any pension benefits left with your former employer on changing jobs have, by law, to be given a degree of inflation-proofing. They must be uprated in line with inflation or by 5 per cent, whichever is less. (This does not apply to Guaranteed Minimum Pensions.) For example, if you left your company scheme in 1991 after five years' service, and your salary at the date of leaving was £15,000, your pension entitlement would be 5/60th of £15,000 – £1,250 a year. This pension, if you leave it with your former employer, must be uprated by the lesser of inflation or 5 per cent.

Much will depend on the level of inflation. If it runs at more than 5 per cent, you will reach retirement age with a pension that has lost its buying power. New legislation has improved the position, although it is still far from perfect. The current situation is as follows:

- If you leave the pension scheme within two years of joining, you are entitled to a full refund of your contributions, provided the scheme allows it. You will not be entitled to contributions made by your employer. If the scheme was contracted out of SERPS, part of the refund is used to buy you back into SERPS, and a tax deduction of 20 per cent will be made from the remainder.
- If you leave after two years, you must be given one or other of the following:

a) A preserved pension. Any Guaranteed Minimum Pension (GMP) which relates to contracting out of SERPs must not be any worse than if you had you remained in SERPS. In addition, if you leave a pension scheme after 1 January 1991, all pension benefits must be revalued by the lesser of inflation or 5 per cent.
b) A transfer value which can be invested in your new employer's pension scheme, a Section 32 'buyout' pension policy, or a personal pension. (Transfers between public sector schemes have different rules.) You cannot transfer the lump sum into the old S226A Self-Employed Retirement Annuities (SERAs).

If you decide on a transfer, it is always better to wait until interest rates are low because the sum of money transferred is then higher. You can ask for a transfer value any time up until one year before retirement.

It is not a good idea to transfer out of any scheme which has guaranteed index-linked benefits, or has, in the past, voluntarily paid index-linked benefits to deferred pensioners. Almost all public sector employees are in index-linked schemes and should on no account transfer out of them.

If you were in a company pension scheme between 1978 when SERPS started and today, a proportion of your frozen pension, known as the Guaranteed Minimum Pension, has to be uprated each year in line with wage inflation. The GMP is the pension you would have earned if you had remained in SERPS. (Most occupational pension schemes are contracted out of SERPS.)

Anyone joining an occupational scheme today will have a substantial measure of inflation-proofing for their pensions, even if they do change jobs. Older employees, particularly those with numerous years of service prior to 1978, will have lost a large proportion of the benefits earned if they have changed jobs a number of times over the years. Clearly, it would be wise to make good any shortfall by making contributions to an AVC or FSAVC scheme, or saving in some other way.

Options on Leaving

If you have been in a company pension scheme for less than two years, the scheme does not have to offer you any preserved benefits; the cost of administering a very small frozen pension would be high. You should, however, be given a refund of your contributions. There may be two deductions made from this sum. If your company scheme was contracted out of SERPS, there will be a deduction to buy you back into SERPS. The second is a deduction of 20 per cent on the balance to take account of the tax relief you have already had on the contributions.

Preserved Pension

After two year's service your former employer is obliged to offer you preserved pension rights if you leave the company. You can, however, claim back all contributions paid by you prior to 1975 if the scheme allows a refund. Whether it is to your advantage to do so will depend on your employer's policy on uprating pension rights to take account of inflation. You will have to ask.

Transfer Payment to a New Employer's Scheme

Your former employer is obliged to offer you a transfer value for your pension rights, but your new employer is not obliged to accept it. Even if he is prepared to do so, the amount of pension it buys is unlikely to be the same as the pension you would have enjoyed if you left it with your former employer. It could be better, but is much more likely to be worse. There could be several reasons for this:

- Your former employer may be mean or generous in the way he calculates the present-day value of your preserved pension benefits (although there are guidelines for calculating some of the benefits).
- The value of the mandatory and promised increases must be included in the calculation, although the value of any discretionary uprating need not be.
- The transfer sum, if accepted by your new employer, may buy better or worse benefits because of the structure of his scheme.

One thing is certain: because of the way transfer values are calculated you will get a larger sum at a time when interest rates are low. If you change jobs when interest rates are high, it will pay you to defer taking a transfer until rates come down.

A good company scheme will offer you independent advice on whether to take a transfer payment or opt for preserved pension benefits. The decision on whether to transfer is difficult and will vary from scheme to scheme. If you are not offered free advice, it will generally pay you to employ a firm of consulting actuaries or pension consultants who will be able to assess the situation and advise you of your best course of action. This might cost from £200 to £300, but is money well spent.

Transfer to a Personal Pension

If you prefer, you can take your transfer sum and put it into a personal pension chosen by yourself. Here again, whether this is better than opting for preserved benefits with your former employer or putting the money into the scheme run by your new employer will depend on a number of factors: your former employer's policy on uprating deferred pension benefits; your new employer's policy on crediting you with pension years of service; and the likely benefits you will earn with a personal pension.

Like all decisions on personal pensions, the benefits earned will depend very much on the investment performance of the fund in which your personal pension contributions are invested. Here again, you will need to take professional advice.

You should also bear in mind that a high proportion of complaints to the Occupational Pensions Advisory Service (11 Belgrave Road, London SW1V 1RB; tel. 071-233 8080) concern the difficulty pensioners have in tracing pensions earned with former employers and getting the firm to pay up. There is an advantage in having all your pension in one place.

Over the course of your career, your former employer may be taken over, pension funds may be merged and benefits policy may be altered. It is not unknown for employers to lose track of what happened to deferred pension benefits earned 20 years ago, so taking your transfer sum and putting it in a personal pension may be the easiest way of keeping tabs on what has happened.

The decision is simpler if your former employer's scheme is not a final salary scheme but a money purchase pension plan. In this case benefits are not linked to your final salary. Your contributions, and any made by the employer, are invested to produce a fund at retirement which is then used to buy an annuity or income for life. This is exactly the same as personal pensions.

The decision to transfer or stay will therefore depend on how the investment performance of the company scheme compares with the investment performance of the best personal pension policies. If it is poor, take the cash transfer value and put it into a personal pension.

Additional Voluntary Contributions

Job-changing almost always affects your pension entitlement from a final salary-linked pension scheme run by an employer, but this may not be the case with a money purchase scheme. There is now a considerable amount of protection for the pension benefits of job changers, but the fact remains that there are many employees now nearing retirement who will not have earned enough pension benefits in their company scheme to retire in comfort.

One answer is to make extra contributions to an Additional Voluntary Contributions (AVC) scheme run by your employer. If the scheme offers benefits which are also final salary linked, this is usually a good bet so long as your salary rises faster than the rate of inflation. You buy 'extra years service'.

For example, Patrick Mahon has been with his current employer for only five years and is due to retire in 10 years' time. Prior to joining his current firm, he had been self-employed and had not been able to afford to put money away in a pension scheme. At the moment he has earned just 5/60ths of his final salary in the company pension scheme, and even if he stays to age 60 when he is due to retire, he can still notch up only 15/60ths of final salary – just a quarter of his earnings. However, he can 'buy' extra years service in the company's AVC scheme, and he is doing this on an annual basis, hoping to be able to boost his pension by purchasing another 10 years' service by the time he retires. This means his pension will be 25/60ths of final salary – almost half his earnings.

Final salary-linked AVCs are, however, relatively rare, and most employers run money-purchase AVCs, often invested in a straight bank or building society deposit.

Since October 1987, employees have enjoyed the absolute right to make contributions to Free-Standing AVC schemes (FSAVCs), not just the AVC run by their employer. This means that you can belong to your company's pension scheme, but buy an FSAVC of your choice from any life company. All FSAVCs are money-purchase and operate like a personal pension – you get what you pay for.

There is one potential drawback with AVCs. If you joined an AVC scheme prior to 8 April 1987, you will be able to take a proportion of the benefits at retirement as a tax-free cash lump sum, just as you can with the main pension benefits. But since that date, anyone taking out a new AVC cannot take any benefits as cash; the contributions can buy only a pension.

In reality, this is only a notional restriction because the pension benefits earned by your AVC are taken into account when calculating the maximum lump sum which can be taken from the main pension scheme.

For example, you may retire on a final salary of £24,000. Your main pension scheme pays you a pension of £8,000. As the pension is less than the Inland Revenue permitted maximum of two-thirds final salary, the lump sum you can take at retirement is restricted to £18,000. The AVC, however, might produce an annual pension of, say, £4,000 a year. This brings total pension benefits up to £12,000 a year and allows the main pension to pay you a lump sum of £27,000, assuming you have no pension from any other source. However, you should check your individual circumstances with the Trustees of your scheme.

You are entitled to full tax relief on contributions to an AVC or an FSAVC. There is a ceiling on the contributions of 15 per cent of earnings (up to £75,000 a year if you joined after 1 June 1989), and you must include in this 15 per cent any deductions made at source from your pay for contributions to the main occupational pension scheme.

A large number of life assurance companies offer FSAVCs, and you can invest in anything from a straight deposit account to the usual range of managed, equity, fixed-interest and property funds. There are also straight building society deposit schemes and with-profits endowment-type AVCs.

The vast majority of employees investing in AVCs should probably choose a straight deposit fund if they are only a few years off retirement, or a with-profits-type arrangement or managed fund if they have more than five years to go. Unit-linked AVCs and FSAVCs should be considered only if you can live with the higher risk and have at least seven to 10 years to go before retirement.

The table below shows the percentage of salary you need to contribute to an AVC or FSAVC at various ages to bring your pension entitlement up to the maximum permitted by the Inland Revenue – two-thirds of final salary.

The figures in the table below assume current earnings of £25,500, rising by 8.5 per cent a year, a retirement age of 65, that the invested contributions will grow by 12 per cent a year and that the member of the scheme will have completed at least 20 years service at retirement age.

Choosing an AVC scheme is very much like choosing a personal pension. There is a wide variety on offer, with differing investment track records. You will need to take advice.

How Much Should I Contribute to an AVC?
Pension Scheme Provides Half of Final Salary

Age next birthday	Pension scheme final salary £	Actual final salary £	Inland Revenue maximum pension £	Scheme pension £	AVC % to fund deficiency %
25	454,890	694,135	462,756	227,445	4.73
30	302,522	461,630	307,753	151,261	5.87
35	201,191	307,005	204,670	100,595	7.44
40	133,801	204,172	136,114	66,900	9.65
45	88,984	135,784	90,522	44,492	12.65
50	59,178	90,302	60,201	29,589	18.54*

* This would exceed the maximum allowable for tax relief.

Personal Pensions

Personal pensions were introduced in 1988 when the government wanted to encourage employees to contract out of SERPS. As the old-style SERAs could not cope with National Insurance rebate and the 2 per cent bonus, personal pensions were introduced to replace SERAs, which you can no longer buy, although if you had one prior to 1988 you can continue to make contributions to it (see below).

Personal pensions are long-term savings contracts designed to provide an income in retirement for those who are self-employed or in non-pensionable employment. You generally cannot take out a personal pension if you are already a member of a company scheme (except for a Minimum Appropriate Personal Pension (MAPP), which can be used to contract out of SERPS if your employer's scheme has not already done so).

People who have more than one job can belong to a company scheme for the main job, and make contributions to a personal pension for, say, income from part-time earnings.

Your contributions are invested in a fund run by the insurance company and the value of the accumulated fund available to buy your pension at retirement age will depend on how well the money has been invested.

There are generous tax concessions to encourage us to save in this way: tax relief is available on your contributions, on the dividends and capital gains made by the funds invested, and on part of the money when it is taken at retirement.

Personal pensions are generally issued by life assurance companies, though friendly societies, unit trust groups, banks, building societies and other financial institutions can offer them too. They can be complex contracts with all kinds of bells and whistles – waiver of premium if you are ill or unemployed and your income falls, the chance to increase, decrease or discontinue premiums, the opportunity to provide dependants' pensions at varying levels, or no dependants' pension at all (if you are single), the ability to switch the underlying investments between different funds, and a host of other options.

They also offer the choice of taking a lower pension in return for a tax-free lump sum at retirement – one quarter of the accumulated fund on a personal pension, usually rather more for the older Self-Employed Retirement Annuities (although the precise amount will depend on your age and the level of annuity rates when you retire).

But one thing that, surprisingly, is not always understood, is that once you have paid your money into a pension scheme, the only way of getting any of it back is to die or retire.

You can in certain circumstances borrow against the pension policy, but you will obviously have to pay interest on this. Money cannot otherwise be withdrawn.

If you are a single person and you die one month after retiring, you get nothing, unless you have opted for protected benefits, i.e. an annuity which guarantees payments for a number of years. The income paid in retirement on a pension policy reflects the fact that some people die younger than others.

How Does a Personal Pension Work?

Personal pensions and their predecessor, Self-Employed Retirement Annuities (SERAs), are 'money purchase' or 'defined contribution' schemes – in other words, what you get out in terms of pension at retirement reflects how much you have put in, and how well that money has been invested. The amount of money available at retirement age to buy your pension will depend on how well these investments have performed over the years.

Most large occupational pension schemes, on the other hand, are 'final salary' or 'defined benefit' schemes, which means that the benefits to be paid at retirement are set out in the trust deed and the employer then has to pay sufficient money into the fund to provide the promised pensions. Your contributions are likely to pay for only a small proportion of the eventual pension benefits.

All personal pension plans operate on the same basis. You pay your contributions into a tax-free pension fund, which may invest in anything from equities to fixed-interest securities and property. Under a with-profits plan a share of the investment profits is allocated to your personal pension policy, and at retirement age the accumulated contributions plus profits are used to purchase the benefits – an annuity, or income for life. You also have the option of taking part of the accumulated fund as a tax-free lump sum, and it is nearly always in your best interest to do so.

You can make regular contributions or one-off lump sums to a personal pension contract. Tax relief at your highest rate paid is allowed on contributions, and the investment fund into which these contributions are paid is also tax-free. This means that investments can accumulate at a faster rate than in, say, a life assurance savings contract where profits and dividends are taxed within the life fund.

The size of the accumulated fund allocated to your pension policy depends on how well the life company invests the contributions over the life of the contract, and what administration charges have been deducted from the value of the underlying investments.

Once paid in, money cannot be withdrawn from a personal pension until you reach retirement age. At retirement you have the option of a pension, which is treated as taxable income, or you can take a lower pension and a tax-free lump sum of up to 25 per cent of the accumulated fund.

With Self-Employed Retirement Annuities (SERAs), which preceded the introduction of personal pensions in 1988, it was possible to take a tax-free lump sum of three times the remaining annuity or income, which was sometimes larger than 25 per cent of the fund. So if you have existing SERAs, it is well worth continuing with them.

If you have dependants, you can arrange for a pension to be paid to them on your death. This typically might be one third, a half, or two-thirds of the main pension. Obviously, there is a price to pay for this. Broadly speaking, to provide a dependant's pension of two-thirds of the basic pension will cost around 20 per cent of the accumulated fund at retirement.

Differences between SERAs (S226) and Personal Pensions

	SERA	Personal pension
Retirement age	60–75	50–75
Tax-free cash	3 times the remaining pension income	25% of fund
Contract out of SERPS	No	Yes
Cash limit	£150,000*	None
Tax relief at source	No	Yes, if employed
Can accept employer's contributions	No	Yes
Transfers from other schemes	No	Yes

* Unless taken out before 17 March 1987.

Where there are no dependants, you can opt for a larger pension at retirement age and for the accumulated contributions plus any increase in their value to be paid to your estate should you die before retirement.

Generally speaking, if you are single and die after retirement, all benefits die with you unless you have opted to protect them – possible for up to 10 years. Here again, there is a price to pay in the form of a lower pension at retirement age.

Inflation today is not the problem it was back in the 1970s, although with the UK's exit from the European Exchange Rate Mechanism, we may well see inflation rise from its current low levels. Bear in mind that it might pay to take a lower pension, but have the benefits index-linked. What may seem a comfortable income when you first retire, could look hopelessly inadequate 10 years later. If you decide to do this, the income you receive initially will generally be around 30 per cent less than for a level pension. At age 65, taking a pension with 5 per cent increases each year, it will take you 14 years to break even.

Who Is Eligible for Personal Pensions?

The self-employed, and those who have earnings but are not members of an occupational pension scheme, are entitled to make contributions to a personal pension plan (or the old-style SERAs).

Employees who belong to a company pension scheme but have other earnings can make contributions to a personal pension in relation to this part of their income. The money you use to make the contributions does not have to come from earnings – you can use savings or an inheritance to pay contributions. This is very useful in later life when you may well have considerable unused pension tax relief.

Non-Earners

If you have no earned income, you are not eligible to make contributions to a pension scheme of any sort. In this situation you will probably have to rely on a spouse or partner to provide. Find out what benefits you may be entitled to.

In a good company scheme a dependent spouse or live-in partner could expect to receive a lump sum of three or four times the earner's gross earnings should he or she die before retirement age. If you are not married, make sure that your partner has nominated you to receive any benefits.

You might also be entitled to a widow's or dependant's pension of half your spouse's or partner's pension if he or she dies either before or after retirement.

If you are a second partner or spouse, there may be another claim on the benefits, particularly if children are involved, depending on what was agreed at the time of divorce. Some company pension trustees use their discretion and either split the benefits between both claimants, or pay both claimants anything from a half to the full dependant's pension.

If your partner or spouse is not a member of an occupational pension scheme, you should ask what pension provision has been made. At the very least, make sure he or she has life assurance which will provide a sensible lump sum of at least four times income on death.

Having checked on the provision made by your spouse or partner, your only alternative course of action if you have no earnings is to save in something like a Personal Equity Plan (PEP) or other long-term saving scheme (see Chapter 6 for full details).

Tax Relief

Pensions are one of the few savings vehicles which still attract tax concessions. They are the most tax-efficient way to save long-term for your retirement because you are entitled to claim relief at your highest rate paid on contributions made. The tables below show the maximum amount which can be contributed at various ages.

In 1989 the Chancellor of the Exchequer put an upper limit on the amount of earnings which could be taken into account when calculating maximum contributions to a personal pension. For 1989–90 it was £60,000, and since then it has been increased in line with inflation to £75,000 in 1992–93, and frozen at that level in 1993–94. There is no tax relief on pension contributions on earnings above this ceiling.

Maximum Contributions to a Personal Pension/Retirement Annuity

| Age on 6 April | % of net relevant earnings | | |
| | Personal pensions | | Retirement annuities |
	1988–89	1989–94	1987–94
35 or less	17.5	17.5	17.5
36–45	17.5	20.0	17.5
46–50	17.5	25.0	17.5
51–55	20.0	30.0	20.0
56–60	22.5	35.0	22.5
61–74	27.5	40.0	27.5
Life assurance*	5.0	5.0	5.0

* Included in the percentage figures, not in addition to them.

Maximum Contribution for Personal Pensions in Cash Terms

| Age on 6 April | Amount of Contribution | | | |
| | 1989–90 | 1990–91 | 1991–92 | 1992–93 and 1993–94 |
	£	£	£	£
35 or less	10,500	11,340	12,495	13,125
36–45	12,000	12,960	14,280	15,000
46–50	15,000	16,200	17,850	18,750
51–55	18,000	19,440	21,420	22,500
56–60	21,000	22,680	24,990	26,250
61–74	24,000	25,920	28,560	30,000
Maximum pensionable earnings	60,000	64,800	71,400	75,000

However, if you have some of the old SERAs, they are well worth maintaining, as there is no income limit on contributions (although the contribution limits are lower) and you can often take a larger proportion of the accumulated lump sum tax-free at retirement.

Anyone with income in excess of the ceiling can top up pension benefits with Personal Equity Plans (PEPs). There is no tax relief on money invested in a PEP, but the income from the investments, and any capital gains, are rolled up within the PEP completely tax-free.

People underestimate the value of this in retirement planning. For example, had you invested the maximum in PEPs from their introduction in 1987-88 to the current 1993-94 year, you could now have up to £43,200 (at their original cost) sheltered from both CGT and income tax – £86,400 for a married couple.

If this PEP investment had been used for pension planning, you could have invested in growth shares while working, converting the investments to high-income shares, unit or investment trusts at retirement, and enjoy a tax-free income. PEPs also have the advantage of allowing you to keep control of your money.

The tax advantages of personal pension contributions, however, are very generous. You can backdate your pension contributions to the previous tax year or the year before, and it may be advantageous to do so if you were paying tax at a higher rate in those years.

You are also entitled to pick up and carry forward unused pension tax relief for up to six years if in previous years you could not afford to make the maximum contributions to a pension scheme – and very few people can. In order to take advantage of this you must have paid the maximum contributions for the current tax year or the previous year. The rules are complicated but any pensions adviser or accountant will make the calculation for you, particularly if you intend investing.

Basic-rate tax relief on personal pension premiums is given in the same way as mortgage interest relief – it is allowed for in the premiums. If you are self-employed, you will pay gross contributions and obtain tax relief through a tax assessment. Higher-rate tax-payers will get further tax relief through a tax assessment, whether employed or self-employed.

When the pension starts to be paid at retirement, it is treated as earned income and is subject to tax in the usual way.

What Size Contributions?

The answer is, whatever you contribute the chances are it won't be enough. If you want to retire on a realistic pension, the sooner you start saving the better. The problem is that in the early years of marriage, when house purchase, school fees and the cost of children often accounts for most of your income, you can generally save very little. Of course, it is absolutely right to ensure that you have protection for your family in the form of life assurance, and shorter-term savings for things like school fees, before you start making heavy commitments to pension provision.

Unlike occupational pension schemes, there is no maximum on the amount of personal pension benefit you can take. The limits are on the level of contributions, but even here, few people can afford to contribute the maximum throughout their working life.

Maximum pension allowable from an occupational pension scheme is two-thirds of final salary, but there are two contributions to an occupational scheme – the employee's and the employer's. If you are making your own retirement provision through a personal pension, the income you receive when you reach 60 or 65 is entirely dependent on the level of your contributions, how well they have been invested and annuity rates at the time you retire.

The table below shows the percentage of earnings you would need to save in a personal pension to achieve the same level of pension as an employee in a good company scheme which pays two-thirds of final salary.

The figures assume that money invested in the personal pension plan shows an average return of 8.5 per cent a year. Salary and contributions are assumed to increase by an average of 6.5 per cent a year, and no cash is taken from the personal pension plan at retirement age.

Another way of looking at the problem is to ask, 'What will my pension contributions buy?' The figures look impressive until you take into account inflation and the real buying power of your pension.

Percentage of Income Needed to Produce a Pension of Two-Thirds Final Salary

Initial salary £10,000

Age now	Retirement age	
	60	65
30	18.9	14.1
35	23.6	17.2
40	30.8	21.6
45	42.6	28.2
50	66.3	39.1
55	129.5	61.1

What Will My Pension Contributions Buy?

Age now	25	35	45	55
Contribution	£50pm	£50pm	£50pm	£50pm
Accumulated fund at age 65	£161,000	£69,200	£27,700	£9,030
Tax-free cash	£40,200	£17,300	£6,920	£2,250
Annual pension	£13,800	£5,964	£2,388	£780
Real Values – Buying Power at Retirement				
Accumulated fund at 65	£22,900	£16,000	£10,400	£5,500
Tax-free cash	£5,710	£4,060	£2,600	£1,380
Annual pension	£1,960	£1,380	£900	£480

Source: Equitable Life

The figures assume 8.5 per cent growth in the value of the invested contributions and an average inflation rate of 5 per cent.

Of course, as your income increases you would expect to put more into your pension scheme. But the table shows the effects of inflation and the necessity to review your pension provision regularly.

As always, the sooner you start saving for retirement the better. The following table shows the effect of delay.

Most saving for retirement will be done after the age of 45 when the cost of providing for children has generally been taken care of. By this time, as the tables show, the sums of money that you need to invest to provide a realistic pension are high, and it is almost impossible to save too much. The figures look even worse for women who retire earlier, live longer and generally have breaks in contributions.

Cost of Delay

Man planning to retire at 65 and investing £50 a month

Age next birthday	Loss in retirement benefits	
	after 1 year's delay	after 2 years' delay
25	11%	21%
35	12%	23%
45	15%	29%

Source: Legal & General

This is the time when inheritance starts to be a consideration, and often you can use a lump-sum inheritance to pay up back contributions.

Endowment (With-Profits) versus Unit-Linked Pensions

Personal pensions come in two basic types: endowments (with-profits), which offer a certain level of guarantee, and unit-linked contracts, which do not.

The former are very like with-profit endowment life policies. Your contributions are held within a fund which invests in a mixture of shares, fixed-interest securities and property. Bonuses are added to your pension policy to reflect the overall, long-term investment performance of the fund, but not all the profits are paid out as bonuses. In the good years, when the fund is showing handsome gains, some are retained so that bonuses can be paid to policy-holders during the leaner years. However, once these bonuses have been declared, they are added to your policy and cannot be taken away. This does not apply to final or terminal bonuses where rates may fluctuate.

These with-profit pension policies offer a comforting level of security; indeed, some offer a guaranteed minimum bonus rate. They also provide a 'smoothing' effect, and avoid too great a degree of volatility. In contrast, unit-linked funds provide no guarantees and are far more volatile.

With a unit-linked policy your contributions are paid into a fund which may invest in shares, fixed-interest securities, property or a mixture of all three. The fund is 'unitized', and a number of units are allocated to your pension plan. The value of your units directly reflects the investment performance of the underlying fund. The total value of the fund is divided by the number of units in issue and the resultant price will be quoted in the daily newspapers. When the underlying investments rise in price, the value of your units will rise correspondingly.

The implications of this and the effect it can have on your pension are important. For example, people coming up to retirement age in the autumn of 1987 might have had widely varying experiences in terms of pension benefits paid out on a unit-linked pension policy.

Those who took their benefits before the stock market crash of October 1987 might well have been 30 per cent or more better off than someone retiring in, say, January 1988. Share prices worldwide dropped dramatically, and this would have been reflected in the value of units held in a unitized pension fund.

It is debatable in the low-inflation 1990s whether we will see the sort of returns from unit-linked and with-profit contracts that we were used to seeing in the 1980s. However, if you decide to take a chance with a unit-linked contract, there are ways of reducing the volatility in the run-up to retirement.

You can crystallize gains made in a unitized pension fund by transferring units into a safe cash or fixed-interest fund once you are within, say, two years of taking your pension.

Unit-linked pension policies offer a choice of funds into which your contributions can be channelled and you are able to switch funds depending on your investment objectives. However, very few individuals do actually switch their money around, although some financial advisers offer a management service, charging a fee to make the switching decisions for you.

The funds offered by the life company will generally include a managed fund, which invests in equities, fixed-interest securities and property, as well as a wide range of specialist funds investing in everything from the Far Eastern markets to the USA, commodity shares to smaller companies. A switch into the gilt or deposit fund just before retirement can lock in gains made in the more volatile equity funds.

The point to grasp is that personal pensions, like savings-type life policies, are all about investment performance. The better the investments perform, the greater the accumulated fund at retirement age, and the higher the benefits. Magazines, such as *Money Management* or *Planned Savings*, give comparative performance figures each month.

The table below shows the accumulated fund from the top ten endowment-type contracts. If you buy a unit-linked personal pension, much will depend on the fund to which contributions are linked. You cannot compare the investment performance of a unit-linked policy investing in a Far Eastern fund with one investing in the UK equity market.

Personal Pensions

Top Ten – Accumulated Fund – 5-year contract from 1.7.88 to 1.3.93*

Male £50 a month	£	Male £600 a year	£	Male £1,000 Single premium	£
Equit. Life	3,542	Sun Life	4,090	Sun Life	1,790
Sun Life	3,499	Equit Life	3,955	Friends Provident	1,772
Scottish Amic Se	3,455	Friends Provident	3,922	London Life	1,713
Friends Provident	3,451	Sun Alliance	3,868	Equitable Life	1,706
Scottish Amic Ee	3,421	Pearl	3,828	Commercial Union	1,673
Scot Equitable	3,421	Prudential	3,814	Clerical Medical	1,646
Pearl	3,414	London Life	3,807	Norwich Union	1,626
London Life	3,399	Scot Equitable	3,795	Pearl	1,607
Prudential	3,397	Scottish Amic Se	3,790	Legal & General	1,600
Legal & General	3,328	Legal & General	3,780	Prudential	1,597

* Figures show retirement fund including terminal bonus, assuming age 61 next birthday at inception, retirement age 65. Plans commenced 1.7.88 with retirement date of 1.3.93.

Top Ten – Self Employed Retirement Annuity – 5-year contract from 1.7.88 to 1.3.93

Male £40 a month	£	Male single premium £1,000 a year*	£	Male £1,000 single premium†	£
Royal London	3,802	Sun Life	2,258	Pearl	12,450
Sun Life	3,596	Royal London	1,963	AXA	11,624
Equitable Life	3,560	Clerical Medical	1,951	Scottish Life	11,134
Clerical Medical	3,527	Pearl	1,924	Clerical Medical	11,097
Eagle Star	3,464	Equitable Life	1,903	London Life	10,929
NPI	3,416	Commercial Union	1,896	Scot Equitable	10,616
Norwich Union	3,407	Standard Life	1,884	Equitable Life	10,524
Standard Life	3,374	Eagle Star	1,883	Scot Provident	10,149
Prudential	3,348	Prudential	1,843	Prudential	9,989
Friends Provident	3,300	Scot Equitable	1,843	Norwich Union	9,742

* Figures show retirement fund including terminal bonus assuming age 60 at inception for monthly premiums and for single premiums (*5 year term) and age 50 for single premium († 15 year term). Retirement age 65.

Source: Money Marketing With Profits Review

Which pension?

The first thing to understand is that you will almost certainly need professional advice when choosing a personal pension. The Society of Pension Consultants (tel. 071–353 1688) can recommend one of its members in your area. Go for the with-profits contract if you are likely to have sleepless nights over the riskier unit-linked type of policy. On the other hand, a belt and braces approach is probably best if you are a worrier. You might decide on a with-profits policy for, say, one third of your pension contributions, and the balance in unit-linked schemes with a broad spread of investments.

Deposit Administration Funds

If you decide on unit-linked schemes, it is sensible to consolidate the accumulated fund as you near retirement, realize units in equity, property and managed funds, and transfer them into a cash-based, deposit administration scheme.

This is like having money on deposit, only held within a personal pension. By doing this you avoid the possibility of a stock-market crash drastically reducing the value of your accumulated fund just before you are due to retire. You will, of course, also miss out on a sudden, last-minute spurt in shares if it takes place just before you retire.

Single Premium or Regular Premium?

You can put your money into a personal pension either as single-premium lump sums, as regular monthly or annual contributions, or as a mixture of the two. Most regular premium policies offer the facility to add lump sums.

Commission on single-premium pension policies at around 4 to 6 per cent of the sum invested are lower than on regular premium contracts where anything up to 52 per cent of the first year's premiums disappear in commission. This is in addition to the insurance companies' charges on the contract. The normal commission of 4 to 6 per cent for single-premium contracts applies if you add a lump sum to a regular premium policy.

Single-premium contracts are also more flexible, allowing you to pay as much or as little as you can afford on a year-by-year basis with no future commitment. This is particularly important for anyone who is self-employed and has fluctuating earnings. And as unused pension tax relief can be carried forward for up to six years, you are not missing out.

Regular-premium contracts have the advantage of imposing a discipline if you are bad at saving. With unit-linked pensions you also get the benefit of 'pound cost averaging' – your contributions buy more units when prices are low, less when they are high. This tends to even out the return.

You could, of course, get the best of both worlds by saving each month in a building society, and once a year transferring the lump sum via a single-premium payment to a personal pension.

If your personal pension is linked to the repayment of a home loan, you will generally find that the lender requires you to make regular pension contributions.

Choosing a Personal Pension

Planning for your retirement is something you should take very seriously. Pensions are complicated and you will inevitably be confronted with a variety of situations to which there is no simple answer. You may not even realize that you have a potential problem or that pensions can provide a tax-efficient solution to many situations not necessarily related to retirement.

For example, perhaps you own your own business. The rules for executive pension schemes and small self-administered pension schemes are very different, and pensions can play a crucial part in running your business, as well as providing income in retirement. (If you come into this category you will definitely need to take advice; it is not possible to cover details of these schemes in a book such as this.)

For example, your small, self-administered pension scheme might own the office block from which you operate, and it can hold shares in the company. Is this a good idea? Surplus profits can be ploughed into an executive pension scheme, but can the company get them back later?

The questions are endless. You may be self-employed now and buying a personal pension, but what should you do about deferred benefits which are locked up in the pension scheme of a former employer?

As a single person do you really need dependants' benefits, and if not, can they be provided later on marriage? What level of dependants' benefits do you need? Is it better for a spouse to make his or her own pension contributions? Do the death benefits form part of your estate for Inheritance Tax purposes?

Clearly, you will need advice and you should definitely consult your accountant, or a pensions adviser, who will be able to analyse your needs and suggest a suitable solution.

Questions to Ask Your Pensions Adviser

1. *What benefits will the plan give me?*
2. *What benefits will it give my dependants?*

Most policies allow you to tailor the dependant's pension to your particular need and will provide a dependant's pension of, say, one third or a half of the main pension. If both you and your spouse are investing in personal pensions, it is better for you each to make contributions in your own name rather than one or other of you relying on the dependant's pension from your partner's pension. The benefits are better.

3. *What happens if I am sick and I cannot afford to make contributions?*

Almost all personal pensions offer a waiver of premiums as an option which will pay the pension premiums during this period. They also offer contribution 'holidays' of anything up to two years or more. This is to cover periods when you suffer a drop in income, or increased demands on your finances, or you may be unable to work because of home responsibilities.

You should also ask if the pension has the option both to reduce and increase premiums. Some policies offer the option of index-linking both premiums and benefits.

4. *What happens if I have the chance to join a company pension scheme at a later date?*

Almost all pension policies allow you to make the policy 'paid up', which means that you make no more contributions, but the benefits are frozen until you retire.

5. *What benefits do my dependants or my estate get if I die before retirement?*

A good pension policy will offer the return of the accumulated fund plus profits up to the date of your death. If you are a single parent, these benefits should be written in trust for the benefit of your children to avoid Inheritance Tax.

6. *What are the charges?*

These will be written into the contract and vary from company to company. If it is a unit-linked policy, you may not have all your contributions allocated to units in the early years. There is almost always an annual management charge of around 1 per cent levied on the fund, and many companies have flat policy fees.

Commission paid to intermediaries is usually up to 6 per cent of the amount invested for one-off, lump-sum single premiums, or up to 52 per cent of the first year's premiums for regular-premium contracts. There are no hard and fast rules, and in some cases the charges and commission could be higher. It is not always easy to see where the charges are being levied, so ask your adviser.

7. *Are there any charges for paying higher or additional, one-off lump-sum premiums?*

This is a useful option if you want to boost your pension with a one-off, lump-sum investment, and you will usually pay the normal commission for a one-off pension payment of 4 to 6 per cent.

8. *What are the penalties if I want to transfer my pension to another company?*

Most personal pension contracts have penalties for taking your money to another company. These can be onerous. If you are not happy with the performance you may well be better off making an existing policy paid up and starting again with a different company.

9. *Can I alter the benefits and have a higher pension for myself if I become a widow or widower and have no other dependants?*

Yes.

10. *When can I retire?*

Between 60 and 75 for the old SERAs, or between 50 and 75 for personal pensions. Some occupations, usually professional sports-persons such as footballers, jockeys and the like, can retire at earlier ages by special concession from the Inland Revenue. You will need to take advice if you come into this category.

If you know absolutely that you want to retire at, say, 60, make sure that the pension plan is written to that age, not older. The higher the age at which you have an option to retire, the larger the pension adviser's commission and the less of your money is invested.

With the old SERAs, retirement can be taken between the ages of 60 and 75. Check whether there is any penalty imposed for early retirement.

11. *What life assurance cover can I include?*
Both personal pensions and SERAs offer tax relief on life assurance premiums written in conjunction with a pension. You can contribute up to 5 per cent of earnings for this benefit. This is very useful for providing dependants' benefits.

12. *Can the policy accept transfer payments from other personal or occupational pension schemes?*
Personal pensions can, the old-style SERAs cannot. You might, for example, have deferred pension benefits in the occupational pension scheme of a former employer which you want to transfer into the personal pension. Check that it has this facility.

13. *What are the options when I reach retirement age?*
Most personal pensions offer a variety of options on retirement. You can take up to 25 per cent of the accumulated fund as tax-free cash (three times the remaining annuity if it is one of the old pre-1988 SERAs).

If you decide that you need protection from inflation, you can opt for an index-linked pension, although this will mean that the benefit will start at about half the usual level. If 5 per cent inflation per annum is assumed, these would be a 30 per cent reduction in the initial pension.

You can also alter the dependant's benefits. Your partner may have inherited some money, for example, and there is no longer a requirement for a dependant's pension. This will mean that you can take a higher pension for yourself.

If you want the payment of pension protected, this is generally an option for anything up to the first 10 years. But you will have to accept a lower initial pension. You can also exercise the 'open-market option' and take your accumulated pension fund to another life company to purchase your annuity.

14. *Can I postpone retirement?*
You usually have the option to postpone retirement, if, for example, you decide to work on, or perhaps interest rates and therefore annuity rates are low.

Most companies now offer 'cluster' policies, which are a series of separate pension contracts. Some policies within the 'cluster' can be used at, say, age 60 to supplement income if you decide to work part-time rather than retire fully. The others are used at a later date. This is also a useful way of organizing your own 'index linking' to take account of inflation.

Options on Retirement

When you reach retirement age (which can vary between 50 and 75, depending on the type and terms of the contract), you will have several options:

- To take the maximum pension offered by the company from which you bought your pension policy. This may be a good or bad idea depending on what the guarantee is and whether it is possible to buy a better pension elsewhere.
- To commute part of the pension as a tax-free cash lump sum (25 per cent of the fund for personal pensions, three times the remaining pension for SERAs), and accept a lower pension.
- To take the accumulated fund and buy an annuity (income for life) from another insurance company (open-market option).

It cannot be emphasized enough that, after the choice of personal pension, the timing of buying your annuity at retirement, if it is of the conventional type, is crucial. If you retire when interest rates are low, annuity rates and therefore your income in retirement will be low and vice versa. Over the past 15 years interest rates have averaged 11 per cent, but this may not be the case in the future.

However, by postponing retirement or phasing it in, you can often obtain a much better return. Do not commit all your pension money to purchasing an annuity when interest rates are low, unless you absolutely have to. You will be locking yourself into a low income for the rest of your life.

Annuity rates vary widely between different companies and at different dates. The answer is to shop around. Two specialist annuity advisers who can advise on all aspects of annuities and phased retirement are: The Annuity Bureau (11–12 Hanover Square, London W1R 9HD; tel: 071–495 1495) and Annuity Direct (Pensions Bureau, 32 Scrutton Street, London EC2A 4SS; tel: 071–375 1175).

There are also other factors which will affect the level of income paid from your annuity:

- Single life or joint life.
- Your age and your partner's age (i.e. life expectancy).
- Frequency of payment (e.g. annually in arrears will provide a higher income than monthly in advance).
- Any guarantees (e.g. guaranteed to be paid for a minimum of five years, even if you die).
- Index-linking.
- Dependants' benefits.

Index-Linking

You will probably have the option to take a lower initial pension but have benefits index-linked to take account of inflation. The problem with this is that index-linking means that you will have to accept a cut of around 30 per cent in your pension at age 65 to provide 5 per cent a year increases, and it will be around 14 years before you break even on the deal.

Open-Market Option

Personal pension policy-holders will also be offered the opportunity to take the accumulated fund at retirement age and shop around for the best annuity rate in order to maximize the pension income. This also has the advantage of offering you the opportunity to consolidate all your pension in one place rather than collecting it from several different sources. You should take independent advice from a pensions consultant on where the best rates can be obtained.

Investing the Lump Sum

As it is tax-free and you do not know when you are likely to die, it is usually advantageous to take the maximum cash lump sum at retirement and invest it yourself. There are tax advantages in using the tax-free lump sum to effect a Purchased Life Annuity. You may decide simply to put it on deposit in the building society, or purchase an income bond. But whatever your decision, you will probably need advice (See Chapter 6 on investing a lump sum).

Personal Pensions versus Occupational Schemes

Advantages

- Personal pensions are portable, can be taken with you from job to job and maintained through periods of self-employment. There is no loss of benefit on changing jobs.
- They are more flexible and can be tailored to your specific needs in terms of both contributions and benefits.
- They can accept transfer payments from the pension scheme run by a former employer, thereby keeping all your pension in one place. A new employer's occupational scheme may not be prepared to accept a transfer from your old company.

Disadvantages

- Personal pensions are inevitably more expensive. To provide a comfortable living in retirement through a personal pension you will have to pay much more than if you were a member of an occupational scheme where your employer usually carries by far the greater proportion of the cost. Most employees in occupational pension schemes pay around 5 per cent of their earnings into a company pension scheme, when the real cost might well be around 15 per cent.
- There is no guarantee that the benefits from a personal pension will be sufficient to live on. They are defined contribution rather than defined benefit schemes. What you pay for is what you get. The income purchased with the accumulated cash sum at retirement age may bear no relation to your earnings at that time. It could be more or less.
- More than nine out of 10 occupational schemes pay benefits linked to your final salary on retirement; the best funds pay increases to pensioners in retirement. The employer guarantees your pension. He has to pay if there is a shortfall on the pension fund and it cannot pay the promised benefits. There is no such guarantee with a personal pension.
- Personal pensions cannot offer the guarantee of life

assurance because you may be a bad health risk and uninsurable. An occupational pension scheme will generally pay three times your annual salary and you are automatically insured through the group scheme, which will cover all employees, regardless of health.

The important point to remember about pension planning is that the sooner you start the better. Pensions are a complicated field and you will undoubtedly need independent financial advice, and a review at different times throughout your working life.

Help

If you have problems with your occupational pension scheme, either when you are employed, after you have left, or in retirement, write to the pension fund managers in the first instance. If this does not produce a satisfactory response, you should then write to the trustees. Finally, if all else fails, you can have the matter referred to the Occupational Pensions Advisory Service, which may refer it on to the Pensions Ombudsman (see Useful Addresses).

If there are difficulties with your personal pension or SERA, write to the company concerned initially, but if this does not produce a satisfactory result, you can ask to have your complaint referred to the Pensions Ombudsman.

Annuities

An annuity is a life assurance contract purchased for a lump sum, which pays an income during the life of the policy-holder. You can buy a single-life annuity, or a couple can purchase a joint-life contract, in which case the income is paid until the second person dies.

Annuities are used most commonly to provide income in retirement, although they are sometimes used to fund premiums on other types of life policies or to pay school fees.

The tax treatment of income paid to you through a 'purchased' annuity is advantageous as part of the income is deemed to be a return of your original capital; the exact proportion depends on your age. A purchased annuity is one you

Life Expectancy

Age	Male	Female
65	80.7	84.7
70	82.6	85.9
75	84.8	87.5
80	87.6	89.5

buy with your own savings, or with the tax-free lump sum you get from a pension scheme on retirement.

It is important to understand that once you have bought an annuity, your money has gone. If you die after only one year, you generally get nothing back at all, although it is possible to purchase 'protected benefits' annuities, where some money is repaid to your estate if you die in the first 10 years.

The life companies use the profits made on the annuitants who die early to pay for the benefits handed out to those who live beyond the normal life expectancy.

Open-Market Option

If you are self-employed and have personal pension plans and the old S226A Self-Employed Retirement Annuities (SERAS), or if you are a member of a money purchase occupational pension scheme, you will have the option when you retire of accepting the annuity offered by the life company which ran the pension plan, or taking the accumulated fund and shopping around for a better annuity elsewhere. This is known as the 'open-market option'.

Some life companies offer especially attractive rates to their existing policy-holders in order to keep them. But whatever the situation, it will pay to shop around before you make a final choice as annuity rates vary widely.

Choosing an Annuity

The level of income paid out by an annuity will depend on several factors:

- Your age, or the age of both you and your partner if you have a joint-life annuity.

- The level of interest rates generally at the time you purchased the annuity.
- The frequency of payment.
- The tax position of the life company.

People coming up to retirement or in retirement during a low-interest-rate period should consider deferring retirement, or only taking part benefits if possible, until such time as interest rates rise. Most personal pension policies offer the option of phasing in retirement by taking only part of the benefits.

Once you buy an annuity, you are stuck with that level of income for the rest of your life, and the variations can be considerable – not just between high-interest-rate and low-interest-rate periods, but also between the rates offered by different life companies at the same time. A difference of 10 per cent is not uncommon between two life companies quoting on the same day. There are a wide range of options which can provide increases – with-profits unit-linked, index-linked and conventional escalating – although the initial annuity will generally be lower.

Generally speaking, it may not be worth buying an annuity with your own savings until you are 70 or more, although this depends on your individual circumstances. The rates are not good under that age. If you are exercising the open-market option on a pension plan, you will have to buy the annuity at an earlier age if you want to retire.

Types of Annuity

There are several different types of annuity available.

Level – the income paid is fixed at the beginning and is paid at the same rate until you die. This type of annuity pays the highest income.

Increasing – the income paid rises each year at a pre-agreed rate, say 5 per cent. In return for these increases, you will have to accept a lower initial income – about 30 per cent less at age 65 – and it will be 13 years before you break even. If you are in poor health, this is not a good deal.

Inflation-linked – the income increases each year in line with changes in the Retail Prices Index, meaning that your annuity retains its buying power. The starting income will, however, give the lowest return of all.

Unit-linked – the lump sum is invested in a unitized fund (like a unit trust), and the income paid each year is expressed as a number of units in the fund, depending on your age and life expectancy. Each year the pre-determined number of units is cashed, but the income will fluctuate, depending on the investment performance of the units in the fund. (Not many companies offer this.)

With-profit annuities – these provide the opportunity for your income to grow. Of course, the amount of income you receive will depend on how well your fund performs. Many people will be familiar with the with-profits approach and such an annuity allows them to continue investing in this medium.

Payments from Annuities

The frequency of payment will affect the return from an annuity. It can be:

- Monthly, quarterly, half-yearly or annually in advance.
- Monthly, quarterly, half-yearly or annually in arrears.

If the payments are made in advance, the income will be lower than if it is paid in arrears.

- Protected benefits – you can opt for the income to be paid for a minimum number of years (anything up to 10), regardless of whether you die during the period, or for the original sum, less any payments made to date, to be returned to your estate on your death. If you choose this option, your starting income will be considerably lower.

Before you can shop around for the best rate you have to decide what type of annuity you want. Do you want:

- Escalating benefits.
- Dependants' benefits.
- Guaranteed or protected benefits.
- Frequency of payment.

In coming to your decision you should take into account the following factors:

- If you are in bad health, opt for the maximum tax-free cash lump sum from the pension plan and take the highest level annuity on offer. You may not live long to enjoy it.

- If there is a history of longevity in the family, or inflation is rampant at the time you retire, consider an index-linked, escalating annuity or phased retirement.
- If you choose a unit-linked-type annuity, will you be able to cope if the income falls?
- Do you need dependants' benefits – in which case you should choose a joint-life policy – or does your spouse have sufficient income in his or her own right?

Finally, if you opt for a lower annuity with escalating benefits, work out how long it will be before you break even on the deal. If it is beyond your normal life expectancy, as is occasionally the case, you probably shouldn't do it.

Tax and the Tax-Free Cash Lump Sum

Almost without exception it pays to take the maximum allowable tax-free cash lump sum from your pension at retirement. Not only does this give you greater flexibility, but it will produce a higher income.

If you use the lump sum to buy a 'purchased' annuity yourself, rather than leaving the entire fund with the pension trustees to purchase a 'compulsory' annuity, the overall income will be higher. This is because the tax treatment of purchased annuities is more advantageous than for compulsory annuities. Income from compulsory annuities is all treated as earned income. Income from purchased annuities is treated partly as earned income and partly as a tax-free return of a portion of the original capital, the exact amount depending on your age at the time of purchase.

For example, Mr Sandelson has an accumulated fund at retirement age 65 of £100,000. If he leaves it all in the fund and allows the trustees to buy a compulsory annuity, this will produce an income payable monthly in advance (guaranteed for five years) of £12,600 a year gross, £9,450 after basic-rate tax at 25 per cent. He can, however, take £25,000 tax-free and invest this in a purchased annuity. The £75,000 invested in the compulsory annuity produces an income of £9,450 gross, £7,102 after tax. But the £25,000 invested in the purchased annuity will produce income of £3,060 gross, £2,685 net, giving him a total after-tax income of £9,787 – an increase of £337 a year.

Basic-rate tax is usually deducted at source from the payments, but you can receive the income gross if you are a non-taxpayer. You will need to complete a form R86 or R89 when you buy the annuity.

6

INVESTMENTS

Surprisingly few people actually plan their investments. They buy a life policy because they have a mortgage, they invest a lump sum because grandparents have offered to pay a child's school fees, and they hang on to a motley parcel of shares because they inherited them.

A recent survey revealed that 56 per cent of adults never take advice, only 26 per cent have a main professional adviser, and 18 per cent take advice from several sources. Even among those who do take advice, just under half had never worked out a financial plan and those who had did not have it reviewed each year.

This simply does not make sense. Whatever your situation – even if you have little or no money to save – you should work out a sensible strategy. For those who have considerable sums to put away, it is important to review the situation regularly. Tax changes and a shift in the investment climate can radically affect decisions made some years ago. For example, many experts believe we are now entering a low-interest-rate era, which will last for some years. If that is the case, it will have a profound effect on everything from mortgages and building society deposits to annuities and income bonds.

In 1990 independent taxation was introduced, which meant that 4.5 million married couples who had investment income but the wife was a non-earner had to rethink their finances. To make the most of the wife's personal tax allowances and basic-rate tax band, it made sense to transfer assets into the wife's name.

These are just two examples of why it is important to analyse your finances and make sensible provision for the future.

Planning Your Strategy

There is a very clear, logical sequence when planning your personal finances. First and foremost, you must have adequate life assurance. Do not be seduced into taking out savings-type policies until you have bought enough life cover (see Chapter 4).

Second, you will need easily accessible cash, probably in a bank or building society high-interest account, in case of emergencies. Around £5,000 is probably about right, but you must be able to get at it in a hurry. By definition, an emergency is something of which you have been given no notice. Do not put your emergency funds into an account requiring notice.

You may need to keep more money readily available if you are self-employed and have a large tax bill (or pension premium) to pay once a year. However, this could go on a longer notice account – say 90 days – and earn extra interest.

Third, you can think about making provision for specific events – school fees, pensions and long-term saving. There is no real distinction between saving and investment, although saving has come to mean putting away regular sums of money on a weekly or monthly basis. Investment is generally understood to mean a lump sum.

There is no lack of choice when it comes to investment; the difficulty is to understand what you are being offered and whether it is suitable for your needs.

Risk

Your attitude towards risk will inevitably shape your choice. If you are the worrying kind, high-risk investments like commodity futures are clearly not for you. If you can't live with the ups and downs of the stock market, a with-profits policy or a guaranteed equity bond is more suitable than a straight investment in unit or investment trusts.

Savings and investment fall into two distinct categories: relatively low-risk interest-bearing investments, and higher-risk equity-based securities.

With interest-bearing investments the risk is that you will get stuck in a low-yielding investment at a time when interest rates are going up, or that inflation will erode your capital.

With equity-based investments the risk lies in the innate

volatility of shares and the ultimate risk that the company could go bust. Your choice will depend very much on the purpose of your saving or investment, and the degree of risk with which you feel comfortable.

When deciding on a particular investment, always ask the sales person or adviser what the risks are. Never forget that the potential return on any investment is in direct proportion to the risk. The old adage, 'You have to speculate to accumulate,' is very true. Nothing ventured, nothing gained.

The totally risk-free investment which provides an attractive income, guaranteed capital gains and a hedge against inflation does not exist. Do not be taken in by extravagant promises in advertisements or sales literature. If interest rates from a building society are generally around 5 per cent after tax, an advertisement offering a return of 10 per cent will either carry a much greater risk, or it is fraudulent.

Inflation

Even with fixed-interest-type securities, such as an income bond, National Savings Certificates, and bank or building society deposits, there is still a risk. Inflation is not the problem it used to be, but there is no guarantee it will not return, and if you are planning long-term you need to take this into account.

Back in the late 1970s returns of up to 16 per cent were obtainable on gilts (government stocks), but inflation hit 27 per cent in 1977, and in spite of the interest payments, gilt-holders were actually eating into their capital at the rate of 10 per cent a year. The following table shows the effect of inflation in terms of buying power.

With long-term savings, such as pensions, inflation is a major factor and should never be ignored. As basic protection against inflation, it is probably a good idea to buy the maximum

What £1,000 Will Buy

Inflation %	Number of years from now			
	5	10	15	20
	£	£	£	£
2	884	781	690	610
5	784	614	481	377
10	621	386	239	149

(£10,000) index-linked National Savings Certificates (and you can invest a further £10,000 if the money comes from other issues of maturing Savings Certificates). The current issue (the sixth) pays 3.25 per cent above the rate of inflation over a five-year term. A husband and wife can therefore have up to £40,000 of savings protected against inflation.

You can also purchase index-linked gilts where both the capital and interest are uprated in line with inflation. This will guarantee that your savings maintain their buying power. However, when planning for retirement a long way ahead, the fact that you are investing with tax relief – at an effective discount of 25 per cent or 40 per cent, depending on your rate of tax – will usually take care of inflation.

It is also worth mentioning here that shares and equity-based investments, like with-profits endowment policies, have generally kept pace with inflation, but over the past five years, since the crash of 1987, this has not been the case. None the less, investment managers confidently predict that equities will return to their more normal performance over the longer term.

Current Value of £1,000 Invested Each Year

Years ago	Building society high-interest account £	UK equity unit trust £
5	6,209	6,025
10	15,244	20,855
15	29,017	570,093

Source: Micropal

A balanced approach, spreading your assets across a wide range of both fixed-interest and equity-based investments, is the best policy.

Advice

The Financial Services Act radically altered the way investment products are bought and sold. An investment adviser now has to make it clear whether he is the tied salesperson of a financial institution – in which case he can recommend only that company's products – or an impartial independent adviser – in which case he is free to choose products from any company from the entire range on offer.

Shopping around for the best return on a bank or building society savings account, or the cheapest interest rate on a credit card, is relatively simple. (*Blay's Guides* monitor all bank and building society accounts, and update the information each month. Copies are available at your public library or you can ring Blays on 0753 880482). But buying any equity-linked investment is very different, and you will almost certainly need to take advice.

Planning Your Savings and Investments

You need to sit down and analyse your saving and investment needs and objectives. Temperament comes into the decision-making process too. Getting into the savings habit is a good idea if you are the sort of person who always spends as much, or more, than you earn. It will stop you squandering your money. If you are disciplined and always set aside the money to pay your tax bill or VAT, your approach will be different.

The type of investment vehicle you choose will depend on a number of factors.

Short- or Long-term Saving?

If you are likely to need your money within two or three years, say, as the deposit on a house or to pay school fees, equity-based investments like shares, unit or investment trusts and equity-based life insurance products, such as with-profit endowments, are not really suitable.

If you are lucky, you can make quick profits short-term in, for example, shares, but there is no guarantee, and you should really take a minimum five-year view of all equity investments. Life assurance-based savings should definitely be viewed as long-term commitments. The surrender penalties with many companies make these poor value for money if they are cashed in within five years.

Investing for Income or Capital Growth?

Most people look for capital growth when saving long-term;

popular investments include unit and investment trusts, direct investment in shares, and with-profit endowments. However, you should not ignore the compounding effects of rolled-up income in something like a TESSA, which pays interest gross. For example, a £1,000 investment that is rolling up at a rate of 10 per cent will be worth £1,100 after one year, £1,210 after two years, £1,611 after five years and £2,594 after 10 years.

There is also a school of investment which says look for income from equities and the capital gains will generally follow.

But on retirement, when savings have to replace earnings, the emphasis is on income. Gilts, income bonds, annuities, bank and building society investments are likely to be your choice. You can, of course, obtain income-like payments, by partial encashment of investments which you have been holding for capital growth. The most common example of this is partial withdrawals from unit-linked bonds. There are risks here and you should consider such schemes carefully. They are usually sold on the basis that you can withdraw, say, 5 per cent a year. However, if the bond does not show capital growth of at least 5 per cent, you will be eating into your capital.

Younger women may also be looking for income if they are widowed or divorced and have a lump sum to invest to replace a husband's earnings. Many women under the age of 40 would, today, expect to return to work on the death of a partner or after divorce. But for a woman widowed relatively early in life and largely or totally dependent on investing the proceeds of, say, a husband's life policy to provide income, it is dangerous to ignore the long-term effects of inflation.

If you are dependent on income from investments to maintain your living standards, you can probably afford to take few risks. But even if you are averse to taking risks, you must make some provision for inflation if both your capital and income are not to diminish in real terms and spending power eroded.

Risk

Long-term there is no doubt that the returns from shares and collective investments like unit and investment trusts have almost invariably outstripped an investment in a bank or building society account. The following table illustrates this point. However, you may not be temperamentally suited to living with the

Current Value of £1,000 Invested Over Varying Periods to 1.7.93

Years	Building society account	Average UK growth unit trust	Average UK growth investment trust	FTSE100
	£	£	£	£
3	1,204.28	1,277.57	1,300.65	1,221.22
5	1,418.50	1,472.46	1,390.28	1,560.76
7	1,619.28	1,891.52	2,302.82	1,757.52
10	2,058.24	3,824.59	5,818.42	na
15	3,182.78	9,340.40	16,689.14	na

Source: Micropal

ups and downs of equity investments. If you are going to have sleepless nights worrying every time the stock market loses ground, think again.

Investment Purpose

The purpose of your savings and investment will dictate whether you save short-term or longer-term.

SHORT TERM (less than 12 months) – Under one year you might be saving for a new car, holidays, Christmas, birthdays or a large item of household equipment, such as a new hi-fi. The self-employed will probably be putting money aside to meet a tax bill, VAT, or pension premiums. It could be that you have expenditure on known upcoming events like medical fees for a minor operation, new school uniforms when the children change schools, or fees for a one-off course of tennis coaching.

Suitable investments – Bank or building society high-interest or notice accounts for taxpayers; gross interest on-shore or offshore bank or building society accounts, or National Savings Investment Account for non-taxpayers.

MEDIUM TERM (one to five years) – This is likely to be the deposit on a first home, a new car, major items of household expenditure, such as a new kitchen or bathroom, loft extension, conservatory, swimming pool, or school fees (although in an ideal world you would be planning for these over a longer time-scale).

Suitable investments – Bank and building society accounts as for short-term saving, plus bank and building society Tax Exempt

Special Savings Accounts (TESSAs). TESSAs are tax-free and pay interest gross, so they are suitable only for taxpayers; non-taxpayers can get gross interest from a bank or building society account. National Savings Certificates, National Savings Capital Bonds, National Savings Yearly Plan, short-dated gilts (government stocks), guaranteed growth bonds or deferred annuities (for school fees, perhaps) are all suitable.

LONG-TERM (five to 10 years or more) – Long-term saving is likely to be for school fees and higher education, retirement, long-term career changes involving a drop in earnings, care of an elderly relative, paying off a mortgage, or a loan used to start a business.

Suitable investments – For savings over five years the entire investment spectrum opens up, ranging from shares, unit and investment trusts, commodities, futures and options, as well as fixed-interest investments as mentioned for shorter-term savings.

If you are going to save regularly through life assurance contracts, such as with-profit endowments and unit-linked policies, you must be prepared to commit your money for at least 10 years. For a savings-type life policy to pay benefits tax-free it has to run for 10 years or more and is known a 'qualifying' life policy. There are potential tax pitfalls for higher-rate taxpayers if you cash in or make them paid up within 10 years, or three-quarters of the term of the policies, if less.

Surrender penalties and charges can be high in the early years, so usually you need to keep the policy in force for at least 10 years to gain the full benefit. If you choose a with-profits endowment, you are arguably best advised to take a 10-year contract with the option to maintain it after the 10 years are up.

Tax and Your Investments

The investments you choose will depend to some extent on whether or not you are a taxpayer. Some, like National Savings Children's Bonds and gross accounts at the banks and building societies, are clearly aimed at non-taxpayers, while TESSAs and National Savings Certificates are designed to give a tax-free return to those who pay tax.

You may not be concerned with the tax treatment of equity-based investments like shares or unit trusts where, with the exception of income funds, the dividend income may be so low as to be negligible. The attraction here is the potential for capital growth.

Non-Taxpayers

To be a non-taxpayer you must have income below the threshold for personal tax allowances.

Tax Allowances 1993–94	
Single person	£3,445
Married couple's allowance	£1,720
Single parent additional relief	£1,720
Widow's bereavement allowance	£1,720
Age allowance*	
Single person 65–74	£4,200
75 and over	£4,370
Married couple 65–74	£2,465
75 and over	£2,505

* Age allowance is reduced by £1 for every £2 of income over £14,200 p.a. down to flat-rate personal allowance figures.

There are an estimated 14 million non-taxpayers in the UK, largely children, non-earning wives, pensioners and other people on very low incomes. The Inland Revenue has calculated that less than half of them are making the most of their non-taxpaying status and investing in accounts which pay interest gross (without deduction of tax).

Separate Taxation

Married couples where one partner has no income should consider transferring income-producing investments into that partner's name in order to make best use of his or her personal tax allowances. The following table shows the amount that can be transferred in this way to make use of personal tax allowances.

Similarly, if one partner pays tax at 40 per cent and the other pays no tax or basic rate only, even more money can be switched to utilize the basic-rate tax band up to £23,700 of taxable income for 1993–94.

Since April 1991 banks and building societies have been able

Gross income from investments (%)	Lump sum to tranfer* 1993–94
1	£344,500
2	£172,250
3	£114,833
4	£86,125
5	£68,900
6	£57,416
7	£49,214
8	£43,062
9	£38,277
10	£34,450
11	£31,318
12	£28,708
13	£26,500
14	£24,607
15	£22,966

* The figures assume that the wife is entitled to the basic single person's allowance of £3,445 (1993–94).

to pay interest gross (without deduction of tax) to those who fill in a simple form on opening the account, declaring that they are non-taxpayers. Almost all children will be non-taxpayers, and so are many elderly people.

There are several interest-bearing investments that cater specifically for non-taxpayers: National Savings Investment Account, National Savings Children's Bonds, National Savings Income, and bank and building society gross accounts (onshore and offshore). All can pay interest gross without deduction of tax. Gilts listed on the National Savings Stock Register and purchased through the Post Office also pay interest gross.

Non-taxpayers should not invest in a TESSA. You will generally get a better return, with fewer restrictions, from an onshore or offshore deposit account paying interest gross.

Taxpayers

Tax relief on most forms of investment has largely gone, the most notable exception being the full tax relief granted on pension contributions and investments of up to £40,000 in Business Expansion Schemes (BES).

Life policies taken out before 14 March 1984 still qualify for tax relief on the premiums, so if you have one of these policies, hang on to it. The returns from qualifying life policies are generally tax-free too.

You can take the interest from a TESSA (Tax Exempt Special Savings Account), or allow it to roll up, tax-free, provided you maintain the investment for the minimum period of five years. The income from a Personal Equity Plan can also be taken or allowed to roll up tax-free.

National Savings Certificates are particularly attractive to higher-rate taxpayers. The current (fortieth) issue offers a tax-free return over the five-year period of 5.75 per cent. To generate that return from a taxed investment a 40 per cent taxpayer would need to earn 9.5 per cent gross, a basic-rate taxpayer 7.6 per cent. Basic-rate taxpayers may sometimes be able to get a better return from a Guaranteed Income Bond or from a bank or building society account. Keep an eye on comparative rates.

Because of the tax breaks on these investments, they should be part of all taxpayers' portfolios, and if you are a higher-rate taxpayer, the benefits are that much greater. Otherwise, the investment vehicle you choose will depend entirely on what you want from your investment as the return is generally taxable. Most have basic-rate tax deducted at source. (See pages 176, 160 and 193 for details of PEPs, TESSAS and BES schemes.)

Timing When to Invest

It is obvious that with interest-bearing investments it pays to lock yourself in when interest rates are high. Sadly, few investors do this, usually because variable-rate investments generally show slightly higher returns when rates are high than fixed-interest investments.

For example, you could have bought an income bond showing a return of nearly 10 per cent net of basic-rate tax back in 1990 when the bank base rate stood at 14 per cent. But at that time the average building society account was paying nearly 11 per cent net of basic-rate tax, so people didn't make the switch. They must be kicking themselves. Those dependent on interest to supplement their income have seen a 50 per cent drop over the past three years. Guaranteed growth bonds are currently showing returns of 6.75 net of basic-rate tax over a five-year period, while the best rate you can get from a building society account is around 5.5 per cent.

The difficulty is in trying to guess when interest rates have peaked, or conversely, when they have bottomed out. At the moment, with bank base rate at 6 per cent, one might assume that rates have fallen as far as they are going to go. But if we really are entering an era of low inflation and low interest rates, as some experts believe, they could go lower still.

However, the general rule is to move into fixed-interest investments, like income bonds, National Savings Certificates, gilts and annuities when interest rates are high. Hold off from investing long-term and stay variable in bank and building society accounts when interest rates are low.

If you are retiring on personal pensions, it may pay to postpone retirement or phase it in over a number of years when interest rates are low. This is because the return from an annuity (which provides your pension once you retire) is affected by interest rates. You could be locking yourself into a low income for the rest of your life.

Conversely, if you are transferring money from a final salary occupational pension scheme into a personal pension or Section 32 Buyout policy, it may pay to wait until interest rates are low because the transfer value is then higher.

A common grouse among bank and building society investors is that they put money into an account because at the time it is being promoted the interest rate is attractive, only to find a year or so later that the institution has launched a better account but has not told existing investors. With a wide variety of fixed-interest investments now on offer, you must keep up to date on rates being paid.

Equity-based Investments

Anyone who bought shares, unit or investment trusts, or other equity-based investments in the summer of 1987 will appreciate how important timing is. During the autumn of that year stock markets around the world fell by 20 to 30 per cent, and investors saw a similar loss on their equity portfolios.

Rises and falls in share prices go in cycles. The following table shows the FTSE all-share index over the past 20 years.

One way of avoiding the worst of these fluctuations is to

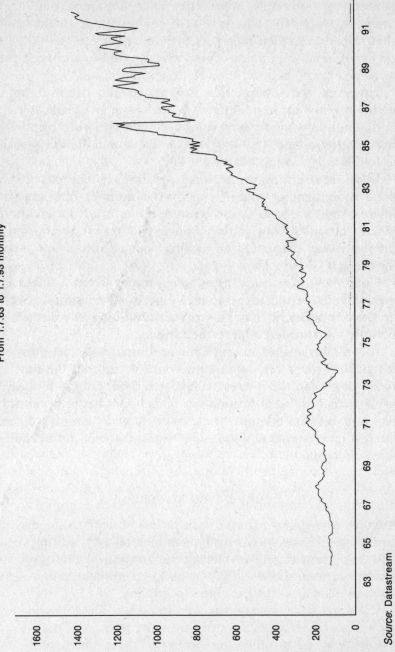

FTA All-Share Price Index.
From 1.7.63 to 1.7.93 monthly

Source: Datastream

invest on a regular basis where you get the benefits of 'pound cost averaging' – when prices are low you get more for your money and vice versa.

Otherwise, if you have a lump sum to invest, try to time it so that you are putting the money into the market at a time when prices could reasonably expect to rise. This is, however, easier said than done.

Shopping Around

You should be able to make a decision about most interest-bearing investments yourself, simply by comparing terms and conditions and shopping around. It definitely pays to keep an eye on the competition because the bank or building society offering the best return now may not be the best buy six months or a year down the line.

Your local library should have a copy of *Blay's Guide* (see Further Reading), which monitors on a monthly basis all the accounts offered by the banks and building societies. This ranges from immediate access accounts to 7-day, 28-day and 90-day accounts. Returns differ, too, according to the amount you have to invest. The guide lists 'best buys' for different types of account and for different amounts.

It is difficult to get advice on interest-bearing investments because the intermediary generally earns no commission for recommending a specific bank or building society account, National Savings securities or gilts.

The Saturday finance pages of the quality newspapers regularly publish tables of bank and building society 'best buys' on investment accounts, as well as the latest National Savings Rates and Guaranteed Income Bond returns. Alternatively, you can consult *Blay's MoneyMaster* in the reference section of most public libraries, although this is not so up-to-date as it is compiled on a monthly basis.

The important thing to remember is that you will always do better if you take an interest in your finances. Nobody will look after your money as well as an interested owner.

Investment Options

Bank and Building Society Savings Accounts

There is a wide range of accounts on offer from banks and building societies with varying terms and conditions. As a rule, the longer you are prepared to commit your savings, the higher the return. You will also get a better rate for larger sums. Some societies do not pay the advertised rate unless you have £20,000 or more in your account. Check precisely what rate your money will be earning.

If you want cheque book, cash and credit card facilities, you generally have to accept a lower rate of return.

The societies offer immediate-access accounts, 7-day, 28-day and 90-day notice accounts, as well as regular savings accounts. Generally speaking, with the notice account, there is a penalty imposed for withdrawing money – usually of loss of interest linked to the notice period; a 7-day notice account will impose a penalty of seven days' loss of interest.

There are also bonds or term shares on offer from time to time, which may lock you in for anything up to three years, but which give you a slightly higher return. These should generally be avoided as there can be hefty penalties for withdrawing your money before the end of the term. The rate is usually variable and you could find yourself trapped when other accounts are offering a better return.

It is a common ploy for a building society to offer an attractive initial rate on a term share to attract investors, dropping it significantly as soon as everyone is locked in. Some accounts have a penalty whenever you withdraw your money. Avoid these.

Most bank and building society investment accounts offer a variable rate of interest; very few pay a fixed rate. Some building societies occasionally offer a guaranteed fixed return, generally over fairly short periods like one year. These, however, are limited offers and you have to move fast if you want to invest. Some offer a fixed rate for only part of the term, and the rate then becomes variable – sometimes at disadvantageous rates – and you are locked in.

The high street banks, however, usually have on offer 7-day, one-month, three-month and sometimes six-month notice ac-

counts which pay fixed rates. This can be an attractive investment if you can afford to lock up your cash for the period, if you
need a guaranteed return over a short term, or if you think
interest rates are likely to fall.

INTEREST from bank and building society accounts may be paid
annually, half yearly, or monthly, the last having obvious appeal
for those dependent on interest to supplement income. It can
also be paid gross (for non-taxpayers) or net of basic-rate tax.

The frequency of payment affects the overall return from
your account.

True Returns

Quoted Rate %	True Rate		
	Half Yearly %	Quarterly %	Monthly %
5	5.06	5.10	5.12
6	6.09	6.14	6.17
7	7.12	7.19	7.23
8	8.16	8.24	8.30
9	9.20	9.31	9.38
10	10.25	10.38	10.47
11	11.30	11.46	11.57
12	12.36	12.55	12.68

MINIMUM INVESTMENT ranges from £1 to £20,000, depending on
the account. Societies are generally trying to deter the really
small saver, and the new postal accounts often have a minimum
of at least £1,000. Some of the best returns are offered by the
smaller societies.

In recent years the banks and building societies have introduced tiered interest rate structures on most accounts: the more
you invest, the higher the return. Make sure that the higher
rates of interest are paid on the total balance, not just the
amount over the threshold.

If you want easy access and perhaps a cash card or cheque
book, go for one of the High Interest Cheque Accounts. Postal
accounts usually offer a better return than over-the-counter
accounts, but if you find this inconvenient, choose one of the
large societies with branches in most high streets.

TAX on bank and building society interest is paid at the basic rate, deducted at source, unless you are a non-taxpayer, in which case you can receive the interest gross, without deduction of tax, provided you sign the requisite R85 declaration when you open the account.

Higher-rate taxpayers will have a further 15 per cent tax liability on all interest received. If you have £50,000 or more to invest, the high street banks will pay you the interest gross, without deduction of tax, regardless of whether you are a taxpayer or not, but the interest is taxable.

Permanent Interest-bearing Shares (PIBS)

These have been issued by some of the larger building societies since June 1991. They have more in common with undated government stocks than building society deposit accounts. PIBS pay a fixed return for an unlimited period of time. Minimum investment varies from £1,000 to £50,000.

PIBS are bought and sold through a stockbroker, like gilts, and the price you pay will reflect interest rates at the time. For example, if a PIB is issued with a 'coupon' or interest rate of 12 per cent and bank base rates fall, the price of the PIB will rise until the yield comes into line with what is available elsewhere in the market. Of course, the reverse is also true.

If the building society were to collapse, PIBS holders are last in line for a payout.

Buy PIBS when interest rates are high and likely to fall. You then lock yourself into a high fixed return and have the benefit of a capital gain as well. There is no guarantee of getting your money back, however.

TESSAs

Tax Exempt Special Savings Accounts are five-year savings plans on which the interest paid is tax-free, provided you leave the capital untouched for the full five-year term. They are run by banks and building societies and anyone over the age of 18 can open a TESSA.

Maximum investment is £3,000 in the first year and up to £1,800 in the four subsequent years, up to an overall maximum of £9,000 per person.

TESSAs were introduced in the 1990 Budget and have been available since January 1991. They are an investment which all taxpayers should consider, provided they can afford to have their money tied up for five years. Non-taxpayers will do better elsewhere.

The interest earned can be left to roll up tax-free, or taken as income, in which case it is paid net of basic-rate tax. For example, if you had earned £400 in interest during the course of the year on your TESSA, you would be allowed to withdraw £300. The £100 basic-rate tax retained remains within the TESSA and is paid out at the end of the five years, provided you have left the capital untouched. If you withdraw any of the capital, you lose the tax concessions.

You are allowed only one TESSA, but you can switch it from one bank or building society to another. Beware of switching penalties imposed by some building societies and banks, and bear in mind that many TESSAs have loyalty bonuses paid after five years, which you will lose if you move.

Most TESSAs pay a variable rate of interest, while a few offer a fixed return – some just for the first year, occasionally for the full five years. You get the best return if you invest the maximum lump sum at the beginning of each year: £3,000 in year one, £1,800 in years two, three and four, and £600 in year five. You can save up to £150 a month, provided the bank or building society offers this facility. Not all of them do.

Some banks and building societies offer 'feeder' accounts into which you pay the full £9,000 and earn taxable interest. The cash is then transferred annually into the TESSA account. If you are not certain that you can commit your savings for five years, choose a TESSA that has no penalties for early withdrawal. You will then be no worse off than if you had invested in a straight net account.

National Savings

All National Savings securities are issued by the government and are on sale through Post Offices. National Savings offers a variety of interest-bearing investments which can be bought over the Post Office counter. The terms and conditions vary, but to obtain the maximum return you must generally hold the investment for the full term. Early encashment will involve penalties.

National Savings interest rates do not change as frequently as interest rates on competing bank and building society accounts.

While this is an advantage when interest rates are coming down, you could end up out of pocket over a period of prolonged interest rate rises.

NATIONAL SAVINGS ORDINARY ACCOUNT is an easy-access account with a minimum investment of £10 and a maximum of £10,000. Anyone can open an account, including children.

Interest is credited annually and the first £70 of interest is tax-free (£140 for a joint account) – the rest is taxable. The rate of interest paid is currently 2.5 per cent or 3.75 per cent on balances of £500 or more if the account has been open for a full calendar year.

At the moment the interest rate for small sums of money is competitive. The building societies are paying similar rates for small sums. In the past, however, the rate paid on a National Savings Ordinary Account has been low compared with building society accounts.

Interest is credited from the 1st of the month following the date of investment and is paid until the 1st of the month prior to withdrawal. In order to maximize the return you should pay in money on the last day of the month and withdraw it on the first.

Up to £250 is available on demand over the Post Office counter; larger sums must be applied for on special forms and take about one week to process. If you withdraw more than £50, your pass book has to be sent back to National Savings Bank headquarters.

NATIONAL SAVINGS INVESTMENT ACCOUNT pays interest gross, without deduction of tax, and is therefore suitable for non-taxpayers. Gross interest is paid automatically and added to your account annually on 31 December. You do not have to make a declaration that you are a non-taxpayer, but the interest is taxable. The rate currently being paid is 6.25 per cent gross.

Anyone can open an account. Minimum investment is £20 with a maximum of £25,000. Money can only be added to the account in amounts of £20 or more. You have to give one month's notice of withdrawal. Children, one of the biggest groups of non-taxpayers, might find this difficult to understand.

Interest is variable, but the rate paid is not always competitive with other gross-paying accounts on offer from the banks and building societies. Minimum investment is £5, maximum £25,000.

NATIONAL SAVINGS CERTICATES are five-year investment certificates paying a guaranteed tax-free return at the end of the period. They do not pay interest. The return is added to the original investment at the end of the five-year term.

Anyone can invest, and you can buy on behalf of your children. You must hold the certificates for the full five years to obtain the maximum return, although you can cash in earlier.

There is usually only one issue at a time on sale, and certificates are withdrawn and a new tranche issued whenever the return gets out of line with comparable investments. The current, fortieth-issue pays 5.75 per cent tax-free. The return is usually pitched at a level to make Savings Certificates attractive to higher-rate taxpayers.

A higher-rate taxpayer would have to earn over 9.5 per cent gross on a comparable investment to equal the tax-free return on the fortieth issue. Basic-rate taxpayers can generally get a better or similar return with fewer restrictions from a building society account. Savings Certificates are not suitable for non-taxpayers as they can also get a better return elsewhere.

Minimum investment in the current, fortieth, issue is £100, and thereafter in multiples of £25. Maximum investment is £5,000, and up to £10,000 in addition if you are reinvesting the proceeds of earlier issues which have now reached maturity.

National Savings Certificates should generally be encashed or reinvested on maturity because the rate of interest paid on mature issues (known as the general extension rate) is only 3.75 per cent. This varies in line with interest rates generally, but you can usually do better by investing elsewhere.

If you have some of the very early issues, the first to sixth, which were on sale between 1916 and November 1939, you are earning only 1.1 to 1.8 per cent on them, so you should cash them in and reinvest.

You can withdraw your money before the five-year term is up but the rate of return will be less. You do not, however, lose the tax benefit. No interest is earned on certificates repaid in the first year.

On death the certificates can be encashed by your heirs or they can transfer them into their own names. To do this you need form DNS904, available from most Post Offices.

INDEX-LINKED SAVINGS CERTICATES offer a return in line with

Return from £25 6th Issue Index-linked National Savings Certificates

Year	Interest paid %	Value at anniversary of purchase £	Effective rate during the year %
1	1.5	26.62	6.5
2	2.0	28.48	6.98
3	2.75	30.69	7.76
4	3.75	33.38	8.76
5	6.32	37.16	11.32

The figures assume a 5 per cent inflation rate.

increases in the Retail Prices Index (RPI), plus a bonus – the sixth issue pays 3.25 per cent a year. The return is totally tax-free. You can invest between £100 and £5,000 in the sixth issue.

Anyone can buy these certificates and married couples can invest £5,000 each. A further £10,000 worth can be held if the money is the proceeds of earlier mature issues of National Savings Certificates.

Index-linked Savings Certificates are obviously most attractive when inflation is low and expected to rise.

When you buy or sell an index-linked savings certificate, the RPI figure that applies is the one announced during the previous month, which in turn reflects inflation in the month before that. The simplest way to find out what your index-linked certificate is actually worth is to look at the chart which is on display in most Post Offices.

If the RPI falls, the value of your certificate goes down in line. You are, however, guaranteed to get back your original investment plus the interest bonuses. If the rate of inflation falls, the value of your certificates is still going up but at a slower rate.

Old index-linked certificates can be kept on maturity and will continue to enjoy increases in line with changes in the Retail Prices Index.

YEARLY PLAN is intended for regular savers who do not have a lump sum to invest in Savings Certificates. You save between £20 and £400 a month by direct debit for a year to buy a Savings Certificate which you must then hold for a further four years to earn the maximum guaranteed return. Anyone can invest, and the current issue of Yearly Plan is paying 5.75 per cent over the five-year period tax-free.

Higher-rate taxpayers who benefit the most from the tax-free return on Savings Certificates are unlikely to need to save regularly. However, Yearly Plan does increase the maximum amount you can invest in savings certificates.

There are more attractive alternatives to Yearly Plan (such as TESSAs) for basic-rate taxpayers.

NATIONAL SAVINGS INCOME BONDS are designed for anyone who needs regular income, and are aimed particularly at elderly people who may need monthly interest to supplement their income.

The rate of interest paid is variable, but is paid gross, without deduction of tax, every month — useful for those who are depending on the interest payments to pay household bills. This makes them an attractive proposition for all non-taxpayers, including children. Interest is, however, taxable if you are a taxpayer.

The rate of interest paid is displayed in Post Offices, and six weeks' notice of any change in the rate is given. The rate at the time of writing is 7.00 per cent gross, which works out at 5.25 per cent for a basic-rate taxpayer. However, you have to give three months' notice of withdrawal, and during times when interest rates are rising fast you could find yourself locked in and unable to earn a better return. Minimum investment is £2,000, and bonds can be added to in multiples of £1,000 up to the maximum of £50,000. Married couples can invest £50,000 each.

The bonds are 10-year investments, and if encashed within the first year, only half the published interest rate is paid. After the first year there are no penalties.

Building society monthly income accounts often offer higher returns, and are more flexible, with shorter notice periods for withdrawal. Most societies offer both gross interest (for a non-taxpayer) and net interest on a monthly income account.

NATIONAL SAVINGS CAPITAL BONDS are suitable for investors who want a guaranteed return but do not need income. They are ideal for parents investing on behalf of a young child, or for those nearing retirement, as they can provide a safe haven for savings with guaranteed capital growth built in.

The bonds pay a guaranteed return which is fixed for the five-year term. At the time of writing, the current issue is paying 7.75

per cent. Interest is paid gross and added to the original investment and paid on maturity although you will have to pay tax on it on an annual basis. They are ideal for non-taxpayers wanting a fixed, guaranteed return.

Anyone can invest, but remember, you have to be prepared to tie up your money for five years. They do, however, offer protection against falling interest rates. Minimum investment is £100 and the maximum is £100,000, including holdings of earlier issues.

Capital Bonds do not tend to offer such good returns as Guaranteed Growth Bonds sold by life assurance companies, and they are less flexible in that you have no choice on the term – only five years. Insurance companies sell guaranteed growth bonds for varying terms of one to five years. Check on what else is available before committing your money.

National Savings Capital Bonds are automatically repaid at the end of the five-year term. You can cash in your bonds at any time by giving three months' notice, but if you cash in before the end of the five years, the return will be lower. No interest is paid if you cash in during the first year.

CHILDREN'S BONUS BONDS, as the name implies, are aimed at children and parents investing on their behalf. They can be bought by an adult for anyone under the age of 16, and they continue to grow in value until the child is 21.

Minimum investment is £25 and the maximum is £1,000, including earlier issues. Returns are tax-free – useful if parents want to invest on a child's behalf.

Generally, if a child has income of £100 or more, derived from money given by parents, any income generated by the investment is treated as though it still belongs to the parent and taxed accordingly. Children's Bonus Bonds get round this problem.

The rate of interest currently being paid is 7.85 per cent tax-free and is guaranteed for five years at a time. After five years, the rate is set again, and if you are happy to continue you need take no action. If you decide to cash in, you need give no notice at the five-year anniversary – otherwise one month's notice is required.

Bonds can be encashed in units of £25. Gift cards are available with the application form for parents and other relatives who want to give a child a present.

PREMIUM BONDS can be bought by anyone aged 16 or over, or a parent, grandparents or guardians can buy them for a child. Minimum investment is £100 for the over-16s, £10 if the bond is bought for a child. Further investments must be made in multiples of £10. Maximum holding is £10,000.

If you are a gambler, Premium Bonds will appeal. They are not investments but a straightforward lottery, so you should buy only for fun. Prizes range from £250,000 to £50, tax-free. Make sure the Bonds and Stock Office has an up-to-date address for you in case you win a prize.

Bonds are not entered into the draw until they have been held for three months. There is no return except the prize money, so when you cash in you get back only your original investment.

Prize money is worked out at a rate of 5 per cent of the total sums which have been invested for at least three months. There are monthly prizes ranging from £50 to £250,000, and weekly prizes of £100,000, £50,000 and £25,000.

SAVE AS YOU EARN is a regular savings plan available only to employees who are entitled to buy shares in their company under an approved Share Option Scheme.

DISCONTINUED INVESTMENTS – National Savings has several investments which are no longer on offer. First Option Bonds were on offer for a few months from July 1992, but have been withdrawn. Index-linked Save As You Earn is also now discontinued, as is the Deposit Bond. If you invested in these things, you are entitled to continue holding these securities. Full details are available from National Savings, 375 Kensington High Street, London W14 8QH; tel. 071–605 9300.

You can get up-to-date rates for all National Savings Securities by telephoning 071–605 9483.

Gilts

Government stocks, or gilts, as they are known, are IOUs issued by the government to fund its overdraft, better known as the Public Sector Borrowing Requirement. They pay a fixed and guaranteed rate of interest for a fixed number of years.

Each £100 nominal of stock is guaranteed to be repaid at face value on the maturity date. Sometimes the maturity date can be from, say, 1999 to 2004 – the government decides exactly when. There are some undated stocks, such as Consols and War Loans, which have no redemption date.

Gilts are traded on the stock exchange, and the price at which you buy reflects the level of interest rates generally. When interest rates are low, as now, it is common for the price of a gilt to be above its maturity value. At the time of writing, most gilts are standing at a premium to their maturity value. When interest rates are high, gilts may be sold at a deep discount to their redemption value. This means that you may have a built-in capital gain or loss.

Gilts offer a fixed rate of return over a fixed period, with the guarantee of the face value back at the end of the term, provided you hold them to maturity.

The government issues them, pitching the interest rate in line with current interest rates available on similar investments elsewhere. However, because gilts can be traded on the stock exchange, the price will fluctuate to reflect current interest rates.

If a gilt was issued with a 'coupon' or interest rate of, say, 10.5 per cent, and current rates are only 8 per cent, the price of the gilt will rise until the yield is in line with interest rates in the market. Had rates risen to 13 per cent, the price of the gilt would fall.

You can only be certain how much money you will get back from an investment in gilts if you are prepared to hold the stock to maturity. If you sell before then, the price you get may be more or less than you paid.

Gilts bought at a discount to their face value – say, £88 for every £100 of stock – have a guaranteed tax-free capital gain if you hold them to maturity. Gilts bought at a premium to their face value – say, £111 for every £100 of stock – have a guaranteed capital loss if you hold to maturity.

For the novice investor wanting to lock into a known interest rate for a fixed period of time, gilts are the only way of doing this for periods longer than five years. Under five years, and you will find it simpler to buy guaranteed income bonds or growth bonds from a life company which offer similar returns.

Gilts are suitable investments for anyone who needs a guaranteed return over a fixed period of time. They have many uses in areas like school fees planning and providing income in

retirement. For example, on retirement you will probably need
to convert most of your savings into income-producing securities. You might decide to put, say, two-thirds of your savings
into long-dated gilts paying 8 per cent. So long as you hold
them, your income will remain constant, and if you keep them
until maturity, you know exactly how much will be returned to
you. The remaining third might be put into an equity-based
investment, like unit or investment trusts, to provide some
capital growth which would offset the effects of inflation on
your static income from the gilts.

In the past it has been possible for parents wanting to provide
school fees at some time in the future to buy a portfolio of 'low-
coupon' gilts maturing in successive years. As the gilts reach
redemption, the proceeds are used to pay the school fees.

Low-coupon gilts offer very little income because the 'coupon'
or interest paid is low. But they are generally bought at a large
discount to the nominal or face value, and have a built-in tax-
free capital gain if held to maturity.

Unfortunately, there are currently only a few low-coupon gilts
in issue, so the scope to adopt this strategy is limited. However,
over the coming few years the government has to fund a
borrowing requirement of some £50 billion a year, so it is likely
that new low-coupon gilts will be issued.

The built-in capital gains works like this. In February 1993
you could buy Funding 3.5 per cent maturing between 1999 and
2004 at around £72 for every £100 of stock. When the stock
matures some time between 1999 and 2004, you will be repaid
£100, showing an £28 tax-free capital gain.

You might decide to invest a lump sum in six gilts which
currently stand at a discount to their redemption value, maturing in successive years to pay all or part of a child's school fees.
This has the advantage of certainty.

UNDATED STOCKS are government stocks which have no maturity
date and are never likely to be repaid. They are bought most
commonly by those requiring a high income from their investments, but the price will fluctuate to reflect the general level of
interest rates in the economy. Try to buy when interest rates are
high for the high yield; sell when interest rates are low for the
capital gain.

Undated Stocks as at 29.5.93

Stock	Price £*	Yield (%)
Consols 2½%	30	8.3
War Loan 3½%	40¼	8.6
Conversion 3½%	61⅝	5.7
Treasury 3%	35⅟₁₆	8.6
Consols 4%	46⁵⁄₁₆	8.6
Treasury 2½%	28²⁵⁄₃₂	8.6

* Parts of a £ are always expressed in fractions rather than decimals.

DIVIDENDS OR INTEREST PAYMENTS on gilts are made twice a year. The months vary from stock to stock, and it is possible to provide a monthly income by choosing stocks with different dividend dates. Dividends are paid with basic-rate tax deducted at source, unless you buy through the National Savings Stock Register, when you can receive your interest gross.

The disadvantage of investing this way is that it is a slow process and can take a couple of weeks, so you will not know the price at which you have dealt, nor the yield. This could be crucial if, for example, there were a bank base rate change in the middle, which would affect both the price and the yield.

REDEMPTION DATES for gilts are split into four groups:

- Short-dated, with a redemption date within five years.
- Medium-dated, with a redemption date between five and 15 years.
- Long-dated, with a redemption date of over 15 years.
- Undated, with no redemption date and the probability of never being redeemed.

PRICES AND YIELDS of government stocks are listed under the above headings in the financial pages of such daily newspapers as the *Financial Times*, *The Times*, the *Independent* and the *Daily Telegraph*. The price quoted will be the price at close of business on the previous day. The quotation will also show the current yield, i.e. the level of income you will receive, and the yield to redemption if you hold it to its maturity date.

The current yield may bear no relation to the coupon or interest rate attached to the stock. For example, Treasury 14 per cent 1996 stood at £120.50 on 24 February 24 1993 for each £100 nominal of stock. It had a current yield of 11.6 per cent gross and a yield to redemption of 6.2 per cent, taking into account the built-in per cent capital loss if the stock is held to redemption.

If a stock is standing at a premium to its redemption value, the running yield (the income you will receive) will be higher than the yield to redemption because you will suffer a capital loss when the stock matures.

If the stock is standing at a discount to its redemption value, the running yield will be lower than the yield to redemption because you will have a built-in capital gain.

The advantages of gilts can be itemized as follows:

- Fixed and guaranteed income.
- Fixed and guaranteed maturity value (except for the undated stocks).
- Fixed investment period (though some gilts mature between known dates, the exact date being decided by the Treasury at the time).

GILT UNIT TRUSTS should be avoided. The charges are high and you would be better off investing direct through the Post Office or buying through your bank or stockbroker.

BUYING AND SELLING GILTS, most of which are now on the National Savings Stock Register, can be done over the counter at the Post Office. The advantage of this is that the interest payments, or dividends, which are made half yearly, are paid gross, without deduction of tax. This is useful for non-taxpayers. The dividends are, however, taxable, although any profits made on selling or redemption are not subject to Capital Gains Tax.

If you buy through your bank or stockbroker, dividends will be paid net of basic-rate tax, and non-taxpayers will have to reclaim the tax deducted at source.

The disadvantage of buying or selling gilts through the Post Office is that you do not know the price at which you have bought or sold because the transaction is carried out by post. When interest rates are moving fast, this is a very real disadvantage since you do not know what the yield, or return, will be.

For example, in February 1993 the bank base rate stood at 6.0 per cent. Treasury 9.5 per cent 1999 was selling at £111.50, showing a current yield of 8.5 per cent gross and a yield to redemption of 7.1 per cent. The yield to redemption is lower because it includes the £11.50 guaranteed capital loss which you will make when the stock matures in 1999.

If the government cuts bank base rates by 1 per cent just as you are purchasing through the Post Office, you might find that the price of this stock has jumped to £126 and the yield has fallen to 7.5 per cent in line with the 1 per cent cut in bank base rate.

If you buy or sell through your bank or stockbroker you can get a price and yield that day, and buy or sell immediately. However, a stockbroker will make a minimum commission charge of around £30; cheap share-dealing services can cut the cost to around £20. The cost of buying £1,000 worth of gilts through the Post Office is £4.

Commission charges if you buy through the Post Office are £1 for transactions not exceeding £250, or £1 plus a further 50p for every additional £25 or part thereof.

Unless you are sure you know precisely what you want to buy and for what purpose, it will pay to take independent advice. Most private-client stockbrokers or your bank will be happy to help.

INDEX-LINKED GILTS, as the name implies, are linked to the rate of inflation as measured by the Retail Prices Index (RPI). They are very useful in retirement planning as they can guarantee an income that will keep pace with inflation without the value of your capital being eroded. Each £100 nominal of stock will be repaid on maturity, plus any increase in the RPI. For example, if the RPI has gone up by 30 per cent over the life of the stock, you will be paid £130.

The stocks generally have a low coupon or interest rate, but the income is also uprated in line with inflation. Over the life of a stock its price, which fluctuates in line with people's expectation of what inflation will be, and is also influenced by interest rates generally, will move up roughly in line with inflation.

TAX ON GILTS varies, depending on where you purchase them. Dividends from gilts bought through a stockbroker are paid net of basic-rate tax, and higher-rate taxpayers will have a further liability. Stock purchased through the National Savings Stock Register pays dividends gross, but this is taxable. If you are resident abroad, some stocks pay dividends gross. All gilts are totally free from Capital Gains Tax.

If you buy through the Post Office, you must sell in the same way. Similarly, if you buy through a stockbroker or your bank, you must sell through the same channel.

Guaranteed Income and Growth Bonds (GIBs)

These bonds are short-term life assurance contracts issued by insurance companies. They guarantee to pay a fixed income for a fixed number of years, and to return your original investment, in full, on maturity.

Like gilts, Guaranteed Income and Growth Bonds (not to be confused with National Savings Income Bonds) provide a guaranteed return over a fixed period of time and are much used in retirement planning. They are available in terms from one to five years.

Guaranteed growth bonds are similar to GIBs, but instead of paying out the income, it is rolled up and paid out at the end of the term with the original investment.

The interest is paid net of basic-rate tax, and this cannot be reclaimed by a non-taxpayer. Generally GIBs are not suitable for those who pay no tax. Higher-rate taxpayers may have a further 15 per cent liability.

USES OF GIBS – Income bonds are bought mainly by elderly people wanting a guaranteed supplement to their pension in retirement, but they do have other uses. Grandparents might buy an income bond to meet school fees or other known expenditure where they cannot afford to take risks, keeping the capital for themselves.

Growth bonds are more often bought by investors in the run-up to retirement, when they are still working and do not need the income. A growth bond has none of the risks of equity-based investments and provides a guaranteed payout on maturity.

Minimum investment is around £1,000 and you can usually get a better rate of return for larger sums of money – sometimes as much as 0.5 per cent more. Once you have invested you cannot get your money back until the bond matures. On death, the bond usually returns your original capital, plus any accrued interest.

BUYING GIBS is mostly done through independent financial advisers. (Some, like Chase de Vere (tel. 071–404 5766) and Baronworth (tel. 081–518 1218) specialize in this area.) The rates paid vary from company to company, so you would be well advised to shop around before committing your cash. The difference can sometimes be as high as 1 per cent.

Local Authority Investments

Local authorities used to raise money from the general public by issuing loan stock and negotiable bonds, very much like gilts. In recent years they have funded their borrowing through the wholesale money markets, and it is no longer possible for private investors to buy local authority loan stock or yearling bonds.

Equity Investment

In your general portfolio planning equity-based investments should be considered once you can afford to commit your money for a minimum of five years – 10 years if the vehicle is a savings-type life policy like a with-profits endowment or a unit-linked life policy. You should have emergency funds readily available, and plenty of life assurance protection, before you consider equities.

The underlying securities in all equity-based investments, whether they are unit or investment trusts, savings-type life policies or Personal Equity Plans (PEPs), are shares in companies. The returns from shares are not guaranteed; prices go up and down, and occasionally companies collapse. Shareholders are last in line in this situation, and there is rarely any payout.

However, as we have seen, the returns from equity investment have – with the exception of the past five years – generally beaten the returns from fixed-interest investments like building society deposits. They have also kept pace with inflation.

With the introduction of Personal Equity Plans, there is now much more incentive for individuals to hold shares directly. You can only use the single company PEP if you are prepared to invest directly in the shares of one company. Income from shares held within a PEP is free from income tax, and any profits made are free from Capital Gains Tax. If you are thinking of buying shares, unit or investment trusts, and you have not used up all your PEP allowance, you will generally be best advised to buy within a PEP.

When you buy shares, you are investing in the performance of that company. As the name implies, you own a share of the business. If the company does well, your income from dividends should go up, and the price of the share will rise to reflect that fact. Conversely, if the business starts to lose money, dividends will be cut (as investors have discovered during this recent recession) and the price of the share will fall. In a worst possible situation you could lose all your money if the company collapses.

Do not invest in shares or unit or investment trusts if this inherent volatility is likely to worry you. The return from shares depends on how good you, the institution or investment manager are at choosing shares with good prospects and avoiding the duds. You can have a lot of fun picking your own shares, provided you understand the risks. But in this situation go slowly; invest only a small proportion of your savings until you see how well you do.

If you are cautious, go for things like the utilities, British Telecom, British Gas, the electricity and water companies. They show a reasonable yield and are unlikely to go bust.

If you have considerable sums to hand – perhaps you have received an inheritance – and do not know how to invest, you would be well advised to consult a stockbroker or other professional adviser.

Most equity-based investment schemes, whether they are unit or investment trusts, savings-type life policies or direct holdings in shares, are in quoted shares – that is, companies whose shares are quoted on a stock exchange.

Buying shares in an unquoted or private company can be very risky for a number of reasons. The proprietors will probably have a controlling interest in the company and can control the market in the shares, so it may be difficult to sell them. To get a quote on the stock exchange a company has to submit to a rigorous financial examination; unquoted companies do not. Most individuals who hold unquoted shares do so because they are part of a family business.

Personal Equity Plans

If you are thinking of buying shares direct, or buying unit or investment trusts, the best route is probably through a PEP. The introduction of PEPs in 1987 has transformed the investment scene for the small private investor because of the income and Capital Gains Tax concessions that PEPs carry.

Dividends from equities held within a PEP are completely free from income tax, while any profits made on selling the securities is free from Capital Gains Tax. The only drawback to PEPs is that if you suffer capital losses, these cannot be offset against gains made elsewhere outside the PEP. Also check charges as these can be high, and cancel out tax concessions on small investments.

Income from a PEP can be taken tax-free or allowed to roll up within the PEP. You can buy and sell the shares or unit and investment trusts as often as you like without incurring any tax liability, provided they remain within the PEP. Since their introduction in 1987, you and your spouse or partner could have, by now, tucked away a considerable sum of money and shielded it from income tax and CGT.

The maximum amount you could have invested has now reached £43,200 for 1993–94, or £86,400 for a married couple – and that is at the original purchase price. The value by now might be considerably more.

Anyone over the age of 18 can invest in a PEP. Up to £6,000 per person can be invested in the current tax year in a general PEP, and £3,000 in a single-company PEP.

Eligible investments are all UK- and EC-quoted shares (just one company for the single-company PEP) and unit or investment trusts. You are allowed only one PEP a year for each of your general and single-company PEPs, and you cannot split the investment between two different PEP managers.

PEPS can be used for any saving: investing for children, school fees, saving for retirement or any long-term commitment. They are also useful if you are prepared to take a chance short-term and just want a flutter with your profits shielded from CGT.

The ability to take tax-free income makes PEPs useful and important tools in retirement planning (see Chapter 5).

Insurance-linked Savings Schemes

The most important thing to understand about with-profits endowments and unit-linked life policies is that they are savings schemes. The amount of life cover offered is minimal, and if you rely on it for protection, you will be desperately under-insured. Make sure you have adequate protection before you take out one of these savings schemes.

The most widely held equity-based investment is undoubtedly the with-profit endowment policy. This is largely because for years they have been used as the repayment vehicle for home loans and have been heavily promoted by the lenders.

For a novice investor there can be no better way to save long-term, provided you can commit your money for at least 10 years and you hold the policy to maturity. The big advantages of this type of savings plan are:

- Investment returns are smoothed over the long term.
- It provides some underlying guarantees.
- It provides a small amount of life cover (but do not rely on this for your total protection – see Chapter 4).
- There is a guaranteed return, albeit usually low.

With-Profits Endowment Policies

Premiums paid by all with-profits policy-holders are pooled by the insurance company and invested in a spread of shares, both UK and foreign, fixed-interest investments and bonds, as well as property. Every year bonuses are declared and added to the value of your policy. These are known as 'reversionary' bonuses, and once added to your policy they cannot be taken away. The level of bonuses paid reflects the long-term investment performance of the fund, both past and future, and the bonus policy of the life company.

In the good years, when the underlying investments do well, not all the profits will be distributed in the form of bonuses. In the bad years, when the investments go down, the fund has surpluses tucked away and is still able to pay out bonuses.

On maturity a 'terminal' bonus may be paid. It is important to understand that this bonus is often a large proportion of the total payout on your policy. You may lose out considerably, therefore, if you cancel or surrender the policy before it matures, although some companies now pay a proportion of the 'terminal' bonus on surrender.

The level of bonuses varies between life companies. Some company actuaries are more conservative than others, preferring to keep more of their profits in reserve against a rainy day when they will have to dip into their surpluses to pay the bonuses.

The split between how much is paid out in annual (or reversionary) bonuses, and the amount paid in terminal bonuses will vary from company to company. The table below shows the maturity value including terminal bonuses on with-profits endowments. There are wide variations in the proportion of the total payout attributable to reversionary bonuses compared with terminal bonuses.

The guaranteed sum assured is the amount which the policy is guaranteed to pay out should you die before the policy matures.

The total payouts reflect three things: the investment expertise of the fund managers, charges levied on the policies, and the bonus policy of the company. With so many policies to choose from you would be well advised to take advice. Sadly, this is rarely forthcoming because most people are sold a with-profits endowment by a bank or building society when they take out a mortgage.

With one or two exceptions, the big financial institutions are all 'tied' to a life company (often their own in-house company), so you will be sold a policy from the tied company unless you stipulate otherwise. Halifax Building Society, for example, is tied to Standard Life, so if you get a home loan from the Halifax, you will be offered a Standard Life Unitized With-Profits policy. Do not be bullied into buying a with-profits endowment from a company you do not want.

CHARGES on with-profits endowments can be high. At the moment it is impossible to find out precisely what they are (although you can ask an intermediary what commission he gets for selling you the policy). The situation, at the time of writing, is under review. It may be that, eventually, life companies will be forced to disclose costs.

You can get some idea what the costs are by looking at the surrender values in the early years. Most of the costs involved

With-Profits Endowment Policies Compared

Actual maturity value results payable on a 10-year endowment policy, maturing on 1 February 1984–93 inclusive.* Male aged 29 at outset. Best results in bold.

Maturing on 1 February 1993	1984 £	1985 £	1986 £	1987 £	1988 £	1989 £	1990 £	1991 £	1992 £	1993 £
Company										
Avon	**2,029**	6,698	6,773	7,303	7,409	7,299	7,074	nd	nd	nd
Axa Equity & Law	1,998	6,870	7,541	7,093	6,599	7,479	8,210	7,767	12,267	11,371
Britannia Life	1,895	6,022	6,027	6,779	7,549	6,754	7,378	6,838	10,885	10,236
Britannic Ass	nd	6,185	6,551	6,702	7,333	7,047	6,971	7,230	12,181	11,211
Clerical Medical	2,136	**7,151**	**8,140**	**8,943**	**8,890**	**8,477**	**8,464**	8,033	**12,730**	**11,681**
Colonial Mutual	1,880	6,124	6,438	6,954	6,669	6,515	7,129	7,162	11,574	9,860
Commercial Union	1,905	6,229	6,838	7,529	7,779	7,634	7,749	7,632	12,628	**12,082**
Co-operative	1,958	6,085	6,489	6,760	6,935	7,019	7,201	7,383	12,437	**12,079**
Crusader	1,980	6,246	6,508	6,616	6,649	6,686	6,563	6,541	nd	nd
Eagle Star	2,002	6,501	6,611	7,091	7,515	7,678	7,756	7,446	11,559	10,150
Ecclesiastical	**2,263**	7,388	7,794	7,794	7,612	7,410	7,410	7,308	10,856	nd
Equitable	2,258	7,297	8,237	8,353	**8,364**	8,223	8,220	8,365	13,693	**12,203**
Friends Provident	2,117	7,271	7,666	8,577	**8,938**	8,513	8,564	8,328	13,108	11,475
General Accident	1,967	6,117	6,430	6,818	7,212	6,952	6,993	7,030	11,837	11,104
Guardian Royal Exchange	1,933	6,183	7,196	7,116	7,060	6,872	6,598	5,887	9,208	nd
LAS	1,866	5,987	6,344	6,313	6,981	7,069	7,037	6,374	11,282	9,164
Legal & General	1,993	6,077	6,510	6,891	7,183	7,410	7,669	7,602	11,854	10,915
London & Manchester	1,965	6,256	6,507	6,676	6,817	6,833	7,108	7,301	nd	10,251
London Life	2,096	6,822	7,073	7,938	7,432	7,150	7,536	7,495	11,689	10,906
MGM	2,067	6,746	6,907	6,970	7,719	6,975	6,919	7,077	10,330	nd
NEL Britannia	1,875	5,818	5,910	6,132	6,209	6,106	6,106	6,823	nd	nd
National Mutual Life	2,073	6,575	7,061	7,257	7,355	**7,808**	7,742	7,724	11,689	10,643
National Provident	1,982	7,016	7,222	7,654	7,653	7,414	7,616	6,997	10,063	9,758
Norwich Union	**2,249**	**7,795**	**7,808**	**8,431**	**8,293**	**8,297**	**8,526**	8,242	12,727	**11,815**
Pearl	1,800	6,124	6,407	6,834	7,416	7,691	**7,995**	8,475	13,392	11,607
Prolific	na	na	5,466	6,350	6,017	6,506	6,517	6,547	11,058	11,093
Provident Mutual	1,984	6,166	6,968	7,035	7,062	7,434	7,388	7,088	11,755	11,125
Prudential	1,991	6,576	6,972	7,149	7,398	7,400	7,162	7,879	12,402	10,952
Refuge Ass	2,227	7,088	7,675	7,675	7,842	7,573	7,658	**8,121**	**12,640**	**12,013**
Reliance Mutual	1,650	5,050	5,009	5,007	6,559	6,950	6,315	nd	nd	nd
Royal Life	1,926	6,195	6,672	7,236	7,242	6,826	7,130	6,781	10,887	9,918
Royal London	1,961	6,088	6,446	6,750	7,156	7,447	7,825	**8,180**	**12,812**	**12,300**
Scottish Amicable	**2,197**	**8,210**	**8,754**	**8,320**	**8,302**	**8,325**	**8,520**	8,096	12,718	10,703
Scottish Equitable	1,989	6,181	6,380	6,523	7,108	6,870	7,239	7,237	12,048	nd
Scottish Friendly	1,710	5,906	6,024	6,177	6,177	6,126	6,126	6,779	11,389	11,298
Scottish Life	2,098	**7,230**	7,543	7,818	7,769	7,505	7,480	7,004	11,536	10,350
Scottish Mutual	2,155	7,139	7,659	7,664	7,745	7,232	7,185	7,192	12,203	11,618
Scottish Provident	1,994	6,351	6,546	7,250	7,703	7,440	7,812	7,456	12,011	11,532
Scottish Widows	**2,235**	**7,762**	**8,321**	**8,977**	**8,794**	**8,512**	**8,607**	7,793	12,276	11,139
Standard Life	**2,255**	**7,902**	**8,843**	**9,024**	**8,958**	**8,869**	**8,958**	8,336	**12,291**	11,522
Sun Alliance	2,120	6,966	7,169	7,369	7,399	6,968	7,014	6,835	11,159	10,113
Sun Life Canada	(2)	(2)	5,224	6,015	7,061	6,600	6,639	6,567	11,024	10,960
Sun Life	1,929	5,904	6,119	6,399	6,546	7,105	7,241	7,260	12,206	**11,754**
Swiss Pioneer Life	na	6,115	6,385	6,159	6,285	6,408	6,484	6,434	11,117	nd
Tunbridge Wells Eq	2,052	**7,308**	**7,813**	**7,847**	**8,215**	6,525	**8,239**	**7,933**	**13,477**	12,151
UK Provident	**2,137**	6,818	6,851	6,629	6,435	nd	6,692	6,555	10,956	nd
Wesleyan Assurance	1,855	5,887	6,004	6,260	7,466	7,780	7,655	7,598	12,193	**11,820**
Highest	2,263	8,210	8,843	9,024	8,958	8,869	8,958	8,475	13,693	12,300
Average	1,939	6,284	6,642	6,942	7,132	7,212	7,424	7,367	11,942	11,105
Lowest	1,650	5,050	6,004	5,007	6,017	6,106	6,106	5,887	9,208	9,164

* Actual results in respect of £10 pm true gross premium prior to 1985; £30 pm gross premium 1985–91; £50 pm gross premium 1992 onwards.
nd – not disclosed.
na – not available.

Source: Money Management

with an endowment savings plan are taken out in the early years. The specialist magazine *Money Management* produces a review from time to time. This shows the projected payout on a with-profits endowment, assuming that all policies added the same percentage bonuses each year. The difference in the total payout accounts for charges.

SURRENDERING OR MAKING PAID UP may sometimes be necessary if you cannot maintain the premiums on your endowment policy. You have several options:

- You can make it paid up. In this case you pay no more premiums but your money remains invested and the proceeds are paid out at the maturity date.
- You can surrender it. The life company will quote you a surrender value, which in the early years may be less, or little more, than the premiums paid.
- You can sell it through a specialist broker. If the surrender value of the policy is more than £3,000 and the policy has run at least a quarter of its term, you may be able to sell it through a broker. If the policy is with a good company, you often get more than if you surrender the policies through the company.

Brokers specializing in buying life policies include Foster & Cranfield, who will auction them for a fee of £50 plus one third of the excess achieved on sale over the surrender value (tel. 071–608 1941), and Policy Network, who value policies and match buyers with sellers (tel. 071–938 3626). Others who will value your policy and make an offer for it themselves, selling it on to another buyer, include Beale Dobie (tel. 0621 851133); Policy Portfolio (tel. 081–203 7221); Policy Plus (tel. 0225 753 643); Policy Register (tel. 061–763 1919).

- You can continue with the premiums but use the endowment policy as security for a loan. Some policies have this facility written into them, and you can borrow from the insurance company, occasionally at preferential rates. Otherwise you will have to borrow through your bank, depositing the policy with it as security. The maximum you can borrow is around 70 to 80 per cent of the surrender value.

Unit-Linked Life Policies

These are savings-type policies which operate like a unit trust. The investment fund is unitized and the value of your units directly reflects the value of the underlying investments.

Unit-linked life policies may show a better return than a with-profits endowment – or they may not. Much depends on your choice of company, the fund in which you invest, the investment climate over the life of the policy, how well the money is invested and the level of the stock market at the time you cash in. The value of unit-linked policies coming to maturity in the months before the crash of October 1987 was probably around 20 to 30 per cent higher than after the crash.

The point to remember is that you have all the risks of direct investment in unit trusts, but with higher charges. The table below shows the relative performances of with-profit and unit-linked policies.

Top 10 With-profits versus Top 10 Unit-linked Policies

Maturity value of a £70 a month regular premium 10-year policy.

With-profits	Total £	Unit-linked*	Total £
1. Equitable Life	19,086	Lond. & Manch.	15,546
2. Tunbridge Wells	18,868	Standard Life	15,469
3. Pearl	18,566	Prolific	15,248
4. Friends Prov	18,352	NPI	14,916
5. Standard Life	17,966	London Life	14,752
6. Scottish Amic	17,918	Norwich Union	14,704
7. Royal London	17,846	AXA Equity & Law	14,680
8. Clerical Medical	17,724	LAS	14,466
9. Norwich Union	17,662	Albany Life	14,040
10. Commercial Union	17,492	Scottish Widows	13,849

* The unit-linked policies are maximum investment plans invested in a UK equity fund. Figures to 1.3.92, based on a non-smoking male aged 29 at inception.

Source: Money Marketing

If you are prepared to live with this degree of risk, you could be better off with a direct investment in unit trusts or investment trusts, particularly if held within a PEP, as it has tax concessions.

The degree of risk with a unit-linked policy is just as great as with a comparable unit trust.

One advantage of unit-linked life policies is that you can switch between the various investment funds on offer without any liability to Capital Gains Tax. However, perhaps even this is not a major consideration. In the past, the ability to switch from one unitized fund to another within a unit-linked life policy, without incurring any Capital Gains Tax liability, was felt to be an advantage in selling these policies. However, this was only ever a problem for the really wealthy because most people can buy and sell shares and unit or investment trusts within the Capital Gains Tax annual exemption (£5,800 for 1993–94).

Now it is possible to enjoy the same CGT advantages by putting your shares and unit or investment trusts into a PEP.

Other Types of Endowment Policies

UNITIZED WITH-PROFITS POLICIES have recently been introduced by some of the big insurers to replace the basic with-profits contracts. These unitized policies have some of the characteristics of a unit-linked policy and a with-profits policy. The fund is unitized and bonuses are declared, expressed as a number of extra units added to your policy. But, like a traditional with-profits policy, once added the bonuses cannot be taken away.

WITH-PROFITS BONDS are lump-sum versions of unitized and conventional with-profits policies and have been heavily sold in recent years. Bonuses are declared and added to the policies as extra units.

LOW-COST ENDOWMENTS are very similar to the straight with-profits endowment. They are usually sold in conjunction with a mortgage and include a certain amount of term or decreasing-term assurance to cover the mortgage should you die before the loan is repaid.

NON-PROFIT ENDOWMENTS are not often sold today. These policies offer a guaranteed return but no bonuses. The sum assured is payable on death or maturity. Generally poor value for money.

The payout from a qualifying with-profit endowment or other savings-type policy is generally tax-free, provided you have paid the premiums for at least 10 years, or for three-quarters of the term of the policy.

The investments will, however, have been subject to tax within the life company's fund. There could be a liability to higher-rate tax on encashment of some non-qualifying life policies, or on early surrender of some qualifying policies. If in doubt, ask your professional adviser.

Unit and Investment Trusts

Unit and investment trusts are equity-based investments. Your money is pooled by the unit trust company with the funds of other investors and spread across a range of securities. The fund may be invested in shares, property, gilts, foreign shares, unquoted companies, or futures and options. The advantage is that for a relatively small sum of money you get a wide spread of investments and your risk is reduced.

Your first equity-based investment should probably be a with-profits endowment. But for the novice investor who has already got a with-profits endowment and wants to take the plunge into direct investment in shares, the safest way to invest is through a unit or investment trust.

If you hold a single share and the company fails, you lose everything. If you invest in 20 different companies, some may do well, others not so well, and one may collapse, but at least you have reduced the risk.

Unit and investment trusts are suitable for your longer-term savings – anything over five years – and can be used in school fees and retirement planning, and to provide income or capital growth to take care of inflation in retirement. If you hold them within a PEP (which you should do if you have not used all your PEP allowance for the year), the income and any capital gains are totally tax-free.

These trusts are also suitable for both lump-sum and regular saving. Most unit trusts, and a significant proportion of investment trusts, offer regular savings schemes.

Unit Trusts

These are open-ended funds. Money from all investors is pooled and a spread of shares or other securities is bought. Each day (sometimes less frequently) the underlying shares in the fund are valued and the total is divided by the number of units which have been issued to investors. The price of these units, whether buying or selling, is determined by the price of the underlying investments, less any management charges.

CHARGES ON UNIT TRUSTS involve a 5 or 6 per cent spread between the offer and bid price, i.e. the price at which you buy (offer price) and the price at which you sell (bid price). If you bought and sold £1,000 worth of units on the same day and there was no change in the unit price, you would lose £50 on your investment, which represents the 5 per cent initial charge.

There is also an annual management charge, calculated as a percentage of the value of the underlying fund. This is usually 0.75 to 1.5 per cent. This is deducted from the dividend income from the underlying shares before the unit trust pays a dividend.

BUYING AND SELLING unit trusts can be done in in two ways:

- Direct through the management company. (Try asking for a discount when you buy because the company will not have had to pay commission to an intermediary.)
- Through a stockbroker, your bank, or some other intermediary (all of whom will earn commission of around 3 per cent of the amount invested).

Investment Trusts

An investment trust is a closed-end fund which invests in shares, property and a number of other securities. It is an investment company whose shares are quoted on the stock exchange. The price of a share reflects to some extent the value of the underlying investments, but it is also affected by the supply and demand for the investment trust shares.

Investment trusts are held extensively by big financial institutions, which often sit on them for many years. If the performance of an investment trust is good, it may be difficult to buy. If it is bad, it may be difficult to sell at anything other than a loss.

In recent years most investment trusts have been trading at a discount to the value of the underlying investments. For example, the assets may be worth 100p per share, but you could buy the investment trust's shares at, say, 90p. But there have been periods when they have traded at a premium. This adds another variable to the equation which has to be taken into account.

CHARGES ON INVESTMENT TRUSTS are taken from the dividend income generated by the underlying investments. The amount may be a percentage of the funds under management, or a flat fee to cover all costs, plus a percentage profit.

Investment trust shares are quoted on the stock exchange, and when you buy and sell you will incur costs – the stockbroker's commission, usually a minimum of £20 per bargain (each order of shares) or around 1.5 per cent. You will also have to pay what used to be known as the 'jobber's turn' – the difference between the price at which the market maker will sell or buy the shares. In some small investment trusts this can be as high as 3 to 5 per cent. However, this will not be apparent as your contract note will simply show the price at which you bought.

BUYING AND SELLING investment trusts must be done through a stockbroker, as they are quoted shares. Your bank or other intermediary will, however, carry out the transaction for you. Most brokers have a minimum fee of £20 to £30. For bargains over £1,000 you will probably pay the old stock exchange rate of 1.67 per cent, diminishing as the size of the investment increases. With the deregulation of the stock exchange, fixed commissions have gone, so it pays to shop around. Generally speaking, the cheapest deals are from 'execution only' brokers, like Sharelink, where the minimum bargain commission is under £20.

Building a Portfolio

Unit and investment trusts come in many different forms and their investment objectives vary widely. Some may invest in a particular geographical area, such as the UK or North America, the Far East or Australia, or in different sectors of the market, such as oil or mining companies, income stocks or recovery situations.

In building up a portfolio of these trusts you will need to choose a selection that varies in content and location. The types of fund available fall into the following categories:

- Income.
- Growth.
- Geographical area. (They may be single country shares,

e.g. Germany or Japan, or regional, e.g. Far East or North
America).
- Specialist sectors (e.g. small companies, electricals,
pharmaceuticals, technology, etc.).

What you choose will depend on a number of considerations:

- Do you want income or growth?
- Are you prepared to live with the double risk of the volatility
of shares, plus currency fluctuations, if you buy overseas
invested unit trusts?
- Do you want blue-chip household-name companies, or are
you prepared to buy smaller company trusts? (These tend to
show greater profits in boom times but fall further when
share prices are going down.)
- Do you have special requirements which would indicate
buying a particular kind of specialist trust (e.g. a high
income trust or a split-level investment trust)?

Split-Capital Investment Trusts

These are specialist investment trusts which have two or more
classes of shares. In their simplest form they offer income shares
and growth shares. The holders of the income shares derive the
income from the entire investment portfolio, while the holders of
the growth shares may get most or all the increase in the value of
the underlying investments.

Most split-capital trusts have a maturity date when the trust is
wound up (although this can be a movable feast) in order that
the capital shareholders are able to realize their investments. For
example, if the dividend yield on a split-capital investment trust
was 6 per cent on the entire portfolio, the income shareholders
may receive a return of 12 per cent, but the growth shareholders
may receive all the capital gain when the trust was wound up.
The exact return will depend on the split between capital and
income shares. Clearly these different classes of shares will
appeal to different types of investors.

There are several other classes of investment trust shares,
each with specific appeal to certain types of investor. You will
need advice if you intend investing in split-capital trusts, as there
are risks which are not immediately apparent, depending on the
structure of the trust.

Unit Trust PEPs

If you have not used your PEP allowance for the current tax year, any investment in unit or investment trusts should be put into a PEP to shield it from income and Capital Gains Tax.

The table below shows the enormous benefits of investing through a PEP because of the tax-free roll-up of income.

Unit Trust and Unit Trust PEP Compared

£6,000 invested each year

Investment made	UK equity unit trust £	UK equity unit trust PEP* £
5 years ago	36,152	37,936
10 years ago	125,135	138,724
15 years ago	342,059	411,684

Figures are calculated to 1.1.93. They assume net income reinvested in the straight unit trust, and gross income reinvested in the same unit trust held within a PEP, had that been possible at the time.
* Hypothetical figures – PEPs not introduced until 1986 and the initial maximum investment was below £6000.

Source: Save & Prosper

How to Buy Unit and Investment Trusts

Both unit and investment trusts can be purchased by lump sum or regular savings. The minimum lump-sum investment is around £500 to £1,500. Regular savings schemes are available from most unit trust groups, and a significant proportion of investment trusts. Minimum investment is around £50 a month.

The Association of Unit Trusts and Investment Funds and the Association of Investment Trust Companies (see Useful Addresses) publish information on which organizations have regular savings schemes. However, a better way to approach the situation may be to choose your unit or investment trust first, and then find out if you can save regularly with it.

The idea of regular savings schemes is to encourage the small investor. They are a very good way of building up an equity holding over a period of time, and are much cheaper and more flexible than with-profits endowment and unit-linked life policies.

Regular savings schemes have the following advantages:

- You can cash in at any time without penalties (just the normal dealing charges).
- You can add a lump sum to your investments at any time.
- You can vary monthly payments, increasing or decreasing them.
- You can take a payments 'holiday' without penalty if you find yourself hard up and temporarily unable to continue.
- You get the benefit of 'pound cost averaging'; this smoothes out the returns because your regular payments buy more units when prices are low, fewer when prices are high.

Choosing a Trust

Unless you are going to take an active interest in your investments, you will be best off taking advice on the choice of trust. Some financial advisers specialize almost exclusively in unit and investment trusts, and will recommend a portfolio of funds tailored to suit your needs. Again, the Association of Investment Trusts and the Association of Unit Trusts and Investment Funds should be able to give you the names of intermediaries who specialize in these areas.

With 1405 unit trusts and 327 investment trusts to choose from, specializing in everything from gold and commodity shares to companies with household names, picking a unit or investment trust is not easy.

The return you get from your investment can vary enormously, depending on the type of trust and the area in which it is invested. The following table shows the wide variation in performances.

If you want to make your own investment decisions, read the personal finance pages of the quality national daily newspapers like the *Financial Times*, *The Times*, the *Daily Telegraph* and the *Independent*. In the Saturday edition they publish special personal finance supplements which regularly look at unit and investment trusts and give details of past performance, as well as recommendations. Study the market for some time before you buy.

Best- and Worst-Performing Unit and Investment Trusts

Value of £1,000 invested over one year to 1.6.93 – net income reinvested

Fund	Value £	Market Sector
Unit trusts – Top 5		
1. Mercury Gold & General	2,439	Commodities
2. Waverley Austr. Gold	1,962	Commodities
3. TSB Natural Resources	1,909	Commodities
4. PM Japan Growth	1,868	Japan
5. Prudential Japanese	1,866	Japan
Unit trusts – Bottom 5		
1. Equitable Special Sits.	926	UK Equity Growth
2. S & P UK Smaller Cos.	919	UK Smaller Cos.
3. PC CAM British Growth	905	UK Equity Growth
4. Thornton American Sm. Cos.	887	North America
5. Aetna Iberian Growth	875	Europe

Sector average over one year: 1,229
Number of unit trusts in the sector: 1,313

Fund	Value £	Market Sector
Investment trusts – Top 5		
1. Jersey Phoenix	2,589	International
2. Oriental Small. Cos.	2,238	Far East*
3. Singapore Sesdaq	2,225	Far East*
4. Abtrust New Thai	2,056	Far East*
5. Gartmore Emerging Pacif.	2,013	Far East*
Investment trusts – Bottom 5		
1. Derby Inc (2003)	758	(SC) Income
2. S & P Linked Inc. (1997)	698	(SC) Income
3. Exmoor Dual Ord (2001)	590	(SC) Highly Geared
4. Greyfriars	502	Venture Cap.
5. Gresham House	307	Smaller Cos.

Sector average over one year: 1,192
Number of investment trust in the sector: 306

Value of £1,000 invested over three years to 1.6.93 – net income reinvested

Fund	Value £	Market Sector
Unit trusts – Top 5		
1. Gartmore hong Kong	2,962	Far East*
2. Prov. Cap. Hong Kong	2,732	Far East*
3. Invesco HK and China	2,504	Far East*
4. Schroder US Small Cos.	2,451	North America
5. James Capel HK Growth	2,370	Far East*

Unit trusts – Bottom 5

1. Baring Europe	785	Europe
2. Kleinwort Ben. Eur. Spec	780	Europe
3. Thornton European Opps.	760	Europe
4. MGM Spec. Sits. Growth	645	UK Equity Growth
5. Aetna Iberian Growth	620	Europe

Sector average over three years: 1,282
Number of funds in sector: 1,147

Investment trusts – Top 5

1. Jersey Phoenix	2,877	International
2. Murray Enterprise	2,717	Venture & Dev.
3. Manakin Holdings	2,319	Venture & Dev.
4. Personal Assets	2,135	International
5. Mezzanine Cap. & inc.	2,082	(SC) Capital

Investment trusts – Bottom 5

1. JF Pacific Warrant	458	Far East**
2. Scottish Nat. Capital	436	(SC) Capital
3. Greyfriars	407	Venture & Dev.
4. Worth	347	Venture & Dev.
5. Gresham House	23	Smaller Cos.

Sector average over three years: 1,280
Number of funds in sector: 249

Value of £1,000 invested over five years to 1.6.93 – net income reinvested

Fund	Value £	Market Sector

Unit trusts – Top 5

1. Gartmore Hong Kong	4,498	Far East*
2. Hypo F & C Small. Cos.	4,497	North American
3. Invesco HK & China	4,179	Far East*
4. Prov. Capital HK	3,907	Far East*
5. Invesco SE Asia	3,880	Far East*

Unit trusts – Bottom 5

1. Cap. House Prop. Shares	804	Property & Financial
2. Aetna Iberian Growth	797	Europe
3. Brown Shipley Recovery	748	UK Equity & Growth
4. Hambro General Prop.	744	Property & Financial
5. MGM Special Sits. Growth	476	UK Equity Growth

Sector average over five years: 1,694
Number of funds in sector: 942

Investment trusts – Top 5

1. Mezzanine Cap & Inc.	3,765	(SC) Capital
2. EFM Dragon	3,506	Far East*
3. Pacific Assets	3,489	Far East*
4. Second Market	3,401	Europe
5. Manakin Holdings	3,149	Venture and Dev.

Investment trusts – Bottom 5

1. Worth	572	Venture & Dev.
2. CSC	557	UK General
3. English & Caledonian	498	Venture & Dev.
4. SUMIT	408	Venture & Dev.
5. Gresham House	21	Smaller Cos.

Sector average over five years: 1,742
Number of funds in sector: 179

* Far East excluding Japan.
** Far East including Japan.
(SC) = Split Capital. Because of the gearing effect of splitting the share capital between two or more classes of shares, the performance of these specialist shares is not directly comparable with the performance of conventional investment trusts. See page 186 for description of split-capital investment trusts.

Source: Micropal

Past performance is not necessarily any guide to the future, but if you want to know how well the funds have performed, the investment returns from all investment and unit trusts are independently monitored by the statistical service Micropal (Trafalgar House, Chalkhill Road, London W6 8DW; tel. 081–741 4100). While this service is too detailed and probably too expensive for the average small investor, it can give you the names of intermediaries in your area who take their service.

Direct Investment in Shares

Direct investment in shares is more risky than buying a unit or investment trust, but it can be more fun as it is easier to identify with Marks & Spencer, for example, and follow the company's fortunes than with an anonymous unit trust. There is more involvement and you can take a real interest in your investments by going along to the annual general meeting.

Stockbrokers are not really interested in small investors, although those who are members of the Association of Private Client Investment Managers and Stockbrokers (see Useful Addresses) are likely to be more sympathetic than others.

If you have relatively small sums to put into shares – say £1,000 at a time – and you want to invest directly, you will either have to pick the companies yourself, or you will need a sizeable lump sum – an absolute minimum of £50,000 – before a stockbroker will be interested in managing a portfolio for you. Below £50,000 virtually all stockbrokers will put you into unit or

investment trusts. However, the introduction of PEPs, particularly single-company PEPs, has encouraged some stockbrokers
to run schemes for their clients, and this is one way of identify-
ing a broker who will deal in small sums.

The Chase de Vere *PEP Guide* (see Further Reading) lists
stockbrokers who run PEPs. If you haven't used your full PEP
allowance for the year (£6,000 in a general PEP and £3,000 in
a single-company PEP), this is the best way to invest in shares
because of the tax advantages.

If you are prepared to take the plunge on your own, there are
several share-dealing services and stockbrokers who offer an
'execution only' service at very cheap rates.

Don't feel intimidated at the thought of having a flutter in
shares, even if you are not entirely sure what to go for. Absolute
beginners can have a lot of fun, provided they realize the risks
involved, treat the exercise a bit like gambling, and deal in
relatively small amounts. Share prices do go up and down,
sometimes wildly, but only a very small proportion of companies go bust and leave you with absolutely nothing.

Guaranteed Stock Exchange-Linked Bonds

These are lump-sum investments where the return is linked to
increases in various Stock Exchange indices, most commonly the
FTSE100 index. In their most common form they guarantee you
a minimum of your money back after five years, or to increase
the value of your original investment in line with the FTSE100
index. If the index has gone down over the period, you don't
lose.

There are several variations which allow you to lock in gains;
you might, for example, see a rise of 30 per cent in the index
over the first four years, followed by a drop of 10 per cent in the
last 12 months. Some of these bonds give you the chance to lock
in at various points. Others offer you a basic minimum return,
say, 3 per cent on your investment, should there be no increase
in share prices.

These bonds are issued by a variety of investment institutions
and their structure varies. But basically your profits are guaranteed by the investment house. Even if they make a loss, they still
have to pay out. For this reason the bonds tend to be issued in
small tranches, and when they are available you might have to

move quickly. Watch for the advertisements in the newspapers. Minimum investment is usually around £1,000. This is a no-lose gamble in shares.

Tax on Trusts and Shares

Dividends on shares and unit and investment trusts are all subject to income tax, and have basic-rate tax deducted at source. A non-taxpayer can reclaim this. However, dividends are tax-free if the securities are held within a Personal Equity Plan, which is the sensible thing to do.

Profits on selling shares and unit or investment trusts, whether lump-sum investments or regular savings, are subject to Capital Gains Tax at either 25 per cent or 40 per cent, depending on the rate of income tax you pay. However, the first £5,800 (1993–94) of profits realized each year is exempt. By using this exemption even those with quite a large portfolio of investments can avoid CGT. Securities held within a PEP are free from CGT.

Business Expansion Scheme (BES)

Investments in the Business Expansion Scheme are among the few on which you still obtain tax relief, but if you want to invest, you will have to move fast. The BES was introduced in 1983 and is due to be wound up at the end of 1993. It was designed to give small investors an incentive to invest in small companies, which generally have difficulty in obtaining finance elsewhere. The schemes have been much modified since, and most of those being issued now are backed by property with a guaranteed buy-out by a big institution.

Currently you can get tax relief at your highest rate paid on up to £40,000 a year invested in BES companies, and any profits on sale after five years are free from Capital Gains Tax.

Higher-rate taxpayers benefit most from the tax concessions, so BES investments are best suited to wealthier individuals. The risks can be high. If you are thinking of investing in a BES, you have very little time in which to do it. Take professional advice.

There are two publications that monitor all the BES issues as they are offered: *BES Magazine* and *BESt Investment*. They evaluate the degree of risk involved and the expertise of the management, as well as the charging structure. If you want to invest in a BES company, you would be well advised to subscribe to one of these publications or to take advice.

Other Investments

There are a host of other specialist investment vehicles, most notably gold, precious stones, other commodities, share options, financial and currency futures, to name just a few. These are used mostly by professional investors and the enthusiastic amateur can get burnt. However, they do provide a means of hedging risks in currencies, interest rates and share price fluctuations.

Unfortunately, in a book such as this, there is insufficient room to cover everything. If you are interested in such investments (and the minimums are usually high), you will need specialist advice, or you will have to read up on the subject in specialist publications.

7

INHERITANCE

During 1991, the last year for which accurate figures are available, some £1,259 million was handed over to the Inland Revenue in Inheritance Tax and its predecessor, Capital Transfer Tax.

No doubt some of this was unavoidable; rising house prices during the 1980s have made us all die richer than we expected. But there is no need to let the taxman take more than is necessary.

However, if you are to avoid paying Inheritance Tax, you need to understand how it is charged and plan ahead.

What is Inheritance Tax?

Inheritance Tax (IHT) is a tax on your wealth when you die. Since none of us can avoid dying, it is better to make provision for this tax and, where possible, minimize the charge.

Broadly speaking, you will pay IHT on death at a flat rate of 40 per cent on the excess of your estate over the £150,000 threshold (1993–94). The threshold is index-linked to the rate of inflation and raised each year unless the Treasury specifically says otherwise – as it did in 1993.

Rapidly rising house prices during the 1980s have put vast numbers of home-owners above the threshold for IHT purposes, and many people, who don't necessarily regard themselves as wealthy, will have an IHT liability when they die.

For the purposes of calculating IHT all your assets at death are totalled, including all gifts (except exempt transfers) made in the previous seven years.

The most efficient way of avoiding IHT, therefore, is to give away your assets and live for another seven years. However, this is usually impracticable, since you will probably need to hang on to some of your assets to provide income, and none of us know precisely when we are going to die. Other steps have to be taken.

Inheritance Tax was introduced in 1984 and was the successor to the earlier Capital Transfer Tax, or Gifts Tax as it was known. It applies to gifts made during your lifetime after 26 March 1974, transfers on death made after 12 March 1975 and settled property.

More importantly, since 17 March 1986 lifetime transfers between individuals and to certain trusts are only liable to Inheritance Tax if you die within seven years of making the gift – a concession which allows many people to avoid the tax, if not completely, then mostly.

IHT is charged – with certain important exemptions and reliefs – on gifts you make within seven years of death, as well as on the value of your estate when you die. However, you can give away assets without limit during your lifetime, and provided you live for another seven years the gifts will be outside your estate on death and there will be no IHT to pay on those gifts.

Gifts made during your lifetime are therefore known as Potentially Exempt Transfers (PETs). They become 'chargeable transfers' only if you die within seven years of making the gift. As a result, the vast bulk of IHT is paid on death – £1,107 million out of a total of £1,259 million in 1990–91.

Wealthy people usually insure their lives at the time a large gift is made, with seven-year term assurance, in order to cover the potential IHT liability should they die within seven years.

If you are domiciled in this country, you have to pay IHT on all your property on death. If you are not domiciled here, it applies only to your assets in this country. (You are deemed to be domiciled in the UK for IHT purposes if you were domiciled here on or after 10 December 1974, and within the three years preceding the date of the transfer which is subject to IHT. You are also deemed to be domiciled here if you were resident here on or after 10 December 1974 and in not less than 17 of the 20 years of assessment, ending with the year in which the gift was made.)

Potentially Exempt Transfers

PETS are gifts made after 17 March 1986 to other individuals, or to accumulation and maintenance settlements, or to life interest trusts, or trusts for disabled persons. This means that IHT will not be payable on these transfers unless you die within seven years.

A lifetime gift by an individual into a discretionary trust is charged at half the rate applicable on death, which currently works out at 20 per cent. If the donor pays this tax, the gift will have to be grossed up. However, if you do die within seven years of making a gift, the PET becomes a 'chargeable event' and liable to IHT, subject to certain reliefs.

The situation regarding trusts and IHT is complicated, so if you are thinking of settling property in trust, you must take professional advice.

How Much Do You Pay?

IHT is chargeable on death on the value of your estate, plus the total of any potentially exempt and chargeable transfers which have been made during the seven years prior to death.

Broadly, IHT is charged on death on all your assets in excess of £150,000 (1993–94) at a rate of 40 per cent for deaths occurring after 9 March 1992. Lower thresholds applied for earlier years. The threshold is indexed in line with inflation each year, unless the Treasury stipulates otherwise.

The current IHT ruling means that you can give away your assets without limit and, provided you live for seven years, they will be outside your estate and exempt from IHT.

Inheritance Tax Rates and Thresholds – Transfers on Death

From 15.3.88 to 5.4.89 –	First £110,000 – nil
	Remainder – 40%
From 6.4.89 to 5.4.90 –	First £118,000 – nil
	Remainder – 40%
From 6.4.90 to 5.4.91 –	First £128,000 – nil
	Remainder – 40%
From 6.4.91 to 9.3.92 –	First £140,000 – nil
	Remainder – 40%
From 9.3.92 onwards	First £150,000 – nil
	Remainder – 40%

Tapering Relief on PETs

Death in years	% of full IHT rate payable
1–3	100
4	80
5	60
6	40
7	20

If you make a PET but die within seven years, the gift is cumulated with other gifts within the seven-year period and with each 'chargeable transfer' within seven years of each PET, and added to your assets on death to determine your IHT liability. There is, however, tapering relief if you die within the seven-year period.

Exemptions

There are a number of important exemptions which can help you to avoid Inheritance Tax. They fall into two categories: transfers which are exempt both during your lifetime and on death, and those which are exempt only during your lifetime.

Transfers Between Husband and Wife

The most important of the exemptions is that all transfers between spouses are exempt from IHT whether during your lifetime or on death. Lifetime gifts between spouses are not included as PETs. If you or your spouse are not domiciled in this country, only the first £55,000 of transfers made to the non-domiciled partner are exempt.

Lifetime Gifts

All gifts made outright, without limit, seven or more years before death are exempt from IHT.

In addition, both you and your spouse can make the following gifts each year:

- Transfers up to £3,000 – any unused portion can be carried forward for one year only.

- Any number of small gifts to different people not exceeding £250.
- Normal expenditure out of income – this must be a regular payment (a grandparent paying school fees for a grandchild, for example). You must be able to show that the expenditure is out of your taxed income and that you are left with sufficient income to maintain your normal standard of living. There are complex anti-avoidance rules regarding life policies, annuities and related transactions.
- Gifts in consideration of marriage – £5,000 if the donor is a parent; £2,500 for grandparents or great-grandparents or between the marrying partners; £1,000 otherwise.
- Certain gifts for the maintenance of the giver's family (for example, an ex-spouse, children under 18 or in full-time education, or infirm relatives).

Other transfers which are exempt if made during your life and on death – they also apply to trusts – include gifts to charities made after 14 March 1983 without limit; gifts to political parties after 14 March 1988 are completely exempt; gifts for national purposes (e.g. to the National Trust, the British Museum, universities, etc.); gifts for public benefit of property deemed by the Treasury to be of outstanding merit (e.g. works of art, manuscripts, etc.); gifts of shares to an employee trust, and gifts to housing associations made on or after 15 March 1988.

If you are thinking of making such a gift or leaving bequests in your will which come into these categories, you will need to take professional advice as they are hedged with qualifications.

There are also complicated rules for IHT relief on business property, agricultural property and woodlands. Here again you will need professional advice.

Gifts Tax-Free on Death Only

- Lump-sum payments from pension schemes, provided the trustees of the scheme have total discretion over who gets the money.
- Refunds of personal pension plan contributions, plus any accrued interest or return of fund, provided they are paid directly to someone else, in trust.

- Lump sums paid out from a life assurance policy, provided it was written in trust for someone else.

Gifts with Reservation

You cannot avoid IHT by giving something away if you still enjoy the benefit of the asset. The most common example of this is where elderly people want to pass on their home to a child or grandchild, but continue to live in it. This will not avoid IHT unless the donor pays a market rent for the property to the recipient – something which most elderly people cannot afford to do.

Quick Succession Relief

If you die having yourself received assets on which IHT had been paid within five years of your death, there is a deduction of a proportion of the tax paid. This is 100 per cent, 80 per cent, 60 per cent, 40 per cent or 20 per cent, depending on whether the period between the transfer and your death is one, two, three, four or five years.

Payment

IHT has to be paid on death, and probate (or letters of administration) will not be granted unless the IHT bill has been settled. If a PET becomes a chargeable transfer because the donor dies within seven years of making the gift, Inheritance Tax has to be paid by the recipient.

In certain circumstances you may be allowed to pay by instalments over 10 years. This applies with assets which are not easily realizable – homes, land and buildings, controlling holdings in shares in companies and certain unquoted shares, as well as business assets. The concession applies only as long as the assets are retained by the beneficiaries; if they are sold, all the tax is due immediately.

On some assets, such as farms and houses, the instalments are free of interest (unless they are paid late). With others, interest is charged on the unpaid tax. However, it is likely to be cheaper to pay the interest on the instalments than to borrow the money to pay the tax in full, even if you intend to pay off the tax bill once probate is granted.

The problem confronting most executors of an estate is that assets cannot be released until probate has been granted, but probate will not be granted until the IHT bill has been settled. How do you find the cash?

Money held in National Savings investments, such as savings certificates, can be drawn upon before probate is granted. The Probate Registry can issue a note when you attend to swear the papers which will allow the appropriate National Savings office to release the cash needed to settle the IHT bill. Similar arrangements have been made by Girobank and many of the larger building societies. However, if this is not sufficient to pay the IHT bill, you will have to borrow the balance.

Valuation

Assets are normally valued at the open-market price at the date you give them away, or the date of death. However, there are complications where the value of assets is affected by the gift – if, for example, you give your child half a set of paintings which are more valuable as a whole. You would be wise to take professional advice on such transfers.

Any liabilities – such as a mortgage on a property – are deducted when assessing the value of your estate for IHT purposes.

What is Included for IHT Purposes?

IHT affects all your property and assets held anywhere in the world: land, houses, other property, shares, bank, building society and other cash deposits, the proceeds of life and pension policies (if not written in trust) and any money owing to you.

You can deduct from this certain exempt transfers, funeral expenses, debts owed by you (except in certain circumstances) and any liability to Income Tax or Capital Gains Tax owing at the date of your death, whether or not an assessment had been raised (but not IHT or Capital Transfer Tax).

Legal fees incurred by you prior to death can be deducted, but not the cost of probate or executors' expenses.

There are exclusions for property held outside the UK if you are not domiciled in this country, including certain UK government stocks where the interest is paid gross to non-residents. If you are non-resident or not domiciled in the UK, you should take advice, as there are a number of double taxation agreements which need to be taken into account.

Final Adjustments

Although the IHT bill has to be paid before probate is granted, there may be adjustments made at a later date. For example, IHT will be payable on any assets overlooked at the time the estate was wound up. The value of a home is not agreed with the district valuer until probate is granted, and nor is the valuation of unquoted shares.

Relief is available, too, if quoted stocks and shares are sold below their probate value within 12 months of the death. You can ask to have IHT based on the sale proceeds instead of the probate value.

Inheritance Tax Planning

Before you can do anything about avoiding Inheritance Tax, you must know just how much you are worth. The best means of doing this is to prepare a summary of your assets, liabilities and income. You could use the following table as a guide.

The best way to avoid Inheritance Tax is to give all your assets away, except the last £150,000, and to survive for another seven years. However, giving everything away is clearly impracticable for most people – particularly when the main asset is the family house. And, of course, none of us know when we will die.

Many elderly people who don't actually need the income generated from their investments are, none the less, reluctant to give assets away in case they become infirm and the money is needed to pay nursing home bills. However, it may well be possible to make provision for any future medical care, and still give away significant amounts to avoid IHT.

The next best method of avoiding IHT, for married couples, is to split the assets between the two partners to reduce or eliminate the potential liability and both make wills leaving at least £150,000 each to the children or other beneficiaries.

For example, a couple may have shares and investments

How Much Are You Worth?

	Capital		Gross Income	
	Self £	Spouse £	Self £	Spouse £
Assets				
Private residence	....	....	....	....
Other property	....	....	....	....
Contents and other chattels	....	....	....	....
Shares in family business	....	....	....	....
Other business assets	....	....	....	....
Agricultural land	....	....	....	....
Woodlands	....	....	....	....
Bank and building society deposits	....	....	....	....
Shares in quoted companies	....	....	....	....
Gilts and other fixed-interest securities	....	....	....	....
National Savings securities	....	....	....	....
Trust funds	....	....	....	....
Lloyds deposits and reserves	....	....	....	....
Loans	....	....	....	....
Other securities	....	....	....	....
Remuneration				
Benefits	....	....	....	....
Investment income	....	....	....	....
Liabilities				
Mortgage on home	....	....	....	....
Bank loans & overdrafts	....	....	....	....
Tax	....	....	....	....
Other borrowings	....	....	....	....
Pensions	....	....	....	....
Life policies	....	....	....	....

worth £300,000 and a house worth another £200,000. When the first partner dies, the assets will pass to the surviving spouse free of Inheritance Tax (provided a will has been made, see page 211 for details of intestacy). However, when the second partner dies, Inheritance Tax at 40 per cent will be payable on the excess over the £150,000 starting point. On the figures given this is £350,000; IHT at 40 per cent will mean a tax bill of £140,000.

If the assets are split between the two partners, both can leave £150,000 to their children or other beneficiaries free of IHT, reducing the excess to £200,000 and the resulting tax bill to £80,000.

Where the only asset is the family home, the two partners can become tenants in common (as opposed to the more usual joint tenants) and each can leave their share of the property to children or other beneficiaries with the express wish that the surviving spouse should be allowed to remain in the property until their death.

How Should You Give Things Away?

Before you give anything away you ought to consider the likely position of both yourself and the recipient after you have made the gift. Gifting money or assets outright is usually the simplest means of passing on your wealth, but it may not always be practicable. For example, you may want to gift assets to a child or to a young person who is not responsible enough to make their own decisions. Or the assets may be shares in the family business which the recipient could sell, perhaps leading to loss of voting control and jeopardizing the business. In these situations transferring assets into a trust might be a better solution.

Bare Trust

This type of trust is often used by grandparents, godparents or other relatives wanting to pass on assets to minor grandchildren, nephews and nieces, or great-grandchildren.

Assets transferred into a bare trust are held by the trustees (usually the parents) for a named beneficiary (or beneficiaries) who has an absolute and unconditional right to both the capital and income. Once the beneficiaries are over the age of 18, they can insist that the assets are transferred into their own name and can then sell them or invest the money in whatever way they see fit. This can cause problems.

However, a bare trust can offer Income Tax benefits for parents wanting to pass assets to minor children. Income in excess of £100 a year from assets given to a child by its parents is treated as though it still belonged to the parent and is taxed accordingly. Income from assets passed into a bare trust is not treated as though it were the parents' income if it is allowed to roll up in the trust until the child is 18, or on earlier marriage.

Accumulation and Maintenance Trust

This gives the donor continuing control over the assets of the trust and can be used for passing on wealth to children or grandchildren. There is no IHT charge when the assets are settled in the trust, and the transfer is treated as a PET – if the donor lives for seven years, it becomes totally exempt.

The rules concerning the beneficiaries and who qualifies are complicated; for example, one or more beneficiaries must, by the age of 25, become entitled to at least an interest in the income of the trust. You will undoubtedly need to take professional advice.

Interest in Possession Trust

This is generally used when the beneficiary is already over the age of 25, but again it allows the trustees to retain control of the trust's assets. It is commonly used where the donor wants the life tenant to enjoy the income from the assets, but wants to pass on the capital to other beneficiaries.

For example, where there are children from a previous marriage, a husband or wife might want to ensure that his or her spouse is provided for, but ultimately wants the assets to go to his or her own children, rather than to the spouse's children from a previous marriage.

Gifts into the trust and out of it escape IHT provided the donor survives for seven years.

Discretionary Trust

This type of trust gives great flexibility, but is the least attractive so far as IHT is concerned. A discretionary trust allows you to give away your wealth but to change your mind at a later date if you need to get at the assets (although you will then not escape IHT on these assets). The tax treatment is complicated, so here again it is essential to take professional advice.

IHT and Capital Gains Tax – the Trap

Where assets are to be passed between husband and wife, it may be better to do this on death rather than in lifetime, particularly

if the assets have huge, unrealized capital gains and both partners are elderly. This is because any liability to Capital Gains
Tax (CGT) can be rolled over when the assets are passed from
one partner to another, but must be paid when the assets are
sold. If they are passed on death, any prior gain is wiped out for
CGT purposes.

For example, Mr Bolton bought shares in 1982 worth
£10,000. By 1991 they were worth £120,000, and he gave them
to his wife Mary in order that she could pass them on to their
grandchildren within the £150,000 nil-rate band for Inheritance
Tax. Mary was a non-taxpayer and the idea was also to transfer
some of their joint investment income to her to escape Income
Tax.

When Mr Bolton died in 1992, the shares were worth
£125,000, and Mary sold them a year later for £150,000. She
was therefore liable for Capital Gains Tax at 40 per cent on the
profit calculated as follows:

Sale proceeds	£150,000
Less cost and indexation	
(£10,000 plus, say, £15,000)	£25,000
Profit	£125,000
CGT at 40%	£50,000

(The actual CGT bill might be reduced by the annual exemption.)

However, had Mr Bolton left the shares to Mary in his will, the
gain up to the date of his death would not have been chargeable
and Mary's CGT on the sale of the shares would be calculated as
follows:

Sale proceeds	£150,000
Probate value plus indexation, say	£131,000
Profit	£19,000
CGT at 40%	£7,600

The CGT liability could be further reduced if part of it is within
the annual exemption. But even if it isn't, the tax bill has been
reduced from £50,000 to £7,600 as a result of the shares having
been left to Mary, rather than given to her.

Which Assets to Transfer

Having decided how you will give away your assets – either directly or in trust – you must then decide which assets to transfer.

Clearly, it pays to give away those assets with the greatest potential for capital growth. However, this may not always be practicable. Look at your total position and see if you can rearrange your assets to ensure that you will have sufficient income during your lifetime, while being able to pass on those assets which are most likely to grow in value.

For example, you might have income in retirement of £10,000 from a portfolio of shares and £12,000 from building society deposits. By using the building society money to purchase an annuity, you might be able to provide the same total income of £22,000 (depending on your age), which would leave you free to pass on the shares to your children or grandchildren.

Shares in a family business have a particularly large potential for capital growth, and it is therefore important to bear in mind the IHT implications when setting up the business. The shares may be virtually worthless when you begin, but if you are successful, they can very rapidly present you with a big IHT problem. Take professional advice when setting up such a venture. This is an extremely complicated area and cannot be dealt with in detail in a general book on investment like this.

You may also be able to reduce your potential IHT liability by changing the mix of your investments to include assets, such as woodlands or business property, which carry IHT concessions.

IHT and Life Assurance

Life assurance products can provide a relatively cheap and painless means of reducing your potential IHT liability. They can also provide the cash to pay any IHT bill if it is not possible to avoid the tax.

First and most important, make sure all your life policies – the sort that pay out a lump sum on death – are written in trust for a named beneficiary; this way the proceeds are outside your estate for Inheritance Tax purposes. This also has the advantage that the proceeds can be paid to the trustee(s) without having to wait for grant of probate. It is, therefore, very important to appoint additional trustees.

The premiums paid (but not the policy proceeds) could, in certain circumstances, be regarded as a PET and liable to tax on your death. However, most policy premiums will fall within the annual exemption of £3,000 or the normal expenditure rule.

For policies taken out after 17 March 1986 the 'gifts with reservation' rules may apply. To avoid this you must surrender entitlement to any benefit from the policy proceeds.

It is also vital to have the policy written in trust where the policy proceeds are designed to pay any potential Inheritance Tax liability. For example, suppose you are a widow and have a house worth £450,000 which you want to pass on to your grandchildren tax-free. Since you cannot give it away during your lifetime and avoid Inheritance Tax if you continue to live in the house (because it is a gift with reservation), there will be an IHT liability when you die of £120,000 on the £300,000 excess value over £150,000.

You may decide that on your death the house can be sold and the IHT paid out of the proceeds. But a common way of dealing with the IHT liability is to insure your life for £120,000, with the policy written in trust for the benefit of the grandchildren. The proceeds are outside your estate for Inheritance Tax purposes and the £120,000 can be used by the grandchildren to pay the tax bill when you die. Of course, the grandchildren, assuming they can show suitable insurable interest, could insure your life for sufficient to cover the IHT liability.

If you take out a whole-life, non-profit policy when you are young, the premiums will be relatively cheap. For example, the cost of a whole-life policy paying out £120,000 on death is around £90 a month if you take it out at the age of 29. By the time you are 65 and thinking about your Inheritance Tax liability, the cost of the same cover has risen to £600 a month.

The difficulty is, of course, that when you are young, you probably have little or no idea what you will be worth and what your potential IHT liability is likely to be by the time you die. Moreover, you probably need all your spare cash to buy your home and educate children.

If the beneficiaries take out a policy on your life to cover the IHT liability (known as a life-of-another policy), the proceeds on your death do not form part of your estate. However, if the beneficiaries predecease you, any surrender value will form part of their estate for IHT purposes.

Married couples often use joint-life-last-survivor policies to cover any potential IHT bill. As the name suggests, they pay out on the death of the second partner, not the first, as transfers between spouses are exempt from IHT.

Using a Life Assurance Policy to Pass on your Assets

This is the simplest and most common means of avoiding IHT. You take out a policy, written in trust for the benefit of named beneficiaries, and the proceeds are outside your estate.

It can be virtually any sort of policy, but is commonly a savings-type policy or a whole-life policy. As long as the premiums fall within the £3,000 annual exemption or 'normal expenditure', there is no liability to IHT on the premiums when you die.

There are all kinds of variations. For example, since you cannot give away the family home and continue to live in it (because this is a gift with reservation), you might decide to give the children the proceeds of an endowment policy and leave the mortgage on the property outstanding until you die.

For instance, the family house might be worth £250,000 with an endowment mortgage of £55,000, and there will be IHT liability when you die. You might decide not to pay off the mortgage when the endowment policy matures, but to pay interest only on the outstanding £55,000 and give the children the proceeds of the maturing endowment policy. If this does not leave you with enough income to pay the interest on the loan, you could use the cash from the policy to pay the interest and the premiums on a whole-life policy to cover the Inheritance Tax liability when you die.

Pensions

The proceeds of any pension fund or pension policy are usually outside your estate for Inheritance Tax purposes, provided the trustees of the fund have discretion as to who receives the benefits. Refunds of personal pension plan premiums and any accumulated interest or capital gains are outside your estate, provided they are paid directly to someone else or in trust.

Inheritance Tax is a difficult area and if you are wealthy enough to have a problem, you can probably afford to take professional advice. You would be well advised to consult both your accountant and solicitor.

8

WILLS AND INTESTACY

An estimated seven out of 10 people have not made a will, yet unless you do, your assets will not necessarily be passed on in the way you would wish. Most married couples do not realize that the surviving spouse does not necessarily inherit everything – and dying intestate can produce horrific problems for your partner. There may be a former wife or husband or grown up children from a previous marriage who may decide to make a claim on the estate. It is therefore important to make a will.

Intestacy – Who Inherits?

	Net Value of Estate		
Beneficiaries	Up to £75,000	£75,000–£125,000	£125,000 +
Spouse with children	Everything	£75,000 + *	£75,000 + *
Spouse without children	Everything	Everything	£125,000†
Children	Equal shares	Equal shares	Equal shares
Others	Equal shares	Equal shares	Equal shares

* All personal chattels plus a life interest in half the remaining estate. This reverts to the children on the death of the second partner. The children also inherit the first half on the death of the first partner.
† All personal chattels plus half the remaining estate. The balance goes to parents or, if they are dead, brothers and sisters, etc. If there is no spouse or children, other beneficiaries in order of priority are: parents of the deceased, brothers and sisters, grandparents, and uncles and aunts, who inherit in equal shares. If there are no known relatives, everything goes to the Crown.

As can be seen from the above table, your assets may not pass to your spouse in full if you die intestate, so it is very important to make a will – doubly so if you are not married but want your assets to pass to a partner with whom you are living. Unless you

211

make a will, a cohabitee is entitled to little or nothing. He or she would have to make a claim for support from the estate.

If you die intestate and minor children inherit, the money or assets will be put in trust until they are 18. This could have unforeseen effects – for example, property must generally be sold and the money invested according to the rules of trust, which are very limiting.

Divorce and Marriage

Marriage invalidates your will, unless you have drawn it up in contemplation of marriage and you do actually marry the person named. Divorce does not completely invalidate your will, but if you have named your former spouse as beneficiary and/or executor, divorce cancels this out and bequests or legacies made to your former spouse fall into the residue of your estate. This is almost certainly not what you intended.

Even if you have made a will, you will generally need to draw up another if you have subsequently married or divorced.

On divorce and remarriage you may well have two families whom you want to benefit. Indeed, if you leave a former wife or husband, or children, out of your will, they may be entitled to make a claim on your estate after you die.

Under the Inheritance (Provisions for Family and Dependants) Act 1975 some relatives and any others who can prove that they were being supported by you, either wholly or in part, can claim reasonable provision. They can also make a claim where there is no will. A lot of legal wrangling can be saved if you forestall these problems by making a will.

Considerations in Making a Will

Most people prefer to let a solicitor draw up a will, but if your affairs are straightforward, there is no reason why you should not do it yourself. You might, for example, want to leave everything to your children in equal proportions, and this is not usually complicated.

If you haven't drawn up a checklist for Inheritance Tax purposes, now is the time to do it. It might look like the table below.

If the value of your estate, minus mortgages, loans, outstanding debts (such as Income Tax and CGT) and other liabilities,

What Are You Worth?

Date	Self £	Spouse £	Documents (where kept)
House	. . . .	. . . .	. . . .
Cash Deposits			
Bank	. . . .	. . . .	. . . .
Building society	. . . .	. . . .	. . . .
Investments			
Gilts	. . . .	. . . .	. . . .
National Savings	. . . .	. . . .	. . . .
TESSAs	. . . .	. . . .	. . . .
Shares	. . . .	. . . .	. . . .
Unit or investment trusts	. . . .	. . . .	. . . .
PEPs	. . . .	. . . .	. . . .
Life assurance	. . . .	. . . .	. . . .
Valuables and works of art	. . . .	. . . .	. . . .
Furniture and personal belongings	. . . .	. . . .	. . . .
Other (e.g. Businesses, money owed to you, any interest in trust funds, etc.)	. . . .	. . . .	. . . .

exceeds £150,000 (1993–94), you will be liable for Inheritance Tax on death on the excess, payable at 40 per cent (see Chapter 7). In this situation you should probably take professional advice.

Who Gets What?

The next step is to decide who should inherit which of your assets. In a very simple will you could simply state that your total assets should be shared equally between your three children. In this situation your estate will be valued on death and it is then up to the executor in consultation with the beneficiaries to decide whether assets should be sold and the proceeds split between the beneficiaries or whether certain assets will be passed to specific beneficiaries. If you think there might be disagreement, or you want named beneficiaries to have specific assets, it might be best to spell this out. It will also help the executor if you keep an up-to-date list of your assets with the will.

Your will can indicate a number of other things apart from who inherits your assets. For example, it might specify who will look after your children (you can appoint guardians), details of your funeral and burial, and preferences about the donation of organs.

You may decide to leave certain of your assets in trust (see Chapter 7), in which case you will definitely need to consult a solicitor or accountant, possibly both, as there can be important tax considerations.

Where the beneficiaries are minor children, the assets will automatically be held in trust by the executors, but unless you stipulate how the assets are to be administered, this can be very restricting. If you have a trust drawn up, you can indicate how the assets are invested and whether certain assets, like the family home, should be retained.

There may be certain tax advantages to leaving assets in trust. For example, in a will trust there is no Capital Gains Tax charge when you make the will, so your assets will be passed on to the beneficiaries of your estate at their value on your death, not the value when you wrote them into your will.

You should probably take professional advice in any of the following circumstances:

- The beneficiaries are minor children.
- Your estate exceeds the threshold for Inheritance Tax.
- You want to leave assets in trust.
- You have a family business or farm.
- You want someone other than your spouse to inherit the family home without a tax liability.

Executors

As the name implies, these are the people named in your will who will execute your wishes on your death. They sort out your estate, obtain valuations, deal with any Inheritance Tax charge, repay debts, obtain probate, distribute all legacies and bequests, and generally wind up your estate.

Up to four executors can be appointed, and anyone can be your executor. However, there are certain points to bear in mind.

- Someone older than you is likely to die first.
- If your estate is anything other than totally straightforward, it is probably better that the executor has some financial knowledge.

- The person who is the major beneficiary of your will can be a good choice as they will have a vested interest in executing it efficiently and at minimum cost.
- Professionals can be very expensive (especially the executorship department of banks), but on the other hand you have the advantage of continuity and not having to worry about the executors dying before you. You will probably need to appoint at least one professional, say a solicitor, if the estate is complicated.
- Remember to ask the person(s) you name as your executors whether they are prepared to take on this responsibility.

Single People, Married Couples and Children

If you are single with no dependants, your will is likely to be straightforward. If you are married, you and your partner may both want to make 'mirror wills' at the same time, leaving everything to each other.

If you are married and/or have dependants, you have to consider the possibility that both you and your spouse might die together (in a car crash, for example). It is absolutely essential to make a will if there are children under the age of 18 and children from a previous marriage as you might want to name guardians for them. You must also consider the ghastly possibility that the entire family, including your children, could die in an accident. Whom would you want to inherit in that event? Your next of kin are your parents, but would it make sense for them to inherit?

Guardians

If you are a single parent, unmarried or widowed, with young children, you will probably want to appoint a guardian in your will. This might be someone who is prepared to look after your children, but, if not, he or she will be responsible for making provision for them, having the legal right to decide on where the children live, their education and other matters. The guardian might also be the executor of your will, in which case, unless you stipulate otherwise, he or she will also be the trustee of your estate until the children reach the age of 18.

Matters are more complicated if you have children from a

previous marriage. You might want to leave your share of the family house to your children rather than your current spouse, while allowing him/her to remain in it until the children grow up.

You might not be happy for your former spouse to assume responsibility for your children, and this could be a very important consideration. The children's surviving natural parent will generally have the right to custody of the children and take precedence over a second spouse, even though the stepfather or stepmother might be a better parent. If you name a guardian, he or she can get the court to decide who has custody of the children.

(Bear in mind here that you might want the children's natural father or mother, your new spouse, or a third party to act as trustee if the proceeds of your life policies are written in trust for the benefit of your minor children.)

With divorce and remarriage now commonplace, the inheritance situation can become very complicated. For example, Jane and Peter have both been married before and have one child each from their first marriages and two from their current marriage.

Peter's first wife died and their child, provided for by grandparents, will inherit a substantial sum on their death. Peter therefore wants Jane and their two mutual children to be the beneficiaries of his will.

Jane's first husband abandoned her, so she wants to leave everything in trust for her first child, the other two being well provided for by Peter. She also wants to stop her former husband from obtaining custody of the child and the use of the assets left to the child.

Clearly, the couple will need to take professional advice as the situation is complicated, but by no means uncommon.

Minor Children

If your children under the age of 18 inherit, unless you stipulate otherwise in your will, the executors will act as trustees of whatever you leave to your children. This is important for the following reasons:

- Any houses or land must be sold and the estate turned into suitable investments according to the laws of trust. This will not be a good idea if the main asset is the family home.

- At least 50 per cent of the cash realized must be invested in safe investments like gilts, bank or building society deposits, or National Savings securities.

The children will become entitled to their share of the trust on reaching the age of 18. Before that date the trustees can advance up to half the share of the capital to which each child is entitled, provided it is used for their maintenance and education. This is why it is important that in this situation you take professional advice. The trustees of money left to minor children have far greater freedom if you stipulate precisely what should happen.

For example, you may want your surviving spouse or the guardian to continue looking after the children in your existing family home, in which case you would not want the property sold. You also might not want the children to inherit any money outright until they are 21 or 25.

How Should You Leave Your Assets?

You might want to leave certain articles like valuables, jewellery, paintings and furniture as specific bequests, with any Inheritance Tax to be paid out of the sale of other assets. This could save considerable squabbling among children after your death, especially if you discuss such bequests with them when making your will. It is surprising how acrimonious disagreements can become about who is entitled to specific items, particularly if they have sentimental value.

You can also stipulate that certain bequests are free from Inheritance Tax. For instance, you might want to leave your home and contents to an only child, tax-free, and have the residue after payment of Inheritance Tax divided among grandchildren or left to a charity.

If the Beneficiary Dies First

In this situation, unless you stipulate otherwise (. . . in the event that Simon Jenkins predeceases me, to his children, Mary and David . . . etc.), the bequest will fall into the residue of your estate. This can be very important if, for example, you want your nephew to inherit, with the residue going to charity. If your nephew dies first and there is no named succeeding beneficiary, everything will go to charity, which might not be your intention.

If the beneficiary is a son or daughter who dies before you, whatever you have left will automatically go to your offspring's child or grandchild.

Drawing Up the Will

You can buy pre-printed will forms from legal stationers, but if after reading this you decide to go ahead and make a DIY will, get hold of a copy of *Make Your Will* (published by the Consumers' Association with Hodder & Stoughton £9.99). This contains full instructions and various types of will form, depending on whether you want to leave everything to one person, stipulate several beneficiaries and bequests, or leave assets in trust.

Witnesses

Having drawn up your will you will need to get two people to witness you signing it. The most important points here are:

- They must not be beneficiaries, nor should their husband or wife be beneficiaries.
- They must not be under 18, blind or mentally deficient.
- Both witnesses must be present when you sign the will, but they need not know what is in it. They do not have to read it.
- Signatures must be handwritten in ink.
- If the will extends to several pages, sign the bottom of each side and get the witnesses to sign also; the same applies to any alterations.
- Put the will somewhere safe, preferably fireproof, and tell the executors where it is. Many people like to leave their will with their bank for safe keeping. You can also deposit it at the Principal Registry, Family Division, Somerset House (Strand, London WC2R 1LP; tel. 071–936 6000).
- If the will is written in general terms leaving everything to be split equally between your children, you might like to leave a list of your assets with the will to make the executors' job easier.

Updating Your Will

Your circumstances will inevitably change over time – assets increase or diminish, or you may decide that the original beneficiaries, say, your children, are now grown up and already well provided for, so you want to make alterations.

- Review your will – probably every three to five years.
- Draw up a new will on marriage, divorce and remarriage.
- Review your will if there are major changes in taxation or trust law.

Any alterations after your will has been signed and witnessed can be carried out by drawing up a new will or by adding a codicil. If the changes are minor, the latter option is probably the simpler course of action, but it must be signed and witnessed in the same manner as your original will. Do not try to alter your will unaided, as the alterations will be ignored and could cause legal problems. If in doubt, get a new will drawn up.

Winding Up Someone's Estate

None of us like to think about it, but sooner or later we will probably have to deal with a death in the family. If the person is old and has died after a full and happy life, it isn't necessarily traumatic. Sorting out the practicalities may be something you prefer to leave to the professionals, but it is not necessarily complicated and you could save a considerable amount of money by doing it yourself.

If the deceased person left a will, the task of sorting out his or her affairs will fall to the executors named in the will. It is the executors' role to apply for probate. This is the legal document that banks and other institutions holding the deceased person's assets require before they release anything.

If there is no will – and 70 per cent of us have still to take this step – administrators apply for Letters of Administration. There is a strict pecking order for who can apply:

- The surviving spouse.
- The deceased's children (or their children if the deceased's own children are already dead).
- Parents, brothers or sisters, or other distant relatives.

Whenever there is no close family, it is worth checking whether you are entitled to act as administrator or not. For this information, contact the Probate Registry (South Wing, Somerset House, Strand, London WC2; tel. 071–936–6000).

Solicitor or DIY?

Surprisingly, only 3 per cent of probate cases each year require the payment of Inheritance Tax. For the remainder it is a case of collecting full details about the dead person's estate and completing a set of relatively easy-to-follow forms and swearing the papers.

Of course, you can use a solicitor. In fact, both the Lord Chancellor's Department and consumer bodies recommend this where the estate is not straightforward. It is probably worth consulting a solicitor if any of the following apply to the estate you are dealing with:

- The deceased's will may not be authentic or could be challenged.
- No will was left, but the relative who should inherit has vanished.
- The deceased was involved in family trusts.
- The deceased owned assets outside the UK.
- The deceased owned a business or farm.
- The major bequests were left to minors.

A good rule of thumb is that if there is anything you cannot readily fill in on the probate form, seek professional advice. Indeed, to find out whether you need professional advice, get hold of the form and see if you could fill it in without too much difficulty.

Finding the Right Solicitor

If you decide you need a solicitor, find one who regularly deals in probate work and check that the charges are acceptable. If the deceased left a will, it is worth contacting the solicitors who drew it up as they are likely to have some knowledge of his or her affairs.

The Law Society (see Useful Addresses) will be able to give you details of local solicitors who actively deal in probate. You will be charged the solicitor's hourly rate, but you might also be charged a fee as a percentage of the total value of the estate, generally around 1½ per cent. Where large sums of money are involved, it will clearly pay to shop around and negotiate charges.

Your solicitor will draw up the relevant papers, and the executors or administrator will swear to their accuracy in his office. Once the papers are lodged, you can expect the sealed Grant of Probate or Letters or Administration to come through in about seven working days.

The DIY Route

If the estate you are dealing with is a simple one, and you are not too emotionally involved, you can almost certainly manage the formalities yourself. There are some simple steps to follow.

STEP ONE: Find out the state of the deceased's financial affairs at the date of death – what assets he or she had, and what debts were outstanding. All assets and debts must be valued as they stood when the deceased died. All subsequent gains or losses will not form part of the estate.

Subtract the debts from the assets to see if the estate is taxable. In the 1993–94 tax year Inheritance Tax is levied at a flat rate of 40 per cent on the part of the deceased's estate above £150,000. If there is tax to pay, you will need to raise the cash before probate is granted.

STEP TWO: Get the forms from your local Probate Registry (you will find this in the telephone book under Probate Registrar). Once you have completed the forms, you will probably get an appointment within two weeks with a probate commissioner.

There are two main forms. The Probate Application Form is very straightforward, but do check that the right person is making the application. The biggest delay in personal applications stems from the wrong people signing the forms.

The second form is IHT44 – 'A return of the whole estate for probate fees and Inheritance Tax purposes' – and this is crucial. It is a snapshot of the deceased person's financial affairs and asks for asset totals under 17 headings for the UK, and a further section for overseas assets.

One classification is for household and personal goods. What is required is their second-hand value, as though they had been sold on the date of death. The probate office will usually accept a low value; roughly a quarter of what the goods were insured for is sufficient. (Many household contents policies now provide new-for-old cover.) You will be asked for formal valuations only if there is an obvious discrepancy in the amount you declare.

While most of the IHT44 form is straightforward, there are several key areas to check:

- Life assurance – Check if the policy actually forms part of the estate. If it was written in trust for someone else, the insurance company can pay out direct to that beneficiary. If it was not written in trust, it will form part of the estate. Where the policy is linked to a debt, often a mortgage on the house, it need not be recorded, but should feature later in the debts section offsetting the outstanding mortgage. The insurance company will be able to give you a 'date of death' valuation.
- Stocks, shares, unit trusts – Details are also required on the separate CAP40 form for the Inland Revenue. Finding the value of these investments can be tricky since it is calculated as the lower 'bid' price for the date of death, plus a quarter of the difference between the lower and the higher 'offer' price as quoted in the Stock Exchange Daily Official List. If that sounds complicated, you may find it easier to write for values to the company registrar of each company in which the deceased had invested. Clearly, if the person used a stockbroker, he can carry out this valuation for you.
- Pensions – In almost every circumstance the lump sum due on death is payable to the surviving spouse or dependants and won't form part of the estate.

Having recorded the assets you then have to set out details of any debts, including mortgages owing and the funeral expenses. The final sections cover jointly owned property, gifts and other transfers, and assets held in trust. It is worth stressing again that if you have difficulty finding the information to complete any of these questions, you are best advised to consult a solicitor.

STEP THREE: Once you have returned the forms, you will be

called for an interview. The person officially entitled to make the application must attend, but if someone else actually worked out all the details, that person should go too. The interview is a fairly painless review of the forms, with the chance for both sides to ask questions. At the end the applicant will be asked to swear to the authenticity of his or her signature and the accuracy of the information in the forms.

STEP FOUR: The Probate Registries are bound by statute to issue Grants of Probate and Letters of Administration within four weeks of your hearing, though you will normally get them sooner. Once you have got the document, you can go ahead and wind up the estate.

Fees

The amount of the fee depends on the size of the estate. For estates up to £10,000 the fee is £10 or less. At £100,000 the fee works out at £250, plus £50 for every additional £100,000, and £1 for every £1,000 thereafter. The Consumers' Association publishes a very useful kit called *How to Sort Out Someone's Will* (price 8.99), available from the Which? Bookshop, 359–361 Euston Road, London NW1; freephone 0800 252100, or from the Consumers' Association, Castlemead, Gascoyne Way, Hertford SG14 1LH.

9

LIVING ABROAD

Retiring abroad has always been a popular option, but with the advent of the European Community and mobility of labour, working abroad is now much easier too, and more people are taking the plunge. Figures are difficult to establish, but the Foreign Office estimates that there are currently 7.8 million UK expatriates living abroad and the number is rising.

Nobody wakes up one morning and suddenly decides to move to a tropical island. The motivation is usually something quite specific – an opportunity to work abroad, retirement for health or social reasons, family commitments – and often there is some knowledge and experience of the place to which the move will be made. Whatever your reasons, there are a number of considerations to take into account before you burn your boats, sell up and move overseas.

Emotional and practical considerations play a larger part than most people realize. For every two families that move abroad, there is one that doesn't like it and returns to the UK. There are two main reasons why people who go to live abroad change their mind: the first is the death of a partner or close relative, and the second is disenchantment. That delightful place where you have spent so many holidays may have a number of unpleasant features that were not apparent to you as a visitor – a repressive political regime, restricted cultural or social life, poor medical services (very important if you are elderly), bad communications and a host of other niggling irritations which make your holiday idyll unpleasant as a permanent residence.

You have to think carefully and ask yourself what is really important to you and which aspects of your life you are happy to change or do without. What is the climate like, in winter as well as summer? Are medical services freely available, adequate and within your means? Families with children of school age will need to know whether the standard of education in the new country of residence is good enough for their offspring to attend local schools, or will they have to board in England? Do the locals speak English or will it be necessary to learn another language? Is it important for you to be able to attend a place of worship?

Surprisingly trivial things assume enormous importance after a few years' deprivation. If you are a keen bridge player, life can be hell if there is no one good enough to play with. And cravings for unobtainable products like Marmite, HP sauce and Jackson's tea are a common feature of expatriate life.

You must also take into account whether it is quick and easy to get back to Britain, and how good communications are generally (very important if you intend working abroad or have children at school in England). Will you want to stay abroad if your partner dies? How difficult will it be to visit or see friends and relatives?

Above all, how will you manage your finances – your home, income, pensions, savings, tax, insurance, and other family assets? For example, many families and couples who retired to Spain in the 1960s and 1970s, because it was sunny and cheap, now find themselves trapped in a country which has one of the highest inflation rates in Europe on incomes that are fixed or falling.

If you are being sent abroad by an employer you may have little or no choice about the matter, other than to resign. But if you are making a free choice about living or working abroad, there are some broad general rules to bear in mind.

- If possible visit the place several times before making the final decision.
- Don't burn your boats: rent a property abroad and let your home in the UK until you are sure the move is permanent.
- If you are retiring abroad, check on State pensions; they are paid in full in EC countries, but in most others (including Canada, Australia, New Zealand, South Africa, Zimbabwe, the United States and Japan) they are frozen at the level in force at the time you leave.
- Check on exchange controls: are there likely to be problems getting UK income remitted to the new country of residence,

or difficulties in getting any income or capital built up there out of the country?

● Will your income be sufficient? If you will be dependent on UK income, will inflation in your new home country, or possible devaluation of the pound, affect your standard of living?

● If necessary, will you be able to work? What is the likelihood of you being able to find self-employment?

● What happens to your assets, both in the UK and overseas, if you die abroad? (This is very important as local regulations can be very onerous.)

● What is the tax situation? Is there a reciprocal agreement with the UK?

● What local taxes will you be liable for in your new country of residence?

Before You Go – General Advice

The longer ahead you plan, the better. There are a number of aspects of your finances and assets which will take time to arrange. Do you intend to let your house in the UK initially, and if so for how long? Are you aiming to be non-resident or even domiciled abroad (much more difficult to achieve and with far-reaching tax consequences)?

The first thing you must do is take professional advice. This is a very complicated area and it is difficult to give specific advice on how you arrange your finances as much will depend on the tax regime of the country to which you intend moving. Consult your accountant, solicitor and, if necessary, a specialist financial adviser who has experience of dealing with expatriates. If you don't have an accountant, you won't go far wrong with one of the medium-to-large UK firms which have a local branch network. If you are going to one of the EC countries or the United States, the larger UK firms may also have a local office. A small firm is unlikely to have the expertise to advise you properly on what is a very complicated matter.

What will you do about savings, life assurance, investments and pensions? Often it is best to transfer them to a safe offshore tax haven like the Channel Islands or the Isle of Man, but, again, you will need professional advice. To make a mistake can be costly, particularly in tax terms. Of course, what you do will depend very much on whether your sojourn abroad is intended to be temporary or permanent. Even if you mean to stay abroad, circumstances may force you to return, so flexibility is essential. For example, an elderly relative may become frail or a child may need special treatment in the UK, which you had not anticipated.

Forward planning is the golden rule as there is a lot which can be done to minimize tax before you leave. For example, interest on money invested in a Channel Island roll-up fund is not liable to tax until it is distributed. If you have by this time moved abroad, this interest will escape UK income tax.

Non-Residence

To establish non-residence in the UK for tax purposes the following rules apply. In any year in which you are present in the UK for 183 days or more you will be considered resident. There are no exceptions to this rule.

Until the tax year 1993–94, you were also considered a UK resident if you had accommodation available for your use during a visit to the UK, however short. This is no longer the case.

You will also be regarded as still resident in the UK if you visit the country in four consecutive years and your annual visits average three months or more.

You will normally be considered non-resident from the day following departure and you may be able to claim a tax rebate of a proportion of income tax already paid. Write to your tax office and request form P85. At the same time it might be useful to get hold of leaflet IR20 ('Residents and Non-Residents' Liability to Tax in the United Kingdom').

If you are granted provisional non-resident status but return permanently to the UK before you have been abroad for a full tax year, you will be considered as never having lost your UK-resident status and your worldwide income will be liable to UK tax. The Inland Revenue is immovable on this. If there is a political or health risk which might force your return, it is worth considering a tax contingency insurance policy.

UK Income

When you become officially non-resident you will have no UK

income tax liability on any overseas income, but income arising in the UK may be taxable, depending on the source. As a general rule it will therefore pay you to transfer as much of your assets as possible offshore to a safe tax haven like the Channel Islands or Isle of Man.

Interest on Bank and Building Society Deposits

This can be paid to expatriates without deduction of tax, but not in the year of leaving and return. This means that if, for example, you left the UK in June 1992, you would be liable for UK tax on the accrued interest in 1993–94. This provision is more important if you return to the UK, particularly if you have amassed savings while abroad. For this reason most people move bank and building society deposit accounts to the Channel Islands or Isle of Man well before they leave so that they do not fall foul of these provisions.

Income from UK Government Stocks

Gilts generally have tax deducted at source, but certain stocks – about a dozen – are exempt if you are non-resident. You apply to receive interest gross on these stocks to the Inspector of Foreign Dividends (Lynwood Road, Thames Ditton, Surrey KT7 ODP; Tel. 081-398 4242).

Other stocks, such as those issued by local authorities and corporate entities, are taxed at source and you generally cannot reclaim the tax unless there is a reciprocal agreement between the UK and your new country of residence.

Most National Savings investments are tax-free, but you will probably be able to get a better return elsewhere once you are no longer liable to UK tax.

Dividends

Generally, you are not able to reclaim tax deducted at source on share dividends. However, you may still be entitled to UK personal tax allowances which would allow you to reclaim tax in the UK up to the level of personal allowances. Check any reciprocal agreement too, as there are often concessions.

Life Assurance

The attraction of UK life policies is that the proceeds of 'quali-fying' policies are usually tax-free. However, UK-based life com-panies pay tax on profits and gains made within the life funds, so on the face of it you might benefit, once non-resident, by saving through an offshore life company in, say, the Channel Islands, which is not liable to tax, and the proceeds of any policy are also tax-free.

However, there are many other untaxed types of investment funds available to the expatriate investor, and the need to save through a life assurance company may well not apply.

Pensions

State retirement pensions are always paid gross without deduc-tion of tax and can be paid anywhere in the world, though they are taxable in your new country of residence. However, if you have other pensions, from earlier employment in the UK for example, your State pension may be taxed by a reduction in your personal allowance.

State pensions are paid in full, plus any subsequent increases, if you move within the EC, but in other countries, most notably the United States, Japan, Australia, New Zealand, Zimbabwe and Canada, they will be paid only at the level in force when you left.

The Department for Social Security, Overseas Branch, New-castle upon Tyne NE98 1YX; tel. 091 213 5000 will deal with specific enquiries.

Private pensions from occupational pension schemes or perso-nal pensions will continue to be liable for tax in the UK and are taxable in your new country of residence. However, there are many reciprocal agreements which allow you, once permission is granted by the Inspector of Foreign Dividends, to receive the

Countries Where You Will Receive Your State Pension In Full

Austria	Belgium	Bermuda	Cyprus	Denmark	Finland
France	Germany	Guernsey	Iceland	Ireland	Italy
Isle of Man	Israel	Jamaica	Jersey	Luxembourg	Malta
Mauritius	Netherlands	Norway	Philippines	Portugal	Spain
Sweden	Switzerland	Turkey	United States		

pension gross and pay tax on it in your new country of residence.

A similar regime applies to government pensions. If you have income from pensions you may also be eligible for personal allowances in the UK, which can be used to offset the liability. Crown employees, former Crown servants and others come into this category. Check with your accountant.

Employment Income

Generally, all income derived from employment in the UK – directorships, part-time employment (even a few weeks a year) and trading – are liable to UK tax. There are exemptions, but the rules are complicated and you will definitely need to consult your accountant if you are likely to find yourself non-resident with income from these sources.

It may be worthwhile transferring the business into an off-shore trust or company, but here again you will need professional advice and the costs may outweigh the benefits.

Rental Income

If you decide to let your house while you are abroad rather than sell it, as most people do until they are sure the move is permanent, you will be liable to UK tax on the rental income and any other rental income you may have. The usual offset for expenses applies, and generally any mortgage or bank interest incurred in order to purchase or improve the property can also be offset against the rental income.

Capital Gains Tax

To avoid CGT you must be not normally resident for at least three complete tax years (one if you are in full-time employment abroad). To be certain of avoiding CGT you should therefore not realize assets until you have completed three years as a non-resident in case you have to return to the UK unexpectedly. (You can insure against this if you want to realize gains earlier.)

Loss-making disposals should be carried out before departure from the UK so that losses can be carried forward and offset against any gains made in the UK, should you resume residence.

This, again, is a complicated area, as much will depend on the CGT rules in your new country of residence, so you should take professional advice.

Inheritance Tax – Making a Will

IHT is much more difficult to avoid because it depends on your domicile, not residence. You acquire a domicile of origin at birth, and non-domicile is extremely difficult to establish if you are born domiciled in the UK. However long you live abroad, you are likely to remain liable to IHT in the UK and will have to pay it when you die.

Domicile is quite separate from residence. It is not defined in UK tax law, but is generally understood to mean your country of ultimate affiliation. It is extremely difficult to persuade the tax authorities that you have changed your domicile just because you have changed your country of residence. Any UK-domiciled person has a potential IHT liability, no matter where in the world his or her assets are located. But this does not necessarily exempt you from paying again in your new country of residence. The consequences of dying abroad can be significant, and since you cannot choose when and where you die, you will also need to take specialist advice on making a will. Local laws can have a devastating effect; in some countries, for example, your assets will be passed on according to strict laws which give a certain proportion to children (when you might want assets to go to your spouse, grandchildren or someone else).

Tax on Your Return

On coming back to live in the UK you will be regarded as resident from the date of return, at which time your worldwide income becomes liable to UK tax. At the same time you become entitled to full personal allowances, even if you have been resident for only part of the year.

It is important to remember that overseas investment income becomes immediately chargeable to UK tax on return on a prior year basis. This means that you could be landed with a tax bill as soon as you set foot on British soil.

Any investments sold or terminated immediately before return will escape tax liability. For this reason you should 'bed and breakfast' all investments, including bank and other deposits. Interest on overseas bank deposits can escape tax if the account is closed just before you return.

If you have income remaining from earnings abroad, you should seek professional advice well before your return as the situation can be complicated, particularly if your return is not permanent. From April 1992 any pension which arises from overseas employment, terminal leave pay, or other payments, whether remitted to the UK or not, is liable to tax, although there is a 10 per cent exemption.

Living Abroad Checklist

Before You Go

- Bring your UK tax affairs up-to-date well before you leave, and check if National Insurance contributions will be necessary. You may want to pay voluntarily as most benefits depend on a full contribution record.
- Open offshore bank or building society accounts and transfer most of your savings. You may need to leave a UK account in existence to deal with UK commitments like income and expenditure on the house.
- Check the cover given in life policies to see if they remain valid once you are non-resident.
- Arrange medical insurance, if necessary.
- Inform your lender if you have tenants in your house and check insurances. Take legal advice on the lease.
- Revise all your savings, pensions, insurance and will, as described earlier.
- Make use of duty-free facilities to buy a car or other household appliances.

On Return

- Take professional advice well before you are due to leave.
- Give ample notice to quit to your local landlord, and to your tenants, if you have them.
- Check local exchange control regulations (ideally, you should have done this before leaving, but they may have changed).
- Close all offshore deposit accounts – in the case of UK accounts, at least one year before leaving.

Which Offshore Tax Haven?

For British expatriates a spell overseas will usually entail dealings with financial institutions in offshore centres, often for the first time. There are more than 30 around the world, and some are better regulated than others. Jersey, Guernsey and the Isle of Man all have investor protection laws, which are at least as good as those in the UK. Most of our household name financial institutions also have offices in these areas.

Clearly, this short chapter cannot cover everything to do

with living abroad and will not deal with your specific problems, although it aims to highlight some of the points that should *always* be considered. Going to live abroad is a subject that requires individual research and professional advice.

10

WHEN THINGS GO WRONG

The 1986 Financial Services Act radically altered the environment in which financial products and services are bought and sold. It brought in a number of changes to protect the consumer, the most important of which are as follows:

- Compensation – Under the Financial Services Act Compensation Scheme any investor who loses money because of the negligence, fraud or failure of an independent financial adviser is entitled to compensation of 100 per cent of the first £30,000 and 90 per cent of the next £20,000 – a maximum of £48,000.
- Polarization – Anyone who sells financial products must identify himself as being either the tied agent or appointed representative of a financial institution (in which case he can sell only that company's products), or an independent financial adviser (IFA) able to give impartial advice and choose a suitable product from the entire range on offer from any financial institution.
- Suitable advice – Any person, whether a tied salesman or an IFA, is obliged to choose a product which is suitable for your need, and in order to do this he must carry out a 'fact find' to establish your requirements. If you are mis-sold a product which is not what you need, you can ask for compensation.
- Regulation and registration – All institutions which sell financial products, and all salespeople, whether tied agents or IFAs, must be registered with one of the Self Regulatory Bodies (SROs):

FIMBRA (Financial Intermediaries, Managers and Brokers Regulatory Authority) – represents most of the independent

financial advisers, although some of the larger firms belong to
IMRO.

IMRO (Investment Management Regulatory Organization) –
members are generally the investment management arms of the
banks, unit and investment trusts, and other financial institutions, plus a few independent intermediaries.

LAUTRO (Life Assurance and Unit Trust Regulatory Organization) – members are the marketing arms of the life assurance and unit trust companies, including their salesforces.

SFA (Securities and Futures Authority) – members are largely
stockbrokers, commodity brokers and futures dealers.

The Securities and Investment Board (SIB) is the overall
watchdog which approves the rules for the other SROs. Many
of the banks and building societies have chosen to be regulated
by SIB direct rather than by one of the SROs, as SIB is not able
to impose fines or penalties – one of the major weaknesses of the
Act. However, the legislation is currently under review, and
when the Personal Investment Authority (PIA) is formed from
the amalgamation of LAUTRO and FIMBRA, it is thought that
the government will lean on the banks and building societies to
join.

It is important to understand the impact this huge change has
had. In the past probably some of the best and safest advice was
given by accountants and solicitors, who were appointed repre-
sentatives of perhaps four or five of the top life assurance
companies. Multi-ties are now illegal and, as a result, many of
these professionals have given up offering advice. They are,
however, allowed to practise as IFAs because they are members
of Recognized Professional Bodies (RPBs), which includes the
accountants' and solicitors' professional bodies.

The limitations of the system are obvious. If you go to a
direct salesman, he can recommend only his company's products, but no single insurance company produces products
which are all the best in their field. Thus, the average person,
who probably needs convertible-term cover, permanent health
insurance, possibly a with-profits endowment policy and a personal pension, is unlikely to find the best of these requirements
in one company. In addition, it is not usually a good idea to
have all your eggs in one basket.

The situation is made even more confusing by the banks and

building societies, most of which are tied to one financial institution (Halifax to Standard Life, for example) or have their own 'in-house' insurance company like Lloyds, Barclays and latterly NatWest. If you do not want their in-house products, they will refer you to their IFA subsidiary, which is able to give impartial independent advice. But independent advice is far from being all it should be. IFAs range from one-man bands to personal finance subsidiaries of big national firms of accountants and financial institutions – NatWest Insurance Brokers, for example.

FIMBRA, which regulates the smaller IFAs, has been criticized for not raising standards, but this will change. In the meantime you could get some dubious advice, or some very good advice, from an IFA.

The trade association, IFA Promotions (tel: 0483 461461, for helpline) is able to provide names of IFAs in your area but gives no indication of their size, competence or expertise. Be aware that IFAs are not obliged to have any professional qualifications, so if you want to play safe, you are probably best advised to consult one of the larger firms of accountants with countrywide branches which has an IFA subsidiary.

A good company offering independent financial advice will be able to advise on all aspects of taxation (usually the starting point for advice), life assurance, investment, pensions and mortgages. It will have qualified staff in each area. A one-man band is unlikely to have the resources to give a complete service.

Alternatively, you could simply buy all your insurance pensions and investment products from one household name insurer. The best companies have better-than-average products right across the board. However, simply being a household name does not guarantee good performance or competitive rates. Some of the worst policies are sold by companies which have been very successful at promoting themselves in the media.

It is worth mentioning here that if investment advice is high on your list of priorities, you should contact the Association of Private Client Investment Managers and Stockbrokers (see Useful Addresses), whose members specialize in dealing with private investors.

IFAs who are also members of the Insurance Brokers Registration Council (IBRC), the British Insurance and Investment Brokers Association and the Society of Pension Consultants must all be professionally qualified.

How to Complain

Banks are the number one target for consumer complaints at the moment, displacing the Inland Revenue as the most disliked financial institution. Hard-pressed customers still paying sky-high interest rates of 20 per cent or more are fed up with 'phantom withdrawals' from supposedly infallible cash machines, missed standing order payments and overcharging on interest. But you don't have to suffer in silence.

Time was when banks, building societies and other financial institutions could treat us all with lofty disdain, and some still do. But with the advent of the 1986 Financial Services Act a plethora of ombudsmen have sprung up to arbitrate in disputes between consumers and financial institutions. If you are frustrated at getting no reply to your letters to the insurance company, tired of hearing from a computer when there is a mistake on your credit card statement, or generally worn down by the bureaucracy of large financial institutions, the ombudsmen offer a welcome lifeline.

The procedure for getting a dispute referred to an ombudsman is the same in each case – you must first complain to the organization concerned, going to a higher authority if the person to whom you have been writing does not give a satisfactory reply (or no reply at all). If all else fails, write to the chief executive. When all channels have been exhausted you can ask the relevant ombudsman to investigate.

There are five ombudsmen, who operate in the fields of insurance, banking, building societies, pensions and investments. They all have powers to make awards of up to £100,000 if they find in your favour, and in each case the service is completely free.

The ombudsman will first decide whether he is able to adjudicate on your complaint (some areas of dispute, such as investment performance or credit decisions, are outside the relevant ombudsman's remit).

In the case of insurance, banking and pensions, the ombudsman's decision is binding on the institution, but you are free to pursue the matter in court if you don't like the decision.

In the case of building societies, the ombudsman's decision is not binding on either you or the society, but the society has to publicize its rejection of the ombudsman's decision and state the reasons why.

If you ask the investment ombudsman to adjudicate, both you and the investment or fund manager will be bound by his decision, and you cannot subsequently pursue the matter in court.

In recent years some of the worst difficulties have arisen where unscrupulous financial advisers and salesmen have sold individuals unsuitable investments or simply disappeared with clients' money. In this case you can complain first to the relevant Self Regulatory Authority (SRO). For independent financial advisers it is likely to be FIMBRA or IMRO. For stockbrokers it will be the SFA. If a salesman for a life office or unit trust company is the cause of your complaint, the SRO is the Life Assurance and Unit Trust Regulatory Authority (LAUTRO). Bad investments can be investigated through the SRO and the ombudsman, but both FIMBRA and the Stock Exchange have a complaints bureau.

(Note that FIMBRA and LAUTRO are soon to be absorbed into the Personal Investment Authority (PIA), currently being established.)

Where there has been incompetence or negligence – obviously bad advice, for example – the SRO can press the member to settle with you. In the event of the failure of an independent financial adviser, compensation of up to £48,000 can be awarded – 100 per cent of the first £30,000 and 90 per cent of the next £20,000.

Other Compensation

Life Assurance

The 1975 Policyholders Protection Act provides compensation of up to 90 per cent of the sum invested without limit if a UK insurance company fails. This would include any bonuses added to a with-profits policy to the date of the collapse, and any increase in unit prices from unitized policies.

The only exception is if the promised benefits are 'excessive', in which case compensation will be reduced. You will not be covered if you invest with an offshore insurance company.

Banks

The 1979 Banking Act provides compensation for bank depositors of 75 per cent of the first £20,000 – a maximum of £15,000 – if a UK bank fails. If you are nervous, keep your money in one of the big five high street banks.

Building Societies

The 1986 Building Societies Act provides compensation up to 90 per cent of the first £20,000 invested – a maximum of £18,000 – in the event that a building society fails. No one has lost money in a building society since the Second World War.

Insurance Brokers

The Insurance Brokers Registration Council (IBRC) has a compensation scheme which should pay out in the event of negligence or the failure of a registered insurance broker. In fact, it has paid out very little because one of the conditions is that all other forms of compensation have first to be exhausted, including the broker's professional indemnity (PI) policy and the FSA scheme. In order for the broker's PI policy to pay out, you must successfully sue him for negligence – something which you probably cannot afford if you have just lost money.

APPENDICES

Useful Addresses

Annuity Bureau
11–12 Hanover Square
London WIR 9HD
Tel: 071-495 1495

Annuity Direct
Pensions Bureau
32 Scrutton Street
London EC2A 4SS
Tel: 071-375 1175

Associated Scottish Life Offices
23 St Andrew Square
Edinburgh EH2 1AQ
Tel: 031-556 7171
Trade association.

Association of British Insurers
51 Gresham Street
London EC2V 7HQ
Tel: 071-600 3333
Trade association.

Association of Consulting Actuaries
PO Box 144
Norfolk House
Wellesley Road
Croydon
Surrey CR9 3EB
Tel: 081-668 8040

Association of Investment Trust Companies
6th Floor
Park House
16 Finsbury Circus
London EC2M 7JJ
Tel: 071-588 5347
Trade association.

Association of Mortgage Lenders
c/o London & Manchester Assurance
Winslade Park
Exeter EX5 1DS
Tel: 0392 282140

Association of Private Client Investment Managers and Stockbrokers (APCIMS)
20 Dysart Street
London EC2A 2BX
Tel: 071-410 6868

Association of Unit Trusts and Investment Funds
65 Kingsway
London WC2B 6TD
Tel: 071-831 0898
Trade association

Bank of England
Threadneedle Street
London EC2R 8AH
Tel: 071-601 4444
Overall banking supervisor.

Banking Ombudsman
Citadel House
5–11 Fetter Lane
London EC4A 1BR
Tel: 071-583 1395

British Bankers Association (BBA)
10 Lombard Street
London EC3V 9EL
Tel: 071-623 4001
Trade association.

British Insurance and Investment Brokers Association
Biba House
14 Bevis Marks
London EC3A 7NT
Tel: 071-623 9043

Building Societies Association and Council of Mortgage Lenders
3 Savile Row
London W1X 1AF
Tel: 071-437 0655
Trade association.

Building Societies Ombudsman
35–37 Grosvenor Gardens
London SW1X 7AW
Tel: 071-931 0044

Building Societies Registry and Commission
15–17 Great Marlborough Street
London W1V 2AX
Tel: 071-437 9992
Overall supervisor of building societies.

Chartered Association of Certified Accountants
29 Lincolns Inn Fields
London WC2A 3EE
Tel: 071-242 6855

Department for National Savings
Charles House
375 Kensington High Street
London W14 8SD
Tel: 071-605 9300

Department of Trade and Industry
1–19 Victoria Street
London SW1H OET
Tel: 071-215 5000
Overall supervisor of insurance companies.

DSS Overseas Branch
Newcastle upon Tyne NE98 1YX
Tel: 091 213 5000

DSS Retirement Forecast and Advisory Service
RPFA Unit
Room 37D
Newcastle upon Tyne NE98 1YX
Tel: 091 213 5000

Finance Houses Association
18 Upper Grosvenor Street
London W1X 9PB
Tel: 071-491 2783
Trade association.

Financial Intermediaries Managers Authority (FIMBRA)
Hertsmere House
Hertsmere Road
London E14 4AB
Tel: 071-538 8860

IFA Promotions
4th Floor
28 Greville Street
London EC1N 8SU
Tel: 071-831 4027; Helpline 0483 461461
Will provide names and addresses of
Independent Financial Advisers (IFAs).

Independent Schools Advisory Service (ISIS)
56 Buckingham Gate
London SW1E 6AG
Tel: 071-630 8793

Inspector of Foreign Dividends
Lynwood Road
Thames Ditton
Surrey KT7 ODP
Tel: 081-398 4242

Institute of Actuaries
Staple Inn Hall
High Holborn
London WC1V 7QJ
Tel: 071-242 0106

Institute of Chartered Accountants of England & Wales
PO Box 433
Chartered Accountants' Hall
Moorgate Place
London EC2P 2BJ
Tel: 071-628 7060

Institute of Chartered Accountants of Ireland
Chartered Accountants' House
87–89 Pembroke Road
Dublin 4
Eire
Tel: 010 3531 680400

Institute of Chartered Accountants of Scotland
27 Queen Street
Edinburgh, EH2 1LA
Tel: 031-225 5673

Insurance Brokers Registration Council
15 St Helen's Place
London EC3A 6DS
Tel: 071-588 4387

Insurance Ombudsman
135 Park Street
London SE1 9EA
Tel: 071-928 7600

International Academy of Matrimonial Lawyers
c/o Miles Preston
Radcliffe & Co
5 Great College Street
London SW1P 3SJ
Tel: 071-222 7040
Association specializing in international divorce.

International Stock Exchange
The Stock Exchange
London EC2N 1HP
Tel: 071-588 2355
Trade association.

Investment Management Regulatory Organization (IMRO)
Broadwalk House
5 Appold Street
London EC2A 2LL
Tel: 071-628 6022

Investment Ombudsman
6 Frederick's Place
London EC2R 8BT
Tel: 071-796 3065

Joint Office of the Superannuation Funds Office and Occupational Pensions Board
Lynwood Road
Thames Ditton
Surrey KT20 0DP
Tel: 081-398 4242
Overall supervisor of pensions.

Law Society of England and Wales
113 Chancery Lane
London WC2A 1PL
Tel: 071-242 1222

Law Society of Northern Ireland
Law Society House
90–106 Victoria Street
Belfast BT1 3JZ
Tel: 0232 231614

Law Society of Scotland
26 Drumsheugh Gardens
Edinburgh EH3 7YR
Tel: 031-226 7411

Life Assurance and Unit Trust Regulatory Organization (LAUTRO)
3rd Floor
103 New Oxford Street
London WC1A 1PT
Tel: 071-379 0444

Linked Life Assurance Group
6th Floor East
Lansdowne House
Berkeley Square
London W1X 5DH
Trade association.

Micropal
Trafalgar House
Chalkhill Road
London W6 8DW
Tel: 081-741 4100

Money Management Register of Fee-Based IFAs
Greystoke Place
Fetter Lane
London EC4A 1ND
Tel: 071-405 6969

National Association of Pension Funds
12–18 Grosvenor Gardens
London SW1W 0DH
Tel: 071-730 0585
Trade association for occupational pension funds.

National Council of One-Parent Families
255 Kentish Town Road
London NW5
Tel: 071-267 1361

National Savings
375 Kensington High Street
London W14 8QH
Tel: 071-605 9300

Occupational Pensions Advisory Service (OPAS)
11 Belgrave Road
London SW1V 1RB
Tel: 071-233 8080

The Office of Fair Trading
15–25 Field House
Breams Buildings
London EC4A 1PR
Tel: 071-242 2858
Licenses credit brokers.

Parliamentary Ombudsman
Church House
Great Smith Street
London SW1P 3BW
Tel: 071-276 2130
Must be referred through an MP – deals with maladministration by government departments including the Inland Revenue.

Pensions Management Institute
4 Artillery Lane
London E1 7LS
Tel: 071-247 1452

Pensions Ombudsman
11 Belgrave Road
London SW1V 1RB
Tel: 071-834 9144

Probate Registry
South Wing
Somerset House
Strand
London WC2
Tel: 071-936 6000

Principal Registry (Family Division)
Somerset House
Strand
London WC2R 1LP
Tel: 071-936 6000

Securities and Futures Authority (SFA)
Stock Exchange Tower
Old Broad Street
London EC2N 1HP
Tel: 071-256 9000

Securities and Investment Board (SIB)
Gavrelle House
2–14 Bunhill Row
London EC1Y 8RA
Tel: 071-638 1240
Overall investment and financial services watchdog.

Society of Pension Consultants
Ludgate House
Ludgate Circus
London EC4A 2AB
Tel: 071-353 1688

Society of Trust and Estate Practioners (STEPS)
c/o George Tasher
42 Princes Boulevard
Bebington
Wirral L63 5LW
Tel: 051-645 6801

Solicitors' Family Law Association
PO Box 302
Keston
Kent BR2 6EZ
Tel: 0689 850227

Terrence Higgins Trust
52 Gray's Inn Road
London WC1X 8LT
Tel: 071-831 0330
Has specialist brokers who can advise about insurance for those considered at risk of Aids.

FURTHER READING

Allied Dunbar Tax Guide, W. I. Sinclair (Longman, £17.99)
Blay's Mortgage Guide and *Blay's Investment Guide* (Blay's Guides Ltd, Blay's House, Churchfield Road, Chalfont St Peter, Bucks SL9 9EW; tel. 0753 880482. Available by subscription only.)
The Equitable Schools Book 1993, Claus Boehm and Jenny Lees-Spalding (Bloomsbury, £14.99)
For Parents Who Live Apart (free from Child Support Agency, PO Box 55, Brierley Hill, West Midlands DY5 1YL; helpline tel. 0345 133133)
Guide to Divorce (Hodder & Stoughton in conjunction with the Consumers' Association, £10.99)
Make Your Will (Hodder & Stoughton in conjunction with the Consumers' Association, £9.99).
PEP Guide (Chase de Vere, 63 Lincoln's Inn Fields, London WC2A 3JX; tel. 071-404 5766. £8.95)
Splitting Up, David Green (Kogan Page, £9.99)
Student Grants and Loans (free from DES, Publications Department, PO Box 2193, London E15 2EU; tel. 081-533 2000.)
Which? Way to Save Tax (Hodder & Stoughton in conjunction with the Consumers' Association, £13.99)

* May be obtained by mail order from the Consumers' Association, freephone 0800 252100.

INDEX

accident and disability insurance, 96
Association of Investment Trust
   Companies, 59, 187, 188
Association of Private Client Investment
   Managers and Stockbrokers, 61–2, 67,
   191, 236
Association of Unit Trusts, 59, 187, 188

bank and building society savings
   accounts, 158–60
Banking Act (1979), 239
Baronworth, 174
Blay's Guide, 69, 148, 157
Blay's Money Master, 157
Blay's Mortgage Guide, 17
Bradford & Bingley Building Society, 18
British Insurance and Investment
   Brokers Association, 97, 236–7
Building Societies Act (1986), 239
Building Societies Association, 25
Business Expansion Scheme (BES)
   investments, 14, 193–4
businesses, remortgaging to finance, 14–15

Chase de Vere, 59, 174
Chase de Vere PEP Guide, 192
Cheltenham & Gloucester Building
   Society, 21
Child Support Agency (CSA), 47
children, 50–70
   higher education, 63–6
      costs, 65
      making provision, 65–6
      mortgage on a property for a
         student to provide finance, 11–12,
         65
      student grants and loans, 64
   investing for children, 66–70
      large sums – trusts, 67

life assurance, 68
special investments, 68
tax and children, 66–7
school fees, 15–16, 50–64
   cost of, 50–1
   deferred annuities, 60
   how to invest, 53
   insurance, 60
   last-minute planning, 61–2
   lump sum or regular saving, 53
   overdraft facilities, 62
   saving, 52
   schemes: Assisted Places Scheme,
      51–2; composition schemes, 57;
      educational trust, 54–7; how they
      work, 54; ten years or more to
      invest, 57–9; under ten years to
      invest, 60–1; with-profit
      endowments, 59–60
   tax on, 52–3
   taxation and, 66–7
   trusts for, 67–8
cohabiting, 31, 34, 38, 48
Council of Mortgage Lenders survey, 8,
   10

deferred annuities for school fees, 60
divorce, 39–48
   Child Support Agency, effect of, 47
   financial considerations, 43–5
   legal aid, 44
   life policies, 44–5, 77
   pensions, 45–8
   tax and maintenance, 42–3
   who gets what, 40–2
   wills, 212

endowment with-profit policies, 59–60,
   177–81